Lifelong Learning as Critical Action

Lifelong Learning as Critical Action

International Perspectives on People,
Politics, Policy, and Practice

André P. Grace

Canadian Scholars' Press Inc.
Toronto

Lifelong Learning as Critical Action: International Perspectives on
People, Politics, Policy, and Practice
André P. Grace

First published in 2013 by
Canadian Scholars' Press Inc.
425 Adelaide Street West, Suite 200
Toronto, Ontario M5V 3C1

www.cspi.org

Canadian Scholars' Press Inc. gratefully acknowledges financial support for our publishing
activities from the Government of Canada through the Canada Book Fund (CBF).

Library and Archives Canada Cataloguing in Publication
Grace, André P., 1954-, author
Lifelong learning as critical action : international perspectives on people, politics, policy,
and practice / André P. Grace.

Includes bibliographical references and index. Issued in print and electronic formats.
ISBN 978-1-55130-546-2 (pbk.).--ISBN 978-1-55130-547-9 (pdf).--
ISBN 978-1-55130-548-6 (epub)

    1. Continuing education. 2. Continuing education--Political aspects. 3. Continuing
education--Social aspects. 4. Continuing education--Economic aspects. 5. Neoliberalism.
I. Title.

LC5215.G73 2013   374   C2013-904567-8   C2013-904568-6

Text design by Ben Craft
Cover design by Em Dash Design
Cover image: MG & Co. © iStockphoto

Printed and bound in Canada by Webcom

MIX
Paper from
responsible sources
FSC® C004071

For My Father, Philip Joseph Grace (1928–2007)

Although his formal education ended when he completed Grade 9, my father was a lifelong and lifewide learner. Dad worked as a fireman, and he fished and farmed as well to supplement our family income. He had the knowledge and skills to perform each of these roles well. As a fisher and farmer, he knew about the migration patterns of fish species, crop rotation, and many other things that those formally educated in studies of zoology, economic botany, and other subjects would learn from books. In particular, I remember many winter nights, watching him as he deftly knit sections of cod traps while I sat at the kitchen table doing my homework in our house in the fishing village of Flatrock, Newfoundland. He was the epitome of the flexible citizen whose daily informal learning and work engagements were inspired by his collective need to be a contributor to his family and community economies. He was a good husband, a good father, and a good provider. I thought about him often as I wrote this book, which has left me with the realization that many ordinary citizens are truly extraordinary.

Contents

Preface

"Stupefying. Dizzying. Deeply unsettling" (p. 1): This is how Coy (2008) described the extraordinary panic that sped through the global financial market from October 6 to 10, 2008. These pivotal dates ushered in a global recession that is sorely testing the economic logic of neoliberalism (Engardio, 2008; Grace, 2009a, 2009b; Mandel, 2008), an ideology that Harvey (2005) describes as a longstanding economic convention and a practical influence on public policy. Many nations, including the United States and many European countries, have been working to rescue their financial institutions and key components of their corporate sectors (Francis & Sasseen, 2008). Indeed, financial rescue by governments and, in some cases, financial rescue of governments in a time of unprecedented unpredictability is now the order of the day. We live incessantly with the fallout of this great economic debacle in uncertain times when "our problems are vaguer and more systematic, not so much a matter of policy as of how we live, and seem to come from every direction at once" (Baird, 2012, p. 31).

Neoliberalism, which promised to advance the social as a corollary of advancing the economic, now appears as a false god whose wrath is choking globalization, keeping it from moving along what was once its apparent sure-footed and prosperous path. In light of this unparalleled global financial crisis, Mandel (2008) suggests that globalization, with its "long accepted patterns of cross-border technological transfer, foreign trade, and global finance[,] ... [is] simply not sustainable" (p. 1). He asks a key question that policy-makers, in response to the current crisis, must answer: "What if we face a wrenching readjustment of the global real economy rather than a crisis of confidence rooted in the financial system?" (p. 1).

What we have learned through the media blitz surrounding the latter-day global financial crisis, and what many citizens have personally experienced, is that neoliberalism has a profoundly dark side, which has led to global economic disaster: "Deregulation, corporate greed, irresponsible lenders, uneducated borrowers, a lack of criminal penalties, and abuse of credit cards and home equity loans are all cited as causes.... The financial system that is coming to an end was based on artificially creating wealth instead of supporting tangibly productive activities" (Kinney, 2008, p. 1). From a US perspective, Engardio (2008) provides further explanation in this synopsis: "What makes this financial crisis so different from many of the others faced in the past three decades is that it did not originate with peripheral emerging markets. It struck the core of global capitalism. And unlike previous US recessions, this crisis cannot be fixed with changes in monetary and fiscal policy. It will require years of financial workouts and restructuring. The fallout, therefore, is likely to radiate out across the globe in countless unforeseen ways" (p. 2).

This has ramifications for lifelong learning, which, for some decades, has become largely technicized and commodified under neoliberalism. It is the profound overemphasis on the economic and the instrumental, and the consequential sidelining of the social, that undergird my call for lifelong learning as critical action that encompasses and nurtures social engagement, political and economic understanding, and cultural work to benefit citizens as learners and workers. The ongoing global economic debacle makes this call even more urgent. In today's uncertain global change culture of crisis and challenge, lifelong learning ought to be an inclusive medium and a set of principles and practices to help individuals learn their way out of life and work conundrums in diverse instrumental, social, and cultural contexts. However, this is an ideal. As many critical, feminist, and other positional educators have frequently and effectively argued (see, for example, Edwards, 2000a; Field, 2006; Grace, 2000a, 2006a, 2006b, 2009a, 2009b; Walters, 2006), lifelong learning, especially as it has evolved under neoliberalism, has been exclusionary and limited in scope. Primarily, it has mandated citizens as learners and workers to engage in vocational and instrumental learning to produce a more skilled, flexible, and mobile workforce. Amid a public to private shift in responsibility for lifelong learning, which is a dynamic that is apparent globally, governments, the Organisation for Economic Co-operation and Development, and others setting policy directions for lifelong learning have expected citizens to take individual responsibility for their own learning and to shoulder the blame when lifelong learning fails. In this milieu, the historically valorized concept of lifelong learning has become highly politicized and corporatized. Its widespread economistic formation, ensconced in recent decades, provides an obvious reason for citizens to question what has happened to the social and what constitutes worthwhile learning, quality work, and the good life.

If lifelong learning is to be a meaningful discourse for today *and* tomorrow, then it ought to have a multi-faceted goal: to prepare citizens as learners for work and for the rest of life as part of more holistic development. To incorporate and delineate these lifewide parameters, I use the idea of *lifelong learning as critical action*. In developing this notion, I provide perspectives on lifelong learning as a multi-dimensional historical and contemporary phenomenon with the potential to address instrumental, social, and cultural concerns within a more holistic approach to learning. I problematize the neoliberal formation of lifelong learning as a predominantly economistic venture as I examine contexts and change forces that have shaped contemporary policy-making and practice in governmental, educational, and other institutional contexts. I provide local, national, and international examples of critical, inclusive, holistic, and engaged lifelong learning that attend to matters of ethics, democratic learning, learner freedom, and justice in civil and economic contexts. These matters, as I see them, are at the heart of lifelong learning as critical action, which aims to be a multi-faceted contextual and relational formation that focuses on developing and actually implementing instrumental, social, and cultural learning projects.

Lifelong Learning as Critical Action is a useful text for university and college courses that focus on the policy-making and practice dimensions of lifelong learning in historical and contemporary contexts in diverse institutions. This book is also well suited to courses on the history and sociology of adult and higher education, which are key domains where lifelong learning as a concept and practice has long had an impact. It is an informative text for courses focused on inclusive education that highlights ethics and social justice, and is a valuable resource for community-based education courses that address democratic practices and learner needs and freedoms in local and larger contexts. It has utility in courses focused on educational theorizing, cultural learning practices, and learning in social movements. *Lifelong Learning as Critical Action* aims to be an instructive text that provides socio-historical, economic, cultural, and political perspectives on the effects of neoliberalism and globalization on education. The book contributes to the knowledge base in education by analyzing lifelong learning in both policy and practice contexts. It provides critical perspectives and challenges readers to engage lifelong learning as a lifewide phenomenon concerned with instrumental, social, and cultural learning. In the end, I hope the book is a stimulus for each reader's own critical action.

Acknowledgements

As an academic, I believe my intellectual identity is caught up in the identities of those who mentored me as I found my way into academe. I would like to thank my two most important mentors: Henry A. Giroux and Michael R. Welton. Henry nurtured my love of theory and theorizing during my post-doctoral studies, challenging me to mediate the tensions inherent in juxtaposing critical and post-foundational perspectives. Like Henry, Michael, my doctoral supervisor, urged me to explore theoretical legacies innervating critical theory and other theoretical discourses today. Michael also nurtured my love of social history and taught me to look back before looking ahead. Their influences are evident in this book, and I am grateful for the opportunities I had to study with them.

André P. Grace
Professor and Director,
Institute for Sexual Minority Studies and Services
Faculty of Education, University of Alberta
Edmonton, Alberta, Canada

List of Acronyms

ABET	Adult Basic Education and Training (South Africa)
AERA	American Educational Research Association
AERC	Adult Education Research Conference (USA)
AI	Amnesty International
ALE	Adult Learning and Education
ALKC	Adult Learning Knowledge Center (Canada)
CCSD	Canadian Council on Social Development
CMEC	Council of Ministers of Education, Canada
CONFINTEA	Conférence internationale sur l'éducation des adultes (French for International Conference for Adult Education)
CCL	Canadian Council on Learning
CLI	Composite Learning Index (Canada)
CPRN	Canadian Policy Research Networks
CRPD	Convention on the Rights of Persons with Disabilities
CQU	Central Queensland University (Australia)
EFA-GMR	Education for All – Global Monitoring Report
FISC	Foro Internacional de la Sociedad Civil (Portuguese for International Civil Society Forum)
GLOBE	Gay, Lesbian, or Bisexual Employees Group (United Nations)
HRDC	Human Resources Development Canada
HRSDC	Human Resources and Skills Development Canada
IALLA	ICAE Academy of Lifelong Learning Advocacy
ICAE	International Council for Adult Education
ICSF	International Civil Society Forum
IFLL	Inquiry into the Future for Lifelong Learning (UK)
IGLHRC	International Gay and Lesbian Human Rights Commission
LGBTQ&A	Lesbian, Gay, Bisexual, Transgender, Queer, and Allies
LLL	Lifelong Learning
MERCOSUR	Mercado Común del Sur (Spanish for Southern Common Market)
NEPI	National Education Policy Investigation (South Africa)
NGO	Non-Governmental Organization
OECD	Organisation for Economic Cooperation and Development

SCUTREA	Standing Conference on University Teaching and Research in the Education of Adults (UK)
TARP	Troubled Asset Relief Program (USA)
TEAC	Tertiary Education Advisory Commission (New Zealand)
UEL	University of East London
UNESCO	United Nations Educational, Scientific, and Cultural Organization
VET	Vocational Education and Training (Australia)
Y2K	Year 2000

Introduction

Moving Beyond Omissions to Achieve Holistic, Proactive, and Inclusive Learning for All

Me in the Lifelong Learning Mix

Since entering the academy, I have engaged in social historical and socio-logical analyses of lifelong learning, focusing on its emergence since the early twentieth century. In this book, I conduct comparative studies of people, politics, policies, and practices shaping lifelong learning, especially in the contexts of OECD (Organisation for Economic Co-operation and Development) countries. Since making *lifelong learning for all* its mantra in the mid-1990s, the OECD has spearheaded various educational policy initiatives focused on lifelong learning that expect the involvement of all sectors of education across adult education, higher education, and public schooling for children and youth. Here lifelong learning has largely functioned within a neoliberal context that emphasizes learning to advance local, national, and global economies. To counter this predominant, albeit narrow, focus, more inclusive life-long-learning initiatives are needed to address social and cultural issues such as the problem of dislocation of vulnerable youth in life, learning, and work contexts. In this regard, I have been interested in delineating what constitutes lifelong learning as critical action where learning is holistic, proactive, and inclusive of all learners across relationships of power and diverse contexts.

Within my research I have included a primary focus on sexual and gender minorities—lesbian, gay, bisexual, transgender, and queer persons—and our issues and concerns regarding social inclusion, social cohesion, and justice in education, health, other institutional contexts, and culture. Throughout my academic career, as academic culture became more inclusive and spaces opened up to engage in sexual and gender minority (SGM) studies, I have been able to expand my SGM-focused research emphasizing political and cultural changes for social transformation. Since the early 1990s, there has been a move to make queer history and culture visible in mainstream, critical, and other arenas in North American adult and higher education. This move counters a history of exclusion in academe that has mirrored exclusion from mainstream culture and society. Even critical forms of education, which emphasize the political ideals of modernity—democracy, freedom, and social justice—and ethical practice, have, for the most part, been complicit in maintaining a heteronormative status quo through the usual omission of queer in theorizing and practice. The cultural politics at play here have worked to keep this heteronormative status quo intact through exclusions, omissions, and enforced silences (Grace, 2001; Hill & Grace, 2009). Recognizing this sorry reality, thematically, my SGM-focused research is concerned with human diversity, social justice, equity, ethics, and democratic and inclusive forms of educational, other institutional, and cultural practices. It involves bringing changes in law and legislation to bear on developing and implementing SGM-inclusive policy and practices in education, other institutions, and culture and society. To conduct this research, I have developed what is emerging as a queer critical theoretical and methodological framework to inform politics and strategies in conducting research and developing and implementing policies that advance respect for and accommodation of sexual and gender minorities. This framework juxtaposes critical theory's emphases on ethics, emancipation, and social justice with queer theory's capacity to investigate the ways that mainstream culture and language as power impact sexual and gender minorities and limit possibilities for our equitable treatment. Queer critical theorizing provides a lens for studying the cumulative impact of the systems, structures, and social forces and responses that influence whether SGM individuals are included in, or excluded from, lifelong learning. In sum, my research to abet SGM inclusion has examined legal, legislative, health, and education issues that affect sexual and gender minorities and demand extensive policy-making as protection in life, learning, and work contexts. My research on sexual and gender minorities has reinforced my belief that inclusive policy-making is crucial to making life better for vulnerable citizens seeking recognition, respect, and accommodation. Such policy-making provides a basis for framing and engaging in ethical educational, other institutional, and cultural practices. With education as an institution expected to replicate the status quo of a larger culture and society that has historically disenfranchised SGM persons, focusing on lifelong learning as critical action that abets inclusion and accommodation is vital and necessary.

In this book I investigate lifelong learning and the politics affecting its formation over time; sexual and gender minorities and other vulnerable populations affected by life, learning, and work transitions; policy studies; and inclusive lifelong-learning practices. In exploring lifelong learning as critical action in conceptual terms and as a cultural practice focused on learning for life and work, I bring theorizing, research, policy analysis, and an understanding of engaged practice to bear on elucidating this idea. Through reflexive analysis, I position lifelong learning as a chameleonic and still emerging concept with a rich history and a complex present shaped by people, politics, policies, and practices in particular times and places. As I explore aspects of the history of lifelong learning to the present moment, I consider the complexity of the notion as well as the diverse conditions and competing discourses that have shaped it. I interrogate the degree to which lifelong learning variously meets the diverse instrumental, social, and cultural needs of citizens as learners and workers who take on multiple and miscellaneous roles at home, at work, and in their communities. I speak to the intricacies of building and sustaining lifelong learning as critical action in life and work contexts where history, politics, and individual and communal dispositions (attitudes, values, and beliefs) permeate and impact relationships of power in the learning process.

In summary then, I consider the eclecticism of lifelong learning in this book, discussing the concept's nature and meaning as well as the contexts, relationships, and change forces that shape lifelong-learning policy-making and practice. I examine the impact that neoliberalism has had on the contemporary position, predicament, and participation of citizens involved in lifelong learning in an ongoing change culture of crisis and challenge. While I primarily use an academic writing style in conducting this analysis, in some places my writing demonstrates my commitment to a contemporary style that intersperses academic writing with poetry, narrative vignettes, and first-person reflection in keeping with communicative styles used in arts-informed and narrative forms of inquiry (Grace, 2006c; Grace & Wells, 2007a, 2007b). This pedagogical strategy disrupts an exclusively formal engagement with lifelong learning by building knowledge and understanding that interweaves the personal, the political, and the pedagogical in ways that lift up voice in the intersection with theorizing. In the turn to theory, my analysis represents my commitment to using multi-perspective critical, feminist, queer, and positional theoretical lenses to guide critique of educational and other social and cultural phenomena that affect citizens and place limits on their lives and work. In this regard, I interrogate the neoliberalization of lifelong learning as a failure to embrace social inclusion, cohesion, and justice in sufficient, overt, and committed ways. Thus this book is not about embracing lifelong learning as some panacea, as many mainstream academics do when they ally with government and corporate interests for such reasons as securing research funding to link lifelong learning to worker performance and productivity. While I draw on various mainstream voices in reviewing the contemporary state of lifelong-learning policy and practice, I mainly focus on diverse critical, feminist, queer, and other positional educators who emphasize equity and social justice in their theorizing and cultural work to problematize the neoliberal formation of lifelong learning. In bringing their voices into deliberations, I show that there is a growing contingent of contemporary lifelong educators whose work in social and cultural contexts represents new directions in theorizing and writing about lifelong learning. In keeping with a post-structural commitment to lift out subjectivities and positionalities and let them stand on their own, I try to capture the perspectives of those I reference and leave them intact, knowing that readers will rewrite my text, make their own comparisons, and offer their own critiques from the politics of their own locations as persons and practitioners. I use the work of this diverse group of theorists, researchers, and practitioners to demonstrate that lifelong learning, even though it has sometimes been a detriment to both the individual and public good, has possibilities for enhancing quality learning, quality work, and quality life.

The Chapters in Conspectus

The chapters in this book are eclectic, weaving together historical and contemporary perspectives on lifelong learning in instrumental, social, cultural, economic, and political contexts. You should anticipate feeling a sense of disruption and dislocation as you move through them. As you read, your feelings of moving to and fro will replicate the feelings of participants in lifelong learning that recasts priorities in seemingly fleeting ways as it moves like a weathervane in response to economic, cultural, and other change forces. As you read, you will need to deal with the winds of change driving lifelong learning in different directions over time.

I open chapter 1 with a narrative vignette that speaks to the contemporary nihilism—a loss of hope and a sense of helplessness and ineptitude—that can consume citizens as learners and workers as they mediate what seems to be relentless adversity and trauma in today's world. I emphasize the importance of deliberating what lifelong learning means in contemporary times, when citizens need learning for life *and* work. As I assert in this introduction, if lifelong learning is to be an antidote for counteracting nihilism, then it needs to be holistic in purpose and intention, energizing possibility and proactivity in the life, learning, and work spaces that citizens inhabit. While I acknowledge that the techno-vocationalizing of lifelong learning contributes to its sum, I maintain that it is insufficient and indeed problematic to cast lifelong learning solely this way. Since learning has to have economic, social, *and* cultural purposes in relation to meeting learners' multiple needs, I call for lifelong learning to be something more than an instrumental formation. I propose that this requires re-articulation of a contemporary culture of lifelong learning steeped in neoliberalism. I end the chapter with vignettes that indicate such re-articulation is urgently needed.

In chapter 2, I consider how lifelong learning has emerged as a policy-driven formation that has only partially met learners' needs since the 1990s. I build this chapter around a central question: Where does contemporary lifelong learning fit in the quest to live a full and satisfying life? As I reflect on this question, I begin with an overview of neoliberalism and its nature and meaning. I consider how the goals of neoliberalism are tied to globalization and corporatism as change forces that endorse privatization, instrumentalism, and individualism to serve business and governmental interests. I explore the economic and social impacts of neoliberalism as a segue to discussing how lifelong learning is constituted as a political and pedagogical project in a neoliberal world. Here I consider whether contemporary lifelong learning is really a panacea or a problem for learners mediating life, learning, and work. I analyze pervasive perspectives and politics shaping lifelong learning and affecting its development in social, cultural, and instrumental contexts. Then I begin the book's central project: to position and frame *lifelong learning as critical action*. I provide an initial explanation and understanding of this concept and practice, exploring ways to think about holistic lifelong learning that critically engages instrumental, social, *and* cultural education. I place emphases on ethics, diversity, inclusion, and the political ideals of modernity—democracy, freedom, and social justice. I also examine matters of context (social, cultural, economic, historical, and political factors impacting the development and implementation of lifelong-learning policy and practice); disposition (attitudes, values, and beliefs shaping lifelong learning); and relationship (how the ways in which individuals are located in demographic and geographic terms affect their access and accommodation as learners). To make a case for engaging in lifelong learning as critical action, I consider examples of learners who lack space and place in the contemporary lifelong learning milieu. I also consider difficulties with the fluidity of lifelong learning as a concept and practice, the contemporary paradoxes marking the reality of lifelong learning, and the way lifelong learning is currently positioned as a mainstream cultural production. I conclude by speaking to the ever-present need of citizens to learn their way out of challenging life and work contexts.

I begin chapter 3 with a reminder: Interest in lifelong learning is hardly new. From this perspective, I turn to the history of the modern practice of adult education, primarily in a North American context, to speak about lifelong learning's long-time location as a fluid and indeterminate concept that some learners have seen as a solution and other learners have regarded as a burden. I identify change forces that have shaped particular purposes and functions of lifelong learning during the twentieth century and into the new millennium. After locating lifelong learning as a concept and practice that has had a number of reincarnations, I speak to its current economistic and instrumental iteration in policy circles, where educational and governmental interests are often made to fit global and corporate interests focused on sustaining the knowledge economy and improving information literacy and technology. In the wake of contemporary neoliberal forces, I emphasize the need for a critical practice of lifelong learning that would engage citizens in holistic instrumental, social, *and* cultural learning. In doing so, I speak to the importance of remembering history. I use the lens of the past as I consider the conceptualization and parameters of contemporary lifelong learning, and as I critique a discernible culture of learner and worker neglect in Canada. Considering the plight of Canadian young adults as an example, I provide critical reflection on federal government policy that abets privatization of lifelong learning and aggravates the situation of citizens as learners by blaming individuals for any failure in lifelong learning. I conclude with a perspective suggesting it may well be time for a critical (re)turn in Canadian adult education to help salvage lifelong learning as a formation and project of the social.

In chapter 4, I consider how the advent of a new millennium provided impetus to review and assess the cultural location and value of lifelong learning as a contemporary formation in different national contexts. I examine three international lifelong-learning events held in Australia, Canada, and the United Kingdom during 2000 and 2001. Each Y2K event broadly focused on conditions and complexities affecting learning for life and work in a neoliberal world. Through the dialogical lenses of these gatherings, which brought together an array of international participants, I examine lifelong learning as a chameleonic concept and versatile practice in education and culture. I consider how participants at the three events framed lifelong learning's parameters and complexities as they discussed perspectives and trends shaping lifelong-learning discourse, policy-making, and practice. In doing so, I discuss three pervasive themes: (1) lifelong learning encompasses instrumental, social, and cultural education; (2) lifelong learning involves mediation of public and private responsibilities; and (3) lifelong learning occupies a precarious and paradoxical position in a world that desires to position it as a permanent global necessity. Using a framework developed by British adult educator and cultural theorist Raymond Williams, I conclude the chapter with a perspective on lifelong learning as a critical practice in a world where culture as knowledge and culture as community vie for space. I locate this practice in inclusive, holistic terms, suggesting that a critical practice of lifelong learning is guided by a key aim: to help persons become responsive and responsible citizens who are able to think, speak, and act in life, learning, and work situations.

I continue to focus on lifelong learning in international contexts in chapter 5, highlighting the pervasive and invasive neoliberal policy consensus that has been driving lifelong-learning policy development globally, certainly since the 1990s. Within this consensus, the notion of citizens as commodities sidelines notions of citizens as social beings and cultural navigators. Against this backdrop, I continue to speak to the need to engage in lifelong learning as critical action as I compare the Canadian lifelong-learning policy culture to those found in Australia, New Zealand, the Republic of Ireland, and South Africa. I consider how lifelong learning has emerged in these nations amid a global neoliberal policy consensus. In doing so, I examine the institutionalization of lifelong learning in Australia, which has required universities to be adaptable in a neoliberal lifelong-learning milieu. I consider tertiary educational tensions between maintaining a liberal educational tradition and advancing learning for the knowledge economy. Next, I consider how the emergence of lifelong learning has followed a somewhat different trajectory in New Zealand. I explore how neoliberalism has impaired social inclusion and cohesion in that country, and I discuss the country's aberrant turn away from lifelong-learning policy throughout the 1990s, when other nations were knee-deep in its development. I then explore lifelong-learning policy culture in the Republic of Ireland where adult learning is the major focus. Here I consider the many challenges to social cohesion that the Irish Republic faces in the wake of the impact of neoliberalism. In a final comparison, I examine the lifelong-learning policy culture in South Africa, questioning why there wasn't a post-apartheid turn to a more critical and holistic form of lifelong learning in the country. I look at the work of South African scholars who have focused on bringing the critical to bear on lifelong-learning policy development and implementation. I end the chapter with a consideration of what ought to constitute lifelong learning as critical action as nations move beyond the current neoliberal policy consensus to link lifelong learning to a revitalization of the social, focused on making a better world.

In chapter 6, I locate lifelong learning and adult education as spaces that have historically excluded sexual minorities. To counter this exclusion, I argue that lifelong learning ought to be revised as a key component of cultural work for social transformation of those whose sexual and gender differences situate them as victims of a moral panic that finds expression as blatant heterosexism (the privileging of heterosexuality), homophobia (the fear of sexual differences), and transphobia (the fear of gender variation and expression). In the spirit of Horton and Freire (1990), who declared that we make the road by walking, I consider how sexual minorities engage in critical learning and action in both developed and emerging nations as they produce, exchange, and distribute knowledge of same-sex rituals and traditions, cross-gender role expressions, and non-heteronormative sexualities. This discussion permeates an exchange with educator and activist Robert J. Hill, which is the focus of this chapter. In this exchange, Hill tells me his stories from the field, exposing the longstanding exclusion of sexual and gender differences from policy-making, knowledge building, and setting the parameters of educational practice. In doing so, Hill locates international adult education as an exclusionary and problematic formation that is prone to systemic degradation of, and symbolic violence toward, sexual minorities. I draw on these stories and various examples of the contemporary global plight of sexual minorities to highlight the need to reform lifelong learning and adult education so they can become more inclusive educational formations that accommodate sexual minorities as historically marginalized and misunderstood global citizens who have a right to learn, a right to know, and a right to be safe, secure, visible, and involved. Here I consider how lifelong learning as critical action can be a site of resistance that assists sexual minorities by using queer public pedagogy to increase global awareness of ongoing persecution and genocide and to make a better world for us. I conclude the chapter with a discussion of the politics and pedagogy that could drive lifelong learning as critical action so it might advance sexual-minority inclusion and accommodation globally. I consider how these politics and pedagogy would engage participants in critical learning focused on being, becoming, belonging, and acting as constituents of an inclusive critical global citizenship.

I revisit the impact of neoliberalism on lifelong learning in the conclusion, beginning by discussing the vast economic debacle of 2008 and what it means for lifelong learning and its future directions. I consider how this global economic crisis unfolded amid a selfish politics of destruction and denial that shook neoliberalism and forced troubled nation-states to act as financial institutions crumbled and citizens experienced burgeoning debt loads and vulnerability in life, learning, and work. I also consider how recurring financial crises resulted in disorientation and uncertainty for markets, governments, and ordinary citizens. Here I ponder Alan Greenspan's perspectives on the emergence of the neoliberal economic model that contributed to what he calls an age of turbulence. I reflect on how this model has profoundly impacted lifelong learning for individuals across the lifespan. I then consider how, in this time of converging crises, we might reframe lifelong learning as critical action by emphasizing education for responsible citizenship. This would involve helping learners to become political change agents who build abilities and capacities to address local and larger needs, thus contributing to possibilities for global homeostasis. To demonstrate this kind of lifelong learning as critical action, I turn to history to explore the politics and pedagogy of Dr. Martin Luther King, Jr., whose notion of *conscience for change* captured his understanding of education for responsible citizenship. This historical reflection is followed by a look at possible futures for lifelong learning. I provide an overview of two recent major studies informative to constructing lifelong learning as critical action: the UK *Inquiry into the Future for Lifelong Learning* (Schuller & Watson, 2009), and the *Education for All Global Monitoring Report 2010: Reaching the Marginalized* (United Nations Educational, Scientific, & Cultural Organization [UNESCO], 2010). I conclude with a historical reflection on the 1996 Delors report, *Learning: The Treasure Within*, as I consider why lifelong learning for all remains to be achieved.

Question Critically

In the late 1990s, I was a SSHRC (Social Sciences and Humanities Research Council of Canada) post-doctoral fellow, studying with Dr. Henry A. Giroux, who at that time directed the Waterbury Forum for Education and Cultural Studies at Pennsylvania State University. Henry is currently the Global Television Network Chair in Communication Studies at McMaster University. During this personally transformative time, Henry nurtured my love for working with multi-perspective theorizing and mediating the tensions of juxtaposing critical and post-foundational ways of knowing and understanding the world. Henry taught me this valuable lesson: It is more important to know how to question critically than it is to have "the" answers. To question critically, as Henry sees it, is to raise key political and pedagogical questions that interrogate the phenomenon at hand and explore its meaning and value (Giroux, 1994). It is a way to (1) engage educators and learners in formal and personal theorizing, (2) encourage dialogue and deliberations in the classroom setting, and (3) promote a collaborative learning atmosphere. Engaged in questioning critically, the educator and learner co-teach and co-learn. I have always encouraged my students to question critically and to value their own theorizing as they build knowledge and understanding.

Extrapolating Giroux's perspective to question lifelong learning critically is to study power relations and how the culture of lifelong learning is shaped, produced, distributed, transformed, and, perhaps most importantly, taken up by learners within particular places and contexts. Thus, as you read this book, I encourage you to question critically as well. To get you started, here are some questions to help you set in motion the deliberative process of building knowledge and understanding of lifelong learning as a complex construct:

A turn to history helps us see how lifelong learning emerged in response to conditions and changes during a particular period.

- How does the turn to the history of lifelong learning in this book speak to the value placed on lifelong learning in different periods?
- When the two are compared, how does lifelong learning today differ from its earlier forms?

Consider lifelong learning in its historical and contemporary formations, as described in this book.

- With regard to instrumental, social, and cultural forms of lifelong learning, to what extent are knowledges and identities (re)produced in the intersection of ethical, political, and pedagogical considerations?
- What enables and what gets in the way of these productions being purposeful and meaningful?
- When is lifelong learning people-centred? When is it not?

Lifelong learning has had different forms and value over time.

- Based on your own lived and learned experience, what takes lifelong learning beyond something necessary to something valuable to you?
- How would you construct lifelong learning as an ideal formation, taking teaching, learning, and the content and form of pedagogy into account?

In contemporary times, there is a symbiotic relationship between neoliberalism as a theory and its everyday, pragmatic practice.

- How has neoliberalism shaped or contextualized lifelong-learning practices today?
- Who benefits and who loses is this process?

We can use contemporary problems to help us define lifelong learning as a multi-faceted educational project in the world today.

- Taking constructs such as culture, economics, ethics, language, agency, and power into account, what problems should we consider in shaping lifelong learning as a transformative process that could help us solve them?
- In shaping lifelong learning as a transformative process, what should we think about in political and pedagogical terms as we establish lifelong learning as a site for problem solving?
- What kinds of knowledge connected to life, learning, and work are needed to inform problem solving?
- What attributes and skills do learners need to be successful in this process?

As this book indicates, neoliberalized lifelong learning that advances economic interests has its own language to communicate what it means and what is expected to be a successful learner.

- Who is a successful learner in neoliberal terms?
- How might a successful learner be more broadly defined in keeping with a more holistic and inclusive understanding of lifelong learning that exceeds neoliberal limits?
- Working within their own language of critique and possibility, what elements might learners include in a checklist that indicates success in lifelong learning for social, cultural, and economic purposes?

Learning is more democratic when educators and learners share agency in developing curriculum and instruction.

- How might both educator and learner histories, experiences, and locations in the world be used to shape the form and substance of lifelong learning?
- Does sharing agency erode educator authority? If so, how? Does this matter?
- What matters more in shaping lifelong learning: an educator's authority or an educator's social responsibility?

Within an ecology of learning, the learning environment in which educators and learners interact also needs to be considered.

- If the learning environment is a site of struggle and resistance, what does it mean for constituents in the teaching-learning interaction?
- Is it too idealistic to situate a learning environment as a site of transformation where possibility is more important than pragmatic practice?

Representations of learners in this book indicate that today's lifelong learners constitute a multivariate population.

- What kinds of lifelong learners are being produced inside and outside of mainstream forms of lifelong learning today?
- What are some examples of learners shaping their engagement in lifelong learning through their own theorizing about their lived situations and experiences?
- What are some examples from this book, and beyond, of lifelong learning as a transformative practice and a counterpedagogy to the neoliberalized practice of lifelong learning?

Engaging in lifelong learning as an ongoing process, especially in the context of work, can be a form of cultural capital.

- How is that cultural capital delineated in neoliberal terms?
- Can one accrue cultural capital by engaging in social forms of lifelong learning? If so, how is it constituted?
- What kinds of cultural capital would learners from vulnerable populations seek to build to aid them in their struggles over issues of representation and belonging in education and culture?

Chapter 1

Positioning Citizens, Situating Contemporary Lifelong Learning

It's Tuesday, November 27, 2007. I am driving to Edmonton International Airport to attend a meeting of the National Advisory Group for the Adult Learning Knowledge Centre that operates under the auspices of the Canadian Council on Learning. The cab driver and I are chatting. He is glad that the snow has come a little later to the city this year. Despite the prospect of another harsh, cold Edmonton winter—locals speak about 30 days of 30 (°C) below—he feels we are lucky. He puts the weather in perspective as he talks about the extreme devastation and numerous deaths that Cyclone Sidr caused when it struck the southwest coast of Bangladesh (his country of origin) about two weeks earlier on November 15th.

The conversation turns, and we talk about the US-hosted Palestinian-Israeli peace summit happening in Annapolis, Maryland. We doubt that the summit's goal to create an independent Palestinian state living peacefully with the state of Israel will happen during our lives. We wonder if there will ever be an end to the conflicts in the Middle East and Afghanistan. The cab driver sighs, "This is the way of the world we know today." His words indicate a sense of hopelessness and helplessness, a sense that we cannot expect the world to get any better. As I silently reflect on his words for a moment, I worry that nihilism has become the common and familiar response to our daily witnessing of extreme violence and the unconscionable disregard for human life. How do we counter the nihilistic tendency that we all can have? We might begin by engaging in critical action that salvages hope and possibility as we mediate life, learning, and work in local and global contexts. As an educator, I see this as an urgent political and pedagogical task.

As the cab driver and I continue our chat, he tells me that he is deeply concerned about global survival. He doesn't talk about personal survival, although surviving and sustaining himself, and likely a family, were probably nestled somewhere in his thoughts, too. After all, driving a taxi in a growing oil city like Edmonton has become a dangerous proposition. It is common for taxi drivers to be assaulted and robbed; some have been murdered. It is also common for the faces of our cab drivers to be immigrant faces. Sadly, many have education credentials that are not recognized in Canada, so access and accommodation in Canada's workplaces are limited. Since the quality of a person's work life deeply impacts the quality of personal and family life, the possibilities for living a full, happy, and satisfying life are also limited. This, too, is the way of the world we know today, a world in which citizens are often precariously positioned as they face life, learning, and work predicaments.

This everyday quandary leaves me grappling with questions about the discourse of contemporary lifelong learning and how hope, healing, and possibility might be incorporated and revitalized through critical action within its parameters. It also leaves me very aware of the need to intersect social and cultural with instrumental considerations as we develop and implement lifelong-learning policy that will have true merit when it is implemented.

The Meaning of Lifelong Learning in Mediating Life and Work

Contemporary conceptualizations of lifelong learning and its constituents including adult education, and the degree to which the importance of educational enterprises is solidified in policy texts, new vocabulary, and everyday practice, are deeply influenced by (1) marketization, as constructed under neoliberalism and globalization; (2) the concomitant importance of knowledge societies as a predominant source of state and global wealth; and (3) supranational organizations including the Organisation for Economic Co-operation and Development (OECD) and the United Nations Educational, Scientific, and Cultural Organization (UNESCO) whose policy scripts emphasize learning in lifelong and lifewide contexts, with the primary goal of advancing economies (Wildemeersch & Salling Olesen, 2012). The importance of these supranational organizations in generating educational paradigms that shape policy-making and the language of learning is key in understanding the predominance of lifelong learning as a pervasive educational force, at least in policy and research circles in many nations in contemporary times. As Milana (2012) relates, these organizations work strategically, as entities and in dynamic interactions with member states, to position lifelong learning within "particular values, meanings and norms about the world that become accepted truths" (p. 106). Moreover, they decide and produce what they deem to be worthwhile and useful knowledge in order to legitimate particular political interests, set policy agendas, and sway nation-states to "rethink the relation between education, work and the economy by the production of 'global imaginaries' (with, however, nuanced meanings)" (Milana, 2012, p. 106). Within this lifelong-learning paradigm favouring education to enable economic interests, techno-vocational education is used to abet worker performativity, holding learners responsible for obtaining marketable skills while showing diminished concern for job security and protecting citizens as learners and workers (Milana, 2012). Within this neoliberal modus operandi, and recognizing that lifelong learning is adopted less by practitioners than by policy-makers and researchers, Milana (2012) points to another key concern: the focus on learner agency casts a shadow over the agency of the educator in the teaching-learning interaction as well as in wider educational relations, which has implications for the politics of education and, indeed, everyday living and working.

This focus on learner agency has been accompanied by a move from emancipation to empowerment in framing educational goals. A focus on emancipation, which found expression in Faure's 1972 report for UNESCO entitled *Learning to Be: The World of Education Today and Tomorrow*, is now replaced by a focus on empowerment, as conceptualized within a narrow focus on individuals, their capacity to learn and work and contribute to society as human capital, and their responsibility to be self-directed in learning to enhance this capacity amid the changes, dislocation, and instability wrought by marketization and globalization (Wildemeersch & Salling Olesen, 2012). This conceptualization of empowerment was evident in the OECD's 1996 report entitled *Lifelong Learning for All* (ibid.). In the period since, we have continued to see lifelong learning shaped within concerns for privatization and individual empowerment that abet learning to fuel economic progress. Wildemeersch and Salling Olesen suggest that this has put adult educators on the defensive as their field of study and practice is sidelined in the turn to lifelong learning. Still, they believe ideas of learning as lifelong and lifewide can create opportunities for adult education to engage in creative experimentation that revitalizes concern with public matters and public engagement:

> Adult education can contribute to such experiments by creating spaces, where education and learning are again connected to societal issues, under the inspiration of old and new values such as democracy, social justice, sustainability, free-

dom, responsibility, equality and solidarity. We assume that this contribution will not be located nicely within educational institutions and organizations, but will rather have their arena in workplaces, in local communities, in single-cause actions and the (new) social movements which have actually to some extent become mainstreamed in new broader concerns for environment, gender relations and social justice. (2012, p. 101)

In this book, I focus on the ways that lifelong learning and its constituents, including adult education, are connected to (or disconnected from) the mediation of life and work as they create learning spaces. I consider how learning and work, at least as they are predominantly constituted in instrumental terms and embedded in technological change and a burgeoning information society, have become inextricably linked. In the face of these dynamics, I speak to the need to emphasize the just and ethical treatment of citizens as they juggle learning, work, and other aspects of life in the face of neoliberalism, globalization, privatization, and other change forces that emphasize performance and productivity. I call for forms of lifelong learning that focus not only on learning for work, but also on learning for life and citizenship.

Lifelong learning needs this holistic composition so it can meet the diverse needs of citizens as they fulfill multiple roles that require learning for social, cultural, and economic purposes, as well as flexibility in the ways and means of learning. These purposes of learning need to be complementary so citizens can become more economically productive *and* socially engaged in order to make their communities and the world better. To increase its sum, lifelong learning ought to be about acknowledging learners' abilities and capacities, nurturing potential and possibilities, building respect and rapport, enhancing access and accommodation, and enabling learning to occur in a range of sites in the home, the workplace, and the community. There should also be recognition that formal education, which can help learners develop such hard skills as technical proficiency, is not enough. For example, the Canadian Council on Learning (CCL) (2008) points out that informal education can assist learners to build soft skills for work and life, such as skills to think critically and make decisions, solve problems, lead groups and engage in teamwork, communicate, adapt, and become entrepreneurial. The CCL maintains that this acquisition of soft skills can positively affect employment and income, job satisfaction, health and well-being, social inclusion, and political participation; still, "informal learning and the significance of its contribution are largely unrecognized by governments and employers" (CCL, 2008, p. 8).

The CCL's more encompassing view of lifelong learning finds parallel in Jarvis's (2007) conceptualization of lifelong learning. As he views it from a sociological perspective, lifelong learning ought to be broadly construed as human learning situated within conscious living:

> Lifelong learning ... [is] the combination of processes throughout a lifetime whereby the whole person—body (genetic, physical and biological) and mind (knowledge, skills, attitudes, values, emotions, beliefs and senses)—experiences social situations, the perceived content of which is then transformed cognitively, emotively or practically (or through any combination) and integrated into the individual person's biography resulting in a continually changing (or more experienced) person. (p. 1)

As we shall see in different examples in this book, this understanding of lifelong learning seems more ideal than real. Indeed, depending on the way it is constructed, lifelong learning may not always be a good thing. Burke and Jackson (2007) call on us to engage lifelong learning as a discursive formation and a site of struggle. This requires us to interrogate diverse constructed and contextualized conceptualizations and definitions of lifelong learning in relation to their meaning and value across relationships of power, and to consider whether particular constructions are socially inclusive, cohesive, accessible, and conducive to the participation of different publics. Burke and Jackson consider this analysis vital because contemporary mainstream lifelong learning as a field of study and practice has become grounded in neoliberal values and assumptions that undergird its exclusionary discourses. Within this hegemony, the subjective, the experiential, and the local are often downplayed in attempts to control and regulate global citizens within a politics of fear emphasizing risk and insecurity in the world today. They provide this description of the mainstream milieu: "In the current hegemonic discourses of lifelong learning, what counts as learning is bound up with particular middle-classed values and perspectives around the decontextualised individual learner: notions of citizenship that are tied in with lifelong learning; neo-liberal constructions of the flexible learner/worker; and learning that happens in the public rather than private sphere of social life" (p. 13). This positioning of lifelong learning raises questions about the meaning, value, and narrow politics of neoliberal discourse and practice. These politics focus on learners without fully considering matters of disposition, relationship, and context except for a frequent emphasis on worker performance related to economic productivity. This emphasis amounts to a focus on "have" learners in educational and economic terms that reduce active citizenship to ensconcing the neoliberal worker as a performer and a producer who primarily contributes to economies rather than communities. Burke and Jackson maintain that this limited neoliberal model of lifelong learning is ineffectual when it comes to conceiving how structural inequalities of power relationships like gender and sexuality function across life, learning, and work contexts. They conclude, "What counts as sensible, rational knowledge takes on legitimacy through a supposed hegemonic truth, yet remains contestable, partial and disempowering for all but dominant groups" (p. 17).

Exploring absences in neoliberal lifelong learning exposes its limits as a dispositional, relational, and integrative experience (Giroux, 2004; Newman, Couturier, & Scurry, 2004). In this regard, the hegemony of largely decontextualized learning for work should prompt us to engage in critical interrogation of what it entails. For example, we should question the place of individualized learning, which, in the instrumental terms advocated by neoliberalism, is usually reduced to matters of participation and pacing so that learners become skilled, performative, and productive. When learners buy into this neoliberal framework for engaging in learning, they, in effect, become part of a sociality preoccupied with credentialism and advancing in the workplace. They accept learning for work as core learning, as the raison d'être for participating in lifelong learning in the first place. However, if learners see lifelong learning as something more, as something with social and cultural as well as instrumental components, then, as individuals, they might experience some degree of dissonance. They may start to resist sole engagement in the decontextualized instrumental learning that they had formerly taken for granted as the learning they needed. The uncertainty and fear that often mark everyday learner experiences in the lifeworld in local and global contexts could prompt such dissonance and resistance. Jarvis (2007) contends that learners may react this way because they "are in a disjunctural situation or else ... [they] have no desire to conform to the expectations placed upon [them]" (p. 7) because they see the bigger picture. While this nonconformity can place individuals at risk and even subject them to censure, it attests to a human need to be agents with destinies that align with the sum of human learning and not just the instrumental component of it.

Taking a similar stance to Jarvis, Lambeir (2005) relates that contemporary lifelong learning is institutionalized and a permanent part of mediating learning for work; it is "a magic spell in the discourse of the educational and economic policymakers" (p. 350). As he sees it, there is synchronicity in the ways that economists and educators work: economists want a "more market oriented supply of courses" and many educators "stress the need to perceive learning as everyone's opportunity, and emphasize the importance of key qualifications, basic skills and primary knowledge" (ibid.). From these perspectives, citizens are supposed to see lifelong learning as a way to move forward when they want a better job and a way out when they are underemployed or unemployed. Lambeir summarizes neoliberalism's educational goal as learning your way toward new or better employment where you can function efficiently in the workplace and contribute to economies in local or larger contexts. He contends that much of this learning sidelines knowledge production and understanding, and emphasizes ongoing "training in information management" (p. 351). He asserts that the citizen's potential for success in work and respect in society depends on achieving in this instrumental learning context. Lambeir concludes that the citizen becomes "a public collection of competences" (p. 352), a commodity, a fabrication, an interchangeable and exchangeable entrepreneur, all of which reduce the learner to an investor and trader in the self.

This neoliberal constriction of learning tends to forget human integrity and our multiple subjectivities. It accentuates the need for lifelong learning to be something more if today's global citizens are to mediate lives in contemporary social and cultural contexts. In this regard, Jarvis (2007) calls for lifelong learning to be more broadly construed as learning that takes place not only in the workplace, but also in learning communities such as homes and volunteer organizations that comprise the lifeworld in local contexts. Moreover, he insists that lifelong learning needs to be located within a wider global context, one that is not necessarily aligned with the dominant neoliberal framework shaping learning within such supranational contexts as the OECD. This expanded view of lifelong learning is necessary in a world marked by rapid change and incessant social, cultural, political, and economic upheaval. There is a push for it from some quarters. For example, since 2004, the International Council for Adult Education (ICAE) has held four sessions of the ICAE Academy of Lifelong Learning Advocacy (IALLA): the first two in Norway (2004 and 2005), the third in Uruguay (2007), and the fourth in South Africa (2008) (International Council for Adult Education [ICAE], 2008). The aim of IALLA IV was to bring adult educators and social movement activists with leadership potential together to engage in a rigorous program focused on self-empowerment and skill acquisition so they could promote adult learning for active citizenship that advances civil society (ICAE, 2008). As the initiator of this residential project that advocates for adult learning, the ICAE (2008) has hoped to consolidate and indeed reinvigorate itself as a global network that revitalizes adult education as social education. This renewal, which nests adult learning and a focus on leadership within a framework of human rights and active citizenship, seeks to challenge the contemporary globalizing model. The ICAE describes this model as "characterized by economic uncertainty, population displacement, war, increasing fundamentalisms, the difficulties regarding multilateralism, and the greater interdependence in relation to all global policies unequally affecting the countries of the world. [Thus] there is a pressing need to rethink deeply and critically the educational proposals at formal and informal levels, for all ages" (2008, p. 3). In offering this challenge, it is important to remember an array of social themes including civil society in action, education as a basic human right, the rights to equality and difference, and the need to keep poverty and gender as central concerns in adult education and indeed in all education.

In another example focused on holistic learning, the Latin American and the Caribbean regional literacy and preparatory conference, which was held in Mexico City in September 2008 in the lead-up to CONFINTEA VI, the Sixth International Conference on Adult Education, produced a final report that paid great attention to the social and cultural contexts of lifelong learning in shaping learning to meet the challenges of the twenty-first century. Identifying *from literacy to lifelong learning* as the great learning challenge, this report proposed broader educational provision that included lifelong learning in family, community, work, media, and active citizenship contexts. It emphasized learning as social participation, and education as a fundamental human and civil right, and as a precursor to good health, well-being, material comfort, quality work, and civic participation. The report characterized the lifelong learner "as the subject of education, as someone who possesses singular and fundamental knowledge, who is a creator of culture, a protagonist of history, capable of producing the urgent changes necessary for building a more just society" (CONFINTEA VI, 2008, p. 1). The report advocated for popular and non-formal as well as formal kinds of education in the production of literate environments. It challenged the individualization of learning, maintaining that the concept of the lifelong learner as the subject of education "surpasses the individualistic vision of learning when it proposes the social construction of knowledge in learning communities which promote inter-cultural, inter-generational and inter-sectoral relationships" (p. 1). This emphasis on social learning, which is linked to cultural and instrumental learning, demands multinational equity in learning as a basis for worldwide social equity, prosperity, and peace. It sets a central task for globalization that requires its rearticulation in the years ahead.

A focus on holistic education that included social education was not universal in all preparatory work for CONFINTEA VI. In 2008, in joint planning for CONFINTEA VI, the US Commission for UNESCO and the US Department of Education released the *National Report on the Development and State of the Art of Adult Learning and Education*. In a review and critique of this report, Hill and his associates (2008) critiqued what they saw as its limited view of adult education. They asserted that the report was thin in substance in advancing the field of study and practice as a public good. Their analysis provides a basis for rethinking adult education as critically progressive social education that focuses on ethics, equity, and inclusivity in learning for life and work, as it positions the educator as advocate and the learner as agent (Grace, 2012). Here learning is viewed as an interactive and reflexive engagement in which participants think, study, and act as they build understanding of issues and engage in problem solving that links practice to policies that enable and enhance it. From this perspective, adult education supports democratic forms of education that attend to learner identities and differences within the ecology of relationships and environments that shape the learning process. In this way, adult education helps to achieve the public good. Hill and his colleagues (2008) provide this summary: Adult education as social education "assists learners in strengthening competencies to participate in political or policy processes, to identify problems, find and debate an array of solutions, and work together for social transformation" (p. 5). They add that the focus on social education can be encompassing, focusing on "popular education; social, economic, and political justice; equality of gender relations; the universal right to learn; living in harmony with the environment; respect for human rights; social justice; and recognition of cultural diversity, peace and the active involvement of women and men in decisions affecting their lives" (p. 30).

The neoliberal emphasis in mainstream lifelong learning remains pervasive in post-CONFINTEA VI progress reports such the Canadian report that the Council of Ministers of Education, Canada (CMEC) (2012) prepared with the assistance of Human Resources and Skills Development Canada and the Canadian Commission for UNESCO. In the Canadian progress report, the

CMEC emphasizes the important link between skill development and national economic progress: "The *Learn Canada 2020* declaration, [which defines lifelong learning,] ... recognizes the link between a well-educated population (for which adult education and literacy play an important part) and a socially progressive society and vibrant knowledge-based economy" (CMEC, 2012, pp. 1–2). Moreover, "the Government of Canada has made it a priority to ensure that Canada has the best-educated, most skilled, and most flexible workforce in the world" (p. 20). This goal puts lifelong learning on a trajectory emphasizing "productivity, competitiveness, [and] economic development" (p. 34). The CMEC even links social cohesion to producing "a well-trained and adaptive workforce" (p. 34).

In painting the larger picture of lifelong learning in Canada, the CMEC (2012) noted that the pan-Canadian definition of lifelong learning that encompasses learning across the lifespan is in keeping with UNESCO's perspective that the boundary between youth education and adult education is blurred in a lifelong-learning paradigm. In Canada's paradigm, there are four pillars of lifelong learning: early childhood learning and development, elementary and high school systems, post-secondary education, and adult learning and skills development. Within this national paradigm, the CMEC views adult education as an important constituent of lifelong learning. Interestingly though, the council notes that Canada has no official national definition of adult education or adult literacy. Moreover, and also problematically, the CMEC relates that there is unevenness in provincial and territorial approaches to adult learning and skill development: While all jurisdictions focus on youth, Aboriginal learners, the unemployed, and persons with disabilities, provinces and territories have been variously selective in focusing on the participation of immigrants, older adults, rural residents, and prisoners. With respect to addressing literacy and essential skills shortages among adults in the wake of CONFINTEA VI, the Government of Canada is promoting such approaches as "*innovation in the [adult-education] delivery method*—[that is,] innovative ways to forge multi-stakeholder approaches and create a sense of ownership among stakeholders, and creative ways of delivering the innovation by promoting participatory and interactive approaches" (p. 47, emphasis in original). The subtext here is that the success of this approach is dependent on the privatization of learning and the involvement of employers. The federal government, in true neoliberal form, is shifting its responsibility for the education of adults to stakeholders whom it sees as benefiting from a more educated and skilled workforce.

Lifelong Learning Now and in the Future

Any attempt to ensconce social and cultural learning as complementary to instrumental learning in future forms of lifelong learning across OECD countries will take tremendous commitment and effort. As demonstrated in chapter 4, since the 1990s the OECD has spearheaded various educational policy initiatives focused on lifelong and lifewide learning. However, hope, healing, and possibility have not been resounding themes in the pervasive instrumental focus framing lifelong-learning discourse during this period when a change culture of crisis and challenge has been prevalent globally. In this culture, it is perhaps more important than ever that lifelong learning help people learn their way out of predicaments in the many and varied spaces in which they live out diverse aspects of their lives. If the promise of lifelong learning is *lifelong learning for all* so that everyone has the opportunity to build a quality life in a better world (Delors, 1996), and if that promise is to be fulfilled, then citizens need to have access to sophisticated learning that includes more than the packaged instrumental learning that has been designed to enhance workplace performativity and productivity. While citizens do need instruction for work so they can put food on the table, they ultimately need to be treated as more than clients and consumers of cyclical, instrumental lifelong learning. They need to experience more broad-based lifelong learning that integrates instrumental, social, and cultural learning as it attends to matters of context, disposition, and relationship. This textured learning would aim to accommodate learners' wholeness and acknowledge their integrity as persons who have multiple subjectivities that are played out in diverse life and work contexts. In other words, citizens need to participate in holistic lifelong learning that is sensitive to the multiple needs they have in relation to the various ways they are located in the world.

Holistic lifelong learning, however, is far from a widespread reality. What we have generally experienced for some time now is more reductionistic lifelong learning with the imprints of neoliberalism, globalization, corporatism, privatization, and individualism that emphasize the economistic and the instrumental (Field, 2006; Giroux, 2004; Grace, 2005, 2007; Jarvis, 2007). This contemporary version of lifelong learning has generally sidelined concerns with the social and the cultural, instead of adequately exploring how these life contexts are embodied and embedded in people's ways of being, becoming, belonging, and acting in the world. Reductionistic lifelong learning commonly shapes non-formal and informal learning, especially in the context of learning for work. It has also become the shared purview of public education (schooling for children and youth), adult education in diverse institutionalized contexts, and higher education in colleges and universities. This suggests that contemporary lifelong learning is not the exclusive property of any one part of the discipline of education; workplace education or other learning venues cannot claim to own it either. Once upon a time, lifelong learning was viewed as a prerogative, a subset of, and a lifeline for adult education, as in the case of the emergence of North American adult education during the 1950s and 1960s (Grace, 2000b). However, this is not the case today. From a more global perspective, Jarvis (2007) contends, "Adult education, in its traditional sense, has begun to disappear as it has been replaced by lifelong learning. [This] reflects the changes that advanced capitalism has been demanding" (p. 63). This marginalization of adult education within lifelong learning is the reverse of a longstanding marginalization of lifelong learning within adult education, evident since 1919 when the Adult Education Committee of the British Ministry of Reconstruction declared that learning should be universal and lifelong (Grace, 2000b, 2005). Still the upshot in contemporary times is that lifelong learning may be emerging as the common thread that connects all learning in the diverse formal, informal, and non-formal spaces and contexts in which it now occurs. Thus it is all the more important that we conceive lifelong learning broadly in contextual and relational terms.

Whatever the future holds for lifelong learning, one thing is certain: Lifelong learning has become a large-scale international policy-and-practice phenomenon. This prevalence positions lifelong learning as a demanding and stressful endeavour that is seemingly omnipresent and unavoidable for many citizens. Still, what passes as lifelong learning is limited in focus. International organizations like the OECD, corporate interests, governments, educational institutions, and even many already educated citizens have predominantly and ardently linked lifelong-learning policy and practice to learning for work, economistic concerns, and the demands of neoliberal politics. With neoliberalism and other interlocking change forces such as globalization and corporatism ascendant, learning for work often appears asynchronous with the kinds of social and cultural learning required for the rest of life or, indeed, for coping with work itself. Moreover, lifelong learning construed in neoliberal terms is negligent in terms of providing access and accommodation to all citizens. This is despite the fact that today's global learning culture is purportedly preoccupied with the buzz phrase *lifelong learning for all* (Delors, 1996). While this phrase expresses the ideal, in reality it denotes a fiction as many citizens struggle amid a curious mixture of calamity and progress in our contemporary change culture of crisis and challenge. The following poetic vignettes help capture the way it is in this culture. They point to the need to engage in a politics and pedagogy of hope, healing, and possibility so we can all learn our way out.

Vignette One

Life
Long
Lifelong
Learning
A white-collar worker
Grabs a suppertime coffee at Starbucks
Before heading off to class at a nearby college
Got to be knowledgeable, skilled, flexible, and mobile
His little girl waits at home for her tired dad
Who spends another evening on the learning treadmill
Building credentials that will help make his work life better for now
Having quality time with family has to come second
And although he's getting ahead
He's still stuck
Mired in the instrumentalism that shapes his lifelong-learning venture
That's the way it is

Vignette Two

Life
Long
Lifelong
Learning
Another worker who is a single mom
Opts out of a stint on the learning treadmill
In an everyday where being a barista at Starbucks helps feed her daughter
One more little girl who waits at home for a tired parent
The single mom has no time to think about being more functionally
     employable

And no time to dream about engaging in quality work
She does not see lifelong learning as her panacea
Because she needs a more immediate way out
She's not getting ahead
She's stuck
Like so many undereducated people occupying the social underbelly
That's the way it is

And so the stories go. They are testimonials to the struggles that ordinary citizens face in today's neoliberal milieu in which greater emphasis is placed on engaging in more vocational and instrumental learning. The intended outcome of this learning is the production of a more knowledgeable, skilled, flexible, and mobile workforce that keeps nations competitive and the global economy strong. Citizens comprising this late capitalist workforce are expected to be more self-reliant, self-sufficient, entrepreneurial, and adaptable as they engage in continuous and often mandatory forms of instrumental lifelong learning. Amid a public to private shift in responsibility for lifelong learning that has been apparent globally under neoliberalism, they are also expected to take individual responsibility for their own learning and to assume the costs involved. These costs include personal overhead in terms of time, effort, money, and the negative impacts on their well-being. Citizens are also expected to take the blame when their engagement in lifelong learning goes awry or is unsuccessful. In this learning-and-work culture that ties knowledge and skills with most worth to performativity, productivity, and learning to advance national and global economies, many feel frustrated, inadequate, and never in sync. They may choose to drop out of what can be construed as an engagement in cyclical lifelong learning primarily focused on learning to keep up at work (Grace, 2007). For many citizens, such learning is perceived as constricting. While there have been times during the last century when lifelong learning was linked to lifewide learning that served broader civil as well as instrumental interests (Grace, 2000b, 2005), in contemporary times lifelong learning for economic purposes has tended to sideline and even subjugate learning for social and cultural purposes. Thus we need to investigate, indeed interrogate, the nature and meaning of lifelong learning. We need to think about how we can reconfigure and revitalize lifelong learning as an interactive and communicative instrumental, social, *and* cultural endeavour in which citizens are agents, acting with lifelong educators and other interest groups to impact the development and implementation of encompassing lifelong-learning policies and practices. The goal of lifelong learning should be to prepare citizens as learners for work *and* the rest of life as part of more holistic development. If it is to have meaning, value, and staying power in the lives of all citizens, then the concept and practice of lifelong learning should be rearticulated and revitalized to include a lifewide focus on building an informed and proactive citizenry that is proficient in learning not just for work, but for all of life.

Chapter 2

Learners' Quests to Live Full and Satisfying Lives

Lifelong learning in its policy-driven forms, developed and inadequately implemented since the 1990s (Field, 2006), has been a partial and primarily instrumental formation with projects predominantly driven by globalization, corporatism, deregulation, privatization, competition, individualism, and progress as defined within neoliberalism and its foci on performance, production, and economic output (Grace, 2006b). With so much at stake in the wake of the impact of these change forces on culture and communities, we cannot afford to view lifelong learning merely as some clinical mastering of knowledge, information, procedures, and skill sets that abet worker performativity and productivity. Contemporary times demand something more: an ecology of lifelong learning that locates learning for enhancing functional employability within a broader spectrum of learning for life and work in instrumental, social, and cultural contexts. Learning should focus on such factors as learner access, accommodation, and costs in terms of time, effort, and money; recognition of prior learning; learning for work; education for citizenship; demographic aspects such as geography and language; and representation, diversity, and inclusion (Adult Learning Knowledge Centre [ALKC], 2007; Kligman, 2003). These factors ought to be considered in a realm where ethics, equity, respect, and choice are intersecting and operative.

Sadly, such an ecological framework for lifelong learning is not predominant today. The contemporary formation of lifelong learning has generally focused on economistic and instrumental concerns, while usually treating social concerns in rhetorical terms that, at best, indicate symbolic rather than real or sustained interest in holistic learning for citizens (Grace, 2007). Shaped within the politics and public pedagogy of neoliberalism, contemporary lifelong learning upholds a key supposition: to advance the economic is to advance the social. This amounts to little more than feigned interest in the social since there is no guarantee of social progress, just the supposition that it will somehow happen as a domino effect in a growing economy. Neoliberalism's relegation of social progress to an effect of economic progress amounts to its abrogation of direct responsibility for the social. This is a key deterrent for citizens in their quest to live full and satisfying lives.

I begin this chapter with a conspectus or synopsis of the nature and meaning of neoliberalism. I consider how neoliberalism's ambition is embodied in globalization and corporatism as change forces that endorse privatization, instrumentalism, and individualism to serve the interests of Big Business and its subsidiary, Big Government. I explore the economic and social impacts of neoliberalism as a prelude to discussing how lifelong learning is positioned as a political and pedagogical project in a neoliberal world. Here I question whether contemporary lifelong learning is really a panacea or a problem for learners striving to live full and satisfying lives. I examine critiques of the pervasive perspectives and politics shaping lifelong learning and guiding (or misguiding) its development in social, cultural, and instrumental contexts. I then begin the book's central project: to position and frame *lifelong learning as critical action*. I provide an initial explanation and understanding of this concept and practice, exploring ways to think about lifelong learning in holistic terms that critically engage instrumental, social, *and* cultural education. I place emphases on ethics, diversity, inclusion, and the political ideals of modernity—democracy, freedom, and social justice. I also examine matters of context (social, cultural, economic, historical, and political factors affecting the development and implementation of lifelong-learning policy and practice); disposition (attitudes, values, and beliefs shaping lifelong learning); and relationship (how the ways in which individuals are located in demographic and geographic terms affect access and accommodation in lifelong learning). To make a case for engaging in lifelong learning as critical action, I consider examples of learners, including women and Aboriginal persons, who lack space and place in lifelong learning as a neoliberal fabrication. I also consider difficulties with the fluidity of lifelong learning as a concept and practice, the contemporary paradoxes marking the reality of lifelong learning, and the way lifelong learning is currently positioned as a mainstream cultural production. I conclude by speaking to the ubiquitous need of citizens to learn their way out.

The Ambition of Neoliberalism and the Corporatist Agenda
Neoliberalism: A Conspectus

Harvey's (2005) brief history of neoliberalism is useful for deepening our understanding of this ideology and the forces that have shaped what he calls "an emphatic turn toward neoliberalism in political-economic practices since the 1970s" (p. 2). During the 1970s, neoliberalism gained ground as an economic convention and a practical influence on public policy in the advanced capitalist world. While Harvey recounts that turbulence, such as that created by the world oil crisis, helped entrench neoliberalism during this time, he singles out two events in 1979 that were pivotal in advancing neoliberalism. First, Margaret Thatcher became British prime minister in May 1979, and immediately committed to a process of neoliberal economic reform that (1) favoured monetarism (the policy of controlling the money supply to keep the economic system viable), competitive flexibility, and other elements of economics as method; (2) touted the values of individualism, privatization, and personal responsibility; and (3) resulted in a dismantling of her country's social democratic state. Second, in October 1979, Paul Volcker, chair of the US Federal Reserve during Jimmy Carter's presidency, shifted monetary policy to address inflation regardless of the effect on employment, which was followed by a dramatic rise in interest rates, a major recession, high unemployment, great damage to unionism, and the growth of corporatism and an economic elite class.

Since then, as Harvey remarks, neoliberalism has "become hegemonic as a mode of discourse" (2005, p. 3); it is oppositional to embedded liberalism (which advocates public responsibility for the welfare of citizens) and the interventionist state. Harvey states that "neoliberalism has meant, in short, the financialization of everything," so that finance has infiltrated state structures and all areas of the economy (2005, p. 33). As discussed in chapter 5, even old-guard social democracies and welfare states such as New Zealand and emerging nations with dire social needs such as post-apartheid South Africa have been contained by neoliberalism. This speaks to the power of neoliberalism's global ambition to liberate the economic from the social, which has led to an economic arrangement, often broadly referred to as globalization that dissolves time and cuts unevenly across geography. Harvey explains: "The uneven geographical development of neoliberalism, its frequently partial and lop-sided application from one state and social formation to another, testifies to the tentativeness of neoliberal solutions and the complex ways in which political forces, historical traditions, and existing institutional arrangements all shaped why and how the process of neoliberalization actually occurred" (2005, p. 13).

As a project that links its pragmatic intentions to ensuring the compliance of citizens, neoliberalism locates the liberation of the economic as the liberation of the individual. From this perspective, Harvey locates neoliberalism as an invasive political project that advocates for strong private property rights, free markets, and free trade. Concomitantly, this economic convention works to reduce state power and influence, limiting the role of the state to setting up and sustaining an institutional framework to abet neoliberalism. The purpose of this framework, as Harvey explains, is to advance the economic using such controls as monetarism and legal, military, and other structures. This affects education in forms such as lifelong learning because the market is expected to infiltrate societal sectors such as education, which are expected to function in ways that enable economic progress. Indeed, "advocates of the neoliberal way now occupy positions of considerable influence in education (the universities and many 'think tanks') and in media, corporate, financial, state, and other sectors" (Harvey, 2005, p. 3). This infiltration aligns with neoliberalism's core belief and its central goal: "The social good will be maximized by maximizing the reach and frequency of market transactions, and it seeks to bring all human action into the domain of the market" (ibid.). Here neoliberalism strongly relies on information technologies to achieve this goal. However, as Harvey points out, there are contradictions inherent in the process of neoliberalization. For example, he notes that neoliberalism's theoretical and political commitment to the ideal of individual freedom is not synchronized with a neoliberal reality that binds citizens in particular ways in learning, work, and other spheres. He also notes that neoliberalism espouses distrust of state power, yet depends on a coercive state to help it to achieve its goals. In light of these contradictions, Harvey calls on us to investigate the tension between neoliberalism as a theory and neoliberalization as a pragmatic practice. He explains: "The process of neoliberalization has ... entailed much 'creative destruction,' not only of prior institutional frameworks and powers (even challenging traditional forms of state sovereignty) but also of divisions of labour, social relations, welfare provisions, technological mixes, ways of life and thought, reproductive activities, attachments to the land and habits of the heart" (ibid.).

Neoliberalism then is a political philosophy that gives primacy to free-market forces as it calls for more private and less public investment to develop individuals and communities in local, national, and global contexts. As a way of viewing progress, neoliberalism insists that economic progress begets social progress, thus apparently reducing the need for nation-states to be welfare states. However, criticalists and others who scrutinize what is happening in culture and society oppose the politics of neoliberalism that seem to forget ethics, equity, and other elements of social democratic progress. They argue that the larger public good and the political ideals of modernity are not primary concerns of neoliberalism as it frames processes in education and other institutions. In a period when corporatism is ascendant (Klein, 2007), criticalists maintain that neoliberalism economically expressed as globalization utilizes privatization, instrumentalization, and individualization as cultural change forces to regulate learning and work. In this regard, they critique globalization as an exclusionary phenomenon that forgets certain individuals who are unable to fulfill their duties as consumers (Bauman, 2005; Jarvis, 2007). In wealthy countries this casts the uneducated, the undereducated, the unemployed, and the underemployed as social outlaws in a consumer society they lack the capital to navigate. In much of the global South, it leaves the poorest citizens with little hope for a better future. Jarvis (2007) blames transnational corporations for this global tragedy, declaring that they build great wealth and power at the expense of disparate creations: a consumer society and a poor world underclass.

As a way out for the world's marginalized citizens, lifelong learning has limitations since globalization has fundamentally positioned it as an economic expression of neoliberalism. Still, globalization itself is much more complex than its economic preoccupation. Pointing to multiple uses and conceptualizations of the term, Jarvis (2007) helps us to understand globalization in terms of its broader contemporary political, cultural, and economic complexity, which can be linked to possibilities for more encompassing lifelong learning. While he notes that economic competition (the market) is at the heart of the global substructure, he offers an expanded definition of globalization from a neo-Marxian perspective. He suggests that a current conception of globalization as courses of action eroding the power of nation-states has to consider both economic institutions (predominantly transnational actors) and technology (including information technology) as core driving forces. As he puts it, "While capital might provide the motive for the sub-structural domination, it is the technology that provides the means through which it is achieved" (p. 57). This has implications for lifelong learning, as technology and information technology have become its movers and shakers. Jarvis also suggests that global power lies with those who control these various driving forces, making globalization a persistent socio-technological trend with far-reaching political and cultural implications. He provides this expanded explanation:

> Globalisation has at least two main elements: the first is the way that those who have control of the substructure in the countries of the dominant West, especially America, have been enabled to extend their control over the substructures of all the other countries in the world, and consequently over their structures and resources; the second is the effects that these substructural changes are having on the superstructure of each society since the common substructure means that similar forces are being exerted on every people and society despite each having different histories, cultures, languages, and so on. (p. 43)

As Jarvis sees it, globalization interwoven with imperialism expressed as Americanization has become a powerful contemporary change force. While he acknowledges that it is difficult to tease out the relationship between US imperialism and globalization (and embedded transnationalism), he concludes, "It is clear that the two work hand in glove in many things" (p. 41). He adds, "American imperialism upholds and supports the socio-technological substructure to such an extent that I would argue that it has become part of it, but that this is but a temporary phase in the development of the world" (pp. 41–42).

The Individual in the Neoliberal Mix

With neoliberalism lauding individualism in relation to citizens' performativity and productivity, criticalists contend that its politics switch responsibility for success in learning and work from the public to the personal/private domain. Giroux (2004) explains how neoliberalism functions as a corporatized discourse that instigates not only economic changes, but also deep-seated changes in cultural politics:

> Public pedagogy in this sense refers to a powerful ensemble of ideological and institutional forces whose aim is to produce competitive, self-interested individuals vying for their own material and ideological gain. The culture of corporate public pedagogy largely cancels out or devalues gender, class-specific, and racial injustices of the existing social order by absorbing the democratic impulses and practices

of civil society within narrow economic relations. Corporate public pedagogy has become an all-encompassing cultural horizon for producing market identities, values, and practices. (p. 106)

As a corporatized discourse, the ambition of neoliberalism, as criticalists see it, is to use economic power to condition and control the individual and the social. Giroux contends that the economic and cultural logic of neoliberalism "both consolidates economic power in the hands of a few and aggressively attempts to break the power of unions, decouple income from productivity, subordinate the needs of society to the market, and deem public services and goods an unconscionable luxury" (p. 105). In this assault on the social, Giroux declares that neoliberalism nurtures popular cultural cynicism, hopelessness, insecurity, despair, and political malaise and withdrawal: "The project of democratizing public goods has fallen into disrepute in the popular imagination as the logic of the market undermines the most basic social solidarities" (p. 105). This nihilism in the public sphere, as Giroux asserts, is conveyed in the "sense of powerlessness that accompanies the destruction of social goods, the corporatization of the media, the dismantling of workers' rights, and the incorporation of intellectuals" (p. 84). These outcomes are signifiers of a neoliberal change culture of crisis and challenge. Bauman (2005) asserts that liquid life in a liquid modern society marks this culture:

> "Liquid modern" is a society in which the conditions under which its members act change faster than it takes the ways of acting to consolidate into habits and routines.... Liquid life [in this society] is a precarious life, lived under conditions of constant uncertainty. The most acute and constant worries that haunt such a life are the fears of being caught napping, of failing to catch up with fast-moving events, of being left behind, of overlooking "use by" dates, of being saddled with possessions that are no longer desirable, of missing the moment that calls for a change of tack before crossing the point of no return. (pp. 1–2)

The subtext here is that living a liquid life in the face of neoliberalism is primarily a problem for "have" citizens seeking to live a full and satisfying life. Indeed, the worries that Bauman links to living a liquid life remain largely unknown to the uneducated, the undereducated, the unemployed, and the underemployed who deal with more basic stressors related to subsistence in a neoliberal change culture of crisis and challenge. Since exclusion from mean-

ingful lifelong learning is their more common experience, they are more concerned with such fundamental issues as having access to useful learning and
being accommodated in institutional contexts in keeping with their life situations. This is because economistic lifelong-learning discourse and practice
have paid insufficient attention to those disenfranchised in life, learning, and
work contexts.

Mutant Neoliberalism and the Disposability of the Social

In a provocative reading of the contemporary corporatist agenda, Klein (2007)
argues that neoliberalism's battering of the social is only getting worse. She
makes the case that a doctrinaire mutation of neoliberalism has used what
she calls *disaster capitalism* to abet economic progress for more than three
decades. Klein asserts that disaster capitalism has equated catastrophes such
as the US invasion of Iraq with market opportunities. She states that these opportunities become realities through extreme social and economic engineer-
ing predicated on calculated assaults on the public sphere in times of fear and
turmoil. Klein refers to the strategy used as remedy under disaster capitalism
as the *shock doctrine*. It involves "three trademark demands—privatization,
government deregulation, and deep cuts to social spending" (p. 10). Enacting
the shock doctrine or "economic shock therapy" (p. 11) has entailed "waiting
for a major crisis, then selling off pieces of the state to private players while
citizens were still reeling from the shock, then quickly making the 'reforms'
permanent" (p. 7). Klein credits the articulation of this "core tactical nostrum"
(p. 7) to Milton Friedman who, until his passing in 2006, was a long-time
defender of deregulated capitalism and unfettered free markets as democratic
lifelines. He "believed history 'got off on the wrong track' when politicians began listening to John Maynard Keynes, intellectual architect of the New Deal
and the modern welfare state" (p. 20). Friedman's version of unbending neoliberalism that is designed to advance purist capitalistic ambitions amounts to
corporatism. The "political trinity" of corporatism, which is about melding Big
Government and Big Business, is "the elimination of the public sphere, total
liberation for corporations, and skeletal social spending" (p. 17). The disaster
in this remedy for catastrophe is the disposability of the social as it relates to
individuals, communities, connectedness, social history, and the need to be
rooted in place. All these social elements are integral to an ecology of lifelong
learning focused on being, becoming, and belonging. Thus the disposability

of the social leads to disaster lifelong learning. Unfortunately, the disposability of the social is inevitable in a corporatist reformation that privatizes war
and disaster, promoting a deceptive process of "'reconstruction' [that begins]
… with finishing the job of the original disaster by erasing what was left of
the public sphere and rooted communities, then quickly moving to replace
them with a kind of corporate New Jerusalem—all before the victims of war
or natural disaster were able to regroup and stake their claims to what was
theirs" (p. 10). This is the modus operandi of a modern-day "'disaster capitalism complex'" (p. 14). As Klein sees it, neoliberals placed the instrumental
value of this complex at par with the economistic elevation of information
technology during the 1990s. Possibilities for lifelong learning as a social venture were lost in this mix.

It can certainly be argued that the shock doctrine and the politics of disaster capitalism have been in play in the midst of the devastation in Iraq since
the early 1990s. McQuaig (2007) relates, "Amid all the death and mayhem, the
Iraqi government … [was] under intense pressure from Washington to implement a proposed new law that would begin the process of parcelling out Iraq's
vast undeveloped oil reserves" (p. 42). McQuaig contends that the Western
spin on this purported oil revenue-sharing law presents it as a blueprint for
ostensibly splitting Iraq's potentially huge oil revenues among its three warring
ethnic groups: the Shiites, the Sunni Arabs, and the Kurds. However, resolving
oil revenue sharing to the benefit of Iraq's 27 million, mostly impoverished
citizens does not appear to be a predominant concern. According to McQuaig,
the proposed law was also about a much larger corporatist concern: "creating
a legal framework for foreign investment in Iraq's oil sector, thereby potentially reviving a dominant role for big multinational oil companies—a role they
have been excluded from since a powerful wave of oil nationalism swept the
Middle East in the 1970s and left the region's bounteous reserves in the hands
of national governments" (p. 42). While the nationalistic fervour of Iraq's citizens, including the Iraqi oil workers' union, translated into recognized intense
resistance to Washington's plan, McQuaig notes that the United States only
saw such resistance as an obstacle that they and Big Oil would overcome. In
the quest to control the world's oil reserves, which is inextricably linked to
dominance in the functioning of the global economy, US imperialism is wed
to the corporatist ambition of Big Oil to ravage a nation, without regard for the
consequences for its largely poverty-stricken population.

In sum, Klein (2007) positions corporatism as a fundamentalist form of purist capitalism that is dangerous to the security of many citizens and the viability of the public sphere. She argues that disaster capitalism depends on tragedy to create the kind of clean slate that gives corporatism its footing. However, she insists that it does not have to be this way.

> It is eminently possible to have a market-based economy that requires no such brutality and demands no such ideological purity. A free market in consumer products can coexist with free public health care, with public schools, with a large segment of the economy—like a national oil company—held in state hands. It's equally possible to require corporations to pay decent wages, to respect the right of workers to form unions, and for governments to tax and redistribute wealth so that the sharp inequalities that mark the corporatist state are reduced. Markets need not be fundamentalist. (p. 24)

Denmark provides a case in point. It is an example of a market-based economy where the public good and attending to social needs are still prioritized. This Scandinavian country boasts one of the highest standards of living in the world, has a far more equitable distribution of per capita income than the United States, and has low unemployment (Fox, 2007; Kiviat, 2007). Each year the World Economic Forum (WEF) ranks the economic competitiveness of nations; that is, the economic position of a country in relation to the productivity of its businesses and its ability to attract outside businesses and investment (Kiviat, 2007). According to the WEF's *Global Competitiveness Report*, Denmark was the third-most competitive economy among the 131 nations ranked in 2007 (Fox, 2007). Still, Denmark is the antithesis of a corporatist nation such as the United States (ranked first). It has "the second highest tax burden in the capitalist world (after Sweden, which is just behind it in the competitiveness rankings), a generous welfare state, a heavily unionized workforce, and at least five paid weeks off every year" (Fox, 2007, pp. 48–49). Still, as Fox (2007) relates, the Danes have managed to create a business-friendly country in which workers have financial security. The Danish way of being competitive challenges the corporatist rhetoric, repeated like a mantra in the United States, which says long hours, low taxes, and minimal government are the keys to economic productivity (ibid.). Ultimately, what the Danes have shown is that governments can be responsive, responsible, accountable, and contributing. They can be role models for workers whom they expect to acquire the same traits.

Of course, the contemporary erosion of the social is indeed more complex than Klein's shock doctrine allows. Not all catastrophes, whether natural or contrived, are marked by suddenness, swiftness, or even unpredictability, as Klein's theory of disaster capitalism requires. Indeed, in some cases we can say that we could see the disaster coming. For example, the issue of urban growth and associated poverty on a global scale did not appear overnight. Quirk (2007) projected 2008 as a watershed year as, for the first time, city dwellers would outnumber those living outside of urban areas. He has linked this global shift to skyrocketing poverty that neoliberalism, in forms such as corporatism, lacks both the inclination and ability to address. He relates that the disaster of escalating poverty, predictable when the economic has the social in a neoliberal stranglehold, is perhaps most apparent in cities in developing nations:

> According to the United Nations Population Fund, the cities of Africa and Asia will double in population between 2000 and 2030, and the poor will continue to flow into shantytowns. Worldwide, the number of slum dwellers has grown from 715 million in 1990 to roughly a billion today, and it's expected to hit 1.4 billion by 2020. When we think of typical poverty or a typical city, we should no longer think of thirsty villagers or Chicago's skyscrapers, but a squatters' settlement. (p. 32)

Still, as Quirk points out, there is an interesting paradox related to cities and poverty: Even though poverty is more intense and visible in urban settings, migration from the countryside into cities in poorer countries seems to curb poverty. Urbanization appears to have its advantages, a variable worth more study and deliberation in lifelong-learning research and policy circles. Quirk also notes that attempts to prevent slum growth as an outcome of contemporary urbanization tend to harm citizens and economies and worsen social conditions in slums. Since growth in the number of city dwellers seems inevitable, Quirk proposes that we heed suggestions in the UN report, *State of World Population 2007*: "Countries serious about slowing the growth of their cities without trapping their citizens in poverty might try a method more effective than demolishing shantytowns. Over half of city growth now comes from natural increase—births less deaths—not from migration.… The best antidote to the ills of urban crowding, over the long term, might be a new emphasis on education, contraception, and women's rights" (Quirk, 2007, p. 33). Here lies an opportunity for lifelong learning as a lifewide venture to engage in a project of social learning to help citizens deal with the ecology of urban sprawl and counter the growing poverty and itinerant communities that have become characteristics of cities in contemporary times. In dealing with this ecology, a focus on women and their rights, including reproductive rights, is crucial.

Lifelong Learning in a Neoliberal World: Panacea or Problem?

It seems logical to present lifelong learning as a way out for citizens as learners and workers. After all, education and re-education—"instilling in the learners new kinds of motives, developing different propensities and training them in deploying new skills" (Bauman, 2005, p. 12)—are still located as panaceas for liquid life-and-work dilemmas. In this regard, Bauman leaves us with an important question: "But will the education and the educators fit the bill?" (p. 12). Perhaps they will not, especially when it comes to meeting the needs of the disenfranchised. If educators find it hard to move beyond the parameters of their own liquid life and perhaps contracted labour, and if the needs and desires of disenfranchised citizens puzzle and confuse them, then maybe the kind of lifelong learning they would provide is not the answer. Why would citizens as learners want to participate in contemporary lifelong learning if it is constructed as a largely info-instrumentalized wasteland that is no longer "a space in which politics is pluralized, recognized as contingent, and open to many formations" (Giroux, 2004, p. 111)? As a corporatist project, such learning, shaped by neoliberal politics and buoyed by the economistic, erodes the idea of a learning society and the social cohesion it could advance. Speaking to this, Jarvis (2006) relates that although the terms *lifelong learning* and the *learning society* have become mainstays in the discourse focused on occupational knowledge, learning for work, and enhanced professionalism, both "are used rather loosely and imprecisely" (p. 205). There is also the presumption that they refer to something good. Jarvis adds, "Since learning carries with it a connotation that it is good and desirable and something that leads to human growth and development, discourse about the learning society has acquired a misleading value orientation—that the learning society is intrinsically a good thing" (ibid.).

With the social expected to come in the back door in neoliberalized lifelong learning, those who need more holistic and embodied learning experience dislocation. From this perspective, it may indeed be time to frame lifelong learning as critical action so citizens can engage in encompassing learning for life _and work._ Certainly, as Jarvis (2000) insists, it is time to return to a more critical analysis of what passes as education these days and what would constitute ethical and valuable lifelong learning. This analysis has to interrogate corporatized learning models in which citizens as learners and workers are valued only if their learning leads to new innovations, new knowledge, and new applications of knowledge. In this regard, Jarvis maintains that much praise of the benefits of continuous training and development actually reduces the idea of education. He challenges us to problematize lifelong-learning policy development and implementation in relation to the options and freedoms that learners have when making choices and decisions in learning engagements. He also challenges us to examine the circumstances under which learning occurs, and to consider who controls the learning in which we engage. In sum, Jarvis wants us to engage in lifelong learning as critical action and involve citizens as learners in a holistic, ethical practice that is "really about lifelong learning and not work-life learning (however important that might be), about people and not profits, about enriching people rather than utilizing human resources, [and] about responding to needs and not meeting targets" (2000, p. 26).

We might begin this engagement with lifelong learning as critical action by asking citizens as learners to join us in investigating "how the very processes of learning constitute the political mechanisms through which identities are shaped, desires mobilized, and experiences take on forms and meaning within those collective conditions and larger forces that constitute the realm of the social" (Giroux, 2004, p. 113). This would locate lifelong learning as a political engagement that weds critical learning to social responsibility (Giroux, 2004). Too much lifelong learning, even when it is well intentioned, is status quo learning devoid of the kind of interrogative political process that Giroux suggests should drive it. For example, this absence is evident in the model of citizenship education that Frideres (1997) designed to develop immigrant capacity and opportunity to participate as citizens of a community and country. In this model he lists participation, awareness, skills, and knowledge, which he reduces to the ingredients required to maintain the status quo, as key dimensions of civic involvement. He indicates that the most common setting for civic involvement is community organizations in which geography and voluntarism intersect to identify local problems and determine public initiatives to address them. Frideres believes this involvement in civil society benefits citizen, community, and nation through interpersonal and interactive problem solving related to an array of social issues including community service delivery, health education, crime prevention, and mental-health service delivery. While such a grassroots focus ought to be good, it can be problematic when it omits emphases on the emergence of larger cultural politics and changes in law and legislation that affect degrees of diversity and inclusion in the immigrant's new nation. Thus, what Frideres misses is a focus on the political nature of citizenship education and the power of mitigating circumstances. Pagé (1997) counters that Frideres' social/civil emphasis, though praiseworthy, needs to be coupled with a political emphasis in the design of citizenship education. Pagé offers this overview of more encompassing citizenship education intended to go beyond abetting the status quo:

> Knowledge which should be acquired [includes] knowledge which can be described as instrumental, on the one hand, indispensable to exercising civic rights and duties—knowledge of government and social institutions, of laws and the parliamentary (or presidential) system; as well as knowledge required to analyze and understand current social realities.... [On the other hand,] citizenship education should not only inform newcomers about the host society's institutions, values and democratic principles, [but] it should [also] make all students aware of the legitimacy of diversity, obstacles to integration and the existence of racism and discrimination. (p. 56)

Such lifelong learning has an ethical heart when participants, including instructors, recognize its political nature, and the power and interests at play that affect the locatedness, agency, and investments of both instructors and learners. Attending to political concerns is essential if lifelong learning is to be an equitable and socially relevant engagement with democratic possibilities for enhancing citizenship. Bagnall (2006) highlights the issue of social relevancy when he calls on us to interrogate the degree to which lifelong learning is a socially responsive and even-handed endeavour attentive to the ethics of individual and institutional involvement. He suggests casting lifelong learning as a social theory to enhance individual and social character by emphasizing the importance of making an informed commitment: "[This is] a commitment to constructive engagement in learning; a commitment to oneself and one's cultural inheritance; to others and their cultural differences; to the human condition and its potential for progress; to practical reason and its contribution to bettering the human condition; to individual and collective autonomy; to social justice; to the non-violent resolution of conflicts; and to democratic governance" (p. 259).

Women as Citizens, Learners, and Workers

In an encompassing critical feminist analysis, Mojab
gnant example of citizens living out much of Bagnall'
mitments as she explores Kurdish immigrant wome
to become resettled learners and workers with the rights of full citi...
in their adopted countries. Mojab turns to Mohanty's theorizing to help her
demonstrate the complexity of these struggles. She locates her analysis in historical materialism and a dialectical examination of the local and micropo-
litical (attending to subjectivity, context, and resistance) and the global and
macropolitical (attending to the global economy and systemic issues arising
from political structures and processes). Mojab argues that "we can unravel
ideological and social relations embedded in *lifelong learning* when we engage in a multilevel analysis of this concept through the lived experiences of
learners, in particular marginalized women" (p. 164, emphasis in original).
She also argues that neoliberalism, despite its apparent drive to privatize and
reduce state influence, actually depends on the state to uphold its interests: "A
strong interventionist state is needed by advanced capitalism, particularly in
the field of education and training—in the field of producing an ideologically
compliant and technically skilled workforce" (p. 165).

Yet, as Mojab demonstrates, providing job training and citizenship education to Kurdish immigrant women was hardly a seamless process of engaging
passive and similar learners. These women, through their experiences of war
and diaspora, have a history of engaging in strategic, distinctive, and informed
learning linked to a situated politics of survival, struggle, resistance, hope, and
healing. Since, as Mojab stresses, this history usually goes unrecognized in
diaspora, the immigrant women faced challenges and uneasiness as they me-
diated their learning against ever-present histories of war and conflict, and
memories of overt physical and symbolic violence in their countries of origin
(Turkey, Iran, Iraq, and Syria). Moreover, lifelong learning in diaspora meant
sorting out new contexts, new contingencies, and new forms of physical and
symbolic violence. A clinical, instrumental view of lifelong learning would not
work for Kurdish immigrant women because of the diverse ways that they
are positioned in diaspora. Mojab emphasizes how important it was to engage the women in dialogue and listen to them so she could work with them
to interrogate conceptions, assumptions, and matters of context, contingency,
disposition, and relationship that placed limits on the utility of contemporary

dard-brand lifelong learning. This dialogic interaction helped Mojab to understand how Kurdish immigrant women have been isolated, racialized, and culturalized in lifelong learning that has not been emancipatory for them. Mojab's work highlights the importance of informing lifelong-learning policy and practice through communicative action that draws on the knowledge and insights of a diverse group of participants who have particular needs, concerns, aspirations, and desires. These citizens as learners and workers need to be positioned as knowledgeable partners and agents who can contribute to the strategic work of creating and enacting viable lifelong-learning programs that attend to the kinds of socio-cultural and instrumental learning they need to move them beyond low-level training and mundane work.

Mojab's research demonstrates the importance of placing emphases on education and women's rights, which, as noted earlier, Quirk suggests is central in dealing with new phenomena such as predominant urbanization. Women remain second-class citizens in so many global jurisdictions where they still lack the privileges of full citizenship. Despite more than a century of waves of feminism, the power of patriarchy has yet to be toppled. Can engagements in lifelong learning help? Blackmore (2007) relates that, in general, lifelong learning for women has been construed as a foundation for gaining employment and building individual success, agency, well-being, and full democratic citizenship within a seamless dynamic that intersects education, training, work, and home. However, much of this conception of lifelong learning is tied to patriarchal, neoliberal values that put barriers to reaching their desired potential in the way of women. Blackmore provides this gendered interpretation of lifelong learning as a powerful idea and seductive discourse and process: "The discourse of LLL [(lifelong learning)] is appealing to women educators and managers, themselves high achievers in LLL, seeking to improve women's opportunities through LLL and to promote social change. The logic of the discourse is seductive and difficult to refute. LLL is a powerful discourse because it penetrates to the soul of educational work about self-improvement, while making individuals more self-managing of their own LLL" (p. 14).

The subtext here is lifelong learning is more the purview of educated, Western women who are pragmatically expected to buy into individualism and its emphases on self-improvement and self-directed learning so they can be citizens who contribute to economies and, consequently, to communities. While lifelong learning ought to benefit all women across cultures and societies, Blackmore tells us that many women still lack minimum educational credentials. Moreover, she points out that women who participate in lifelong learning find it does not provide an even playing field in terms of the outcomes of engaging in learning: internationally, women still lag behind men in terms of rewards and benefits accrued. This indicates that lifelong learning is not the panacea that the rhetoric about deliverance (read as enabling economic prosperity and social cohesion) suggests. Disenfranchisement and dislocation still mark the life-and-work realities of many women. Moreover, many women are left out of lifelong learning altogether.

The promise of lifelong learning as a holistic, democratizing, empowering, and inclusive idea, discourse, and process remains to be fulfilled. Individual integrity and homeostasis that abet satisfaction and well-being are still not guaranteed in learning that predominantly focuses on work. It is from this perspective that Blackmore interrogates contemporary lifelong learning that is mainly about the upskilling and training of workers who are expected to become more flexible, mobile, and able to accommodate to serial jobs. This neoliberal formation of lifelong learning has been "mobilised at a time when education is now delivered through a complex set of contractual, consensual, competitive, and cooperative arrangements, bewildering for both providers and users alike in their multiplicity, contradictions and array of choices" (p. 14). She concludes, "The discourses of LLL and how they are mobilised with particular subjects in mind, whether 'at risk' youth, middle managers, or women not in paid work, cannot be de-contextualised from the cultural and structural re-formation of the education-work nexus during the past two decades in most Western nation states" (p. 2). In strengthening the education-work connection, these Western nation-states have not relinquished control, which is contrary to the neoliberal design to minimize state presence and privatize learning and work. Indeed, nation-states probably exercise even greater control over what and how citizens currently learn. Within the present politics of state involvement, learning is government regulated to ensure corporate interests are considered so both business and industry perpetuate their investment in national economies. Blackmore provides this assessment:

> Paradoxically, while there is a desire by government [in many Western nation states] to divest responsibility in provision of education and training, there has been a push to introduce and re-regulate private and public providers.... LLL providers, informally connected during the 1970s and 1980s, are now governed through national frameworks of certification and accreditation ... and converg-

ing modes of curriculum "delivery." ... Informal education has been replaced by multiple gradations of certification. Yet certification can mean fewer benefits in terms of accessing employment due to the rise of credentialism, while options for informal and nonformal education are reducing. (p. 5)

Thus rather than reducing their involvement in lifelong learning, most Western nation-states exercise control, particularly at the level of policy development, in ways that regulate lifelong learning to keep the current marriage of Big Business and Big Government stable. This marriage emphasizes efficiency, accountability, and performativity, and places citizens in a panopticon, not a learning society. In regulating learning, surveillance involves technologies of performativity, including performance indicators, performance management, and quality audits (Blackmore, 2007). Assessment as an expression of neoliberal instrumentalism reduces good citizenship to the equivalent of individual information and skills prowess and economic productivity. Blackmore suggests: "A pessimistic reading is that the lock step approaches of competencies/outcomes have normalising tendencies [and] intensify government control. [These approaches are] usually driven by strong externally defined standards that treat learning as a set of discrete outcomes and not as situated and multi-dimensional (emotional, personal, cognitive, etc.), while viewing curriculum and pedagogy as vocational tools to produce learner-earners not citizens" (p. 7).

In the end, Blackmore's overview tells us that the public good, often discussed in terms of social cohesion, is a secondary concern in neoliberalized lifelong learning. Indeed, social cohesion is reduced to an expected outcome of economic prosperity, and it is not guaranteed. In this dim light, Blackmore cautions us to question contemporary assumptions about lifelong learning. Paying particular attention to the needs of women as citizens, learners, and workers, she suggests that we expand possibilities for lifelong learning by revising policy development: "Policies that take seriously the differential benefits of LLL need to protect the family-work balance rather than undermine it; create conditions of work and learning that facilitate LLL; develop more sophisticated indicators of what counts as educational success; and realise LLL is about building social as well as economic capital" (p. 15).

Aboriginal Lifelong Learning

According to the 2006 Census, Canada's Aboriginal population is growing much faster than the non-Aboriginal population, with children and youth aged 24 and under constituting 48 percent of the Aboriginal population compared to 31 percent of the non-Aboriginal population (CMEC, 2012). Nearly 1.2 million Canadians identified themselves as Aboriginal—First Nations, Métis, or Inuit (CMEC, 2012). Between 1996 and 2006, Canada's Aboriginal population increased by 45 percent, while the non-Aboriginal population grew at a much lower rate of 8 percent (Saskatchewan Ministry of Education, 2008). This rapid population growth has implications for Aboriginal learning as a lifewide engagement across the lifespan. Aligning with Bagnall's (2006) social theory of lifelong learning that includes emphasizing cultural inheritance, it reinforces the need to attend to Aboriginal cultural contexts in framing lifelong learning. In the Canadian context, mainstream lifelong learning, especially with its neoliberal emphases on instrumentalism and job performance, has been inadequate in providing culturally sensitive learning engagements for the Aboriginal population. The CMEC (2012) acknowledges that ensuring that education and training for Aboriginal learners is culturally appropriate has been a challenge. This challenge can be compounded by such factors as access problems for rural and remote learners and poor learner disposition based on previous inadequate learning experiences.

To respect the integrity of Aboriginal peoples, lifelong learning has to recognize, appreciate, and accommodate Aboriginal identities, histories, languages, and cultures. When it involves education for citizenship, lifelong learning needs to incorporate Indigenous values and perspectives on being, becoming, and belonging as Aboriginal persons. In contemporary nation building in Canada, history must be front and centre; it must interrogate how the valorized settler or pioneering spirit has subjugated the Aboriginal spirit within a politics of Euro-Canadianization enacted as taking, loss, and deprivation. This history must also acknowledge that Aboriginal peoples have long engaged in lifelong learning as contextual, relational, and dispositional experiential learning. While there are distinct cultural and historical differences among First Nations, Métis, and Inuit populations, and great diversity in the communities in which they live, there remains a common thread in their learning process: Aboriginal learning has been historically constituted as a holistic lifelong and lifewide—intellectual, spiritual, physical, and emotional—engagement involving intergenerational learning via traditional ceremonies, storytelling, spiritual experiences, observation, and imitation (Canadian Council on Learning [CCL], 2009). The Canadian Council on Learning (2009) speaks to Aboriginal learning as an integrated, holistic, and regenerative process:

Aboriginal Peoples in Canada have long advocated their own values, cultural traditions and ways of knowing. Their perspective on learning reflects an enduring philosophy and way of living that integrates all knowledge and experience throughout each stage of a person's life. [Moreover,] Aboriginal learning is a highly social process that nurtures relationships within the family and throughout the community. These relationships serve to transmit social values and a sense of identity, and also serve to ensure cultural continuity. As a result, the value of individual learning cannot be separated from its contribution to collective well-being. (p. 10)

In speaking to the encompassing and holistic nature of Aboriginal lifelong learning, Battiste (2002) starts with a sorry reality. She describes the decline of Indigenous knowledge as a marker of the resilience, self-reliance, and traditions of Aboriginal peoples in Canada. Battiste lists three key causal factors for this decline: (1) federal government– and church-instigated assimilation and acculturation as tenacious and destructive phenomena, (2) the sidelining of Indigenous knowledge and pedagogy in education, and (3) the displacement and erosion of Aboriginal heritages and languages—the main ingredients in the structuring and survival of Indigenous knowledge—as a consequence of the modernization and urbanization of Aboriginal peoples. This destruction has worked against community building and possibilities for Aboriginal lifelong learning as a biopsychosocial and spiritual process grounded in a traditional ecological structure that integrates the self, others, and the environment. In Aboriginal pedagogy, as Battiste notes, value is placed on experiential learning, as well as learning that takes place in such contexts as talking or sharing circles, meditation, ceremonies, and learning by observing and doing. Contesting the neoliberal notion of knowledge as commodity, and situating knowledge as "a resourceful capacity of being that creates the context and texture of life" (2002, p. 15), Battiste provides this synopsis of the Aboriginal learning paradigm:

Learning is viewed as a life-long responsibility that people assume to understand the world around them and to animate their personal abilities. Knowledge teaches people how to be responsible for their own lives, develops their sense of relationship to others, and helps them model competent and respectful behaviour. Traditions, ceremonies, and daily observations are all integral parts of the learning process. (pp. 14–15)

As Battiste relates, in educating for health, wholeness, and harmony, building Indigenous knowledge is crucial to building and sustaining people and communities. In essence, it is an engagement in transformative learning. Graveline (2000) provides further elucidation of this viewpoint in her discussion of conducting Indigenous research as a reflexive engagement, which she captures in a poetic narrative. She explores Aboriginal ontology and experience, and exposes the complexities of working within an Aboriginal research paradigm where adaptations are part of the investigative process that must keep tradition at its core. Here Graveline speaks to the importance of First Voice as a pedagogical and methodological device in the search for authentic meanings:

My ongoing lifework
    Transforming contemporary challenges
        by invoking Aboriginal Tradition. ...
My own Consciousness was/is Shaped by Aboriginal teachings
    Influenced by interactions with Western colonial realities. ...
As a Métis woman, scholar, activist, teacher and healer
I enact First Voice as pedagogy and methodology.
Observing my own lived experience as an Educator
    Sharing meanings with Others
        Create collective context....
Consciousness
    Context
        Community
            Change
                Visions
Talking Circle as Methodology Enacted....
An egalitarian structure
    each voice acknowledged
        heard in turn....
Circle builds community....
(pp. 361–365)

Graveline deftly writes from the politics of her personal and cultural locations, providing perspective for informing Aboriginal lifelong learning as a political and pedagogical practice. For her, the research process is ecological, and brings the researcher, the researched, and the place of engagement to bear on knowledge building amid the tensions of using the "Circle as Methodology" in academe, which is steeped in Eurocentric traditions. In terms of minority politics, the challenge in dealing with these tensions is how to have Aboriginal participants constitute a strong and distinct counterpublic contesting a history of disenfranchisement without the group falling prey to isolationist or segregationist stances that limit possibilities for networking and coalition building with non-Aboriginals. Drawing a parallel to engaging in lifelong learning where similar tensions exist, we might ask: Are there possibilities for coalition building across differences for learners from Aboriginal, European, Asian, and other traditions innervating Canada's cultural mosaic? Moreover, are there possibilities for building transcultural communities where deliberations across differences become the fuel for socio-cultural learning and acting in the world?

Due to the complexity and dynamics of Aboriginal ways of knowing, learning cannot be measured conventionally since such gauging generally ignores Aboriginal needs, desires, and cultural variations. According to the CCL (2009), conventional measurement frameworks (1) focus on measuring learning deficits; (2) fail to consider Aboriginal social, cultural, and political contexts; (3) do not measure lifelong learning in holistic or lifewide contexts; and (4) do not give sufficient weight to experiential learning. Thus it is important that governments and researchers know what Aboriginal learners consider to be markers of their successes. Historically, these external groups have used the high-school dropout rate to measure the success of Aboriginal learners. These rates, which reflect mainstream conventions instead of Aboriginal cultural differences and values, are therefore high. The CCL records the "familiar and concerning" (p. 6) statistics that 40 percent of Aboriginal young adults aged 20 to 24 have not completed high school compared to 13 percent of the non-Aboriginal population. The rates of non-completion jump to 61 percent for First Nations young adults living on reserves and 68 percent for Inuit young adults living in remote communities. How would these rates change if indicators consistent with success in an Aboriginal learning paradigm were used to measure the learning of these young adults?

There is a clear and present need to focus on culturally sensitive ways to gauge the success of Aboriginal learners by using Aboriginal perspectives on learning to frame the determination. In developing a new basis for measuring Aboriginal learning, the CCL has proposed the Holistic Lifelong Learning Measurement Framework, which incorporates elements of First Nations, Métis, and Inuit lifelong-learning models. Aboriginal learning specialists from across Canada developed these models, which were published by the CCL in 2007. These models "highlight the fact that learning from—and about—culture, language and tradition is critical to the well-being of Aboriginal people" (CCL, 2009, p. 5). This is because such learning as an everyday occurrence in Aboriginal communities is a very social and relational process. This holistic learning incorporates informal and experiential learning, is enhanced by strong family and community ties, and includes involvement in social, cultural, and recreational activities. This locates community as an interactive place to relate to and learn from others. Aboriginal youth can be motivated to learn in this context, building Indigenous knowledge and skill sets through exchanges with other community members (Little Bear, 2009).

In presenting the Holistic Lifelong Learning Measurement Framework, the CCL (2009) provides an overview of its three main components, each of which has measurement indicators. The first is sources and domains of knowledge, whereby "an individual learns from and about: people (family, Elders, community), languages, traditions and ceremonies, spirituality, and the natural world" (p. 14). The second is the lifelong-learning journey, which involves learning in formal and informal contexts in a range of environments across the lifespan. The third is community well-being, which is an individual and collective responsibility in social, cultural, political, economic, corporeal, and health contexts. As the CCL notes, these indicators reflect Aboriginal perspectives, focusing on learning across the lifespan and across settings including the school, home, community, workplace, and the land. The CCL asserts that the dynamic relationship between learning and well-being in Aboriginal lives is embodied and embedded in the framework. Staying true to this framework when measuring Aboriginal learning presents two main challenges: (1) attending to demographic and contextual factors including geography or place, and (2) avoiding falling into a neoliberal mindset when gauging the impact of social and economic factors on learning successes. For example, functional employability in neoliberal terms and work success from Aboriginal perspectives would necessarily have different indicators. Moreover, understandings of work and productivity would be differently construed from cultural versus economic perspectives. If the Holistic Lifelong Learning Measurement Framework is used with an awareness of these factors and attention to the centrality of Aboriginal culture in framing lifelong learning and measuring its success, then it has the potential to inform social policies and programming that enhance possibilities for Aboriginal learning and its contributions to Aboriginal communities and the larger Canadian culture.

Elders play a key role in the success of holistic Aboriginal lifelong learning, as they "teach about the importance of responsibility and relationships within the family and the community; all of which reinforces inter-generational connections and identities" (CCL, 2009, p. 5). They motivate others to learn across the lifespan, and contribute significantly to the health and well-being of community members. Perhaps most importantly for children and youth, Elders make the traditional classroom come alive for Aboriginal learners: "Historically, the traditional Aboriginal classroom was made up of the community and the natural environment surrounding it. In this context, adults were responsible for ensuring that every child learned the specific skills, attitudes and knowledge they needed to function in everyday life. Given the importance of the natural world in everyday life, learning from the land was a critical part of the Aboriginal 'classroom'" (ibid., p. 24).

Today, Elders are respected community educators who transmit cultural knowledge and engage in cultural affirmation in both word and action. They provide children, youth, and, indeed, the whole community with ways to know, be, become, and belong. Here, both the land and Aboriginal language play central roles. It is the land, not time, that is a core referent in the Aboriginal mindset: (1) it nurtures life; (2) it is central in Aboriginal ecology; and (3) it is integral to Aboriginal identity formation (Little Bear, 2009). The importance of the land speaks to the centrality of a politics and pedagogy of place in Aboriginal learning. Little Bear (2009) addresses the importance of place: "It is not enough to only know about places, [their] history or narrative, but a learner must experience them both physically and emotionally, achieved through rituals, and visitations.... Aboriginal people suffer when absent from the land. Place must be an integral part of any curriculum" (p. 21).

Aboriginal language is also inextricably linked to cultural continuity and vitality (CCL, 2009; Environics Institute, 2010). With a growing population, Canada's urban Aboriginal peoples feel that cultural sustainability is quite dependent on passing on language coupled with transmitting customs and traditions and protecting Aboriginal culture from external influences (Environics Institute, 2010). The CCL notes that Aboriginal language is important for making meaning and sense of cultural experiences and passing on cultural knowledge through intergenerational sharing. It is also a medium for sharing values for living and relating in community. Little Bear (2009) asserts that language guides Aboriginal people in building relationships and in engendering social healing and progress. In sum, Aboriginal language is central to holistic living, identity construction, knowledge building, and honing an Aboriginal worldview.

Post-Secondary Education for Aboriginal Students

Emphases on the importance of land/place and language also need to guide post-secondary education for Aboriginal students as a constituent of Aboriginal lifelong learning. Higher education works well for these students when it attends to Aboriginal culture, disposition (values and beliefs), and learning contexts as matters of accommodation. The Saskatchewan Ministry of Education (2008) provides this synopsis of successful educational encounters: "Success is reflected within those post-secondary institutes and programs which manifest First Nations and Inuit self-determination. Success is also exemplified in programs that accommodate transitional supports, the wisdom of Elders, Aboriginal resources, Aboriginal instructors and staff, community-based programs, and curricula as well as andragogy [or learning for adults] that mirrors Aboriginal languages, cultures, beliefs and values" (p. 4). The ministry considers the focus on post-secondary education for Aboriginals a vital necessity for redressing economic and social inequities and making progress in the province. Of course, this requires addressing the tainted history of post-secondary education for Aboriginal students in Canada. Historically, government policy used post-secondary education as a vehicle for assimilating Aboriginal students into Euro-Canadian society. Within a politics of assimilation, engaging in higher education was to experience learning as dislocation, as separation from culture, beliefs, values, language, the land, and other constituents in Aboriginal identity formation; indeed, post-secondary education as assimilation constituted an assault on Aboriginal integrity.

Part of the way forward, as the Saskatchewan Ministry of Education (2008) points out, is involving stakeholders in the Aboriginal community in the governance of post-secondary education so policy-making, program planning, curriculum development, and the coordination of resources and supports are informed by Indigenous philosophy and values, as well as cultural and community practices. The ministry also relates that the post-secondary culture of learning, including teaching-learning dynamics, needs to be informed by the following core elements of the Aboriginal learning paradigm: (1) Aboriginal pedagogy's emphasis on holistic, co-operative learning in community and the use of such methods as storytelling, group discussion, demonstration, modelling, and observation; and (2) the ways Indigenous language shapes modes of communicating. The ministry describes the First Nations University of Canada, with campuses in Regina, Saskatoon, and Prince Albert, Saskatchewan, as a leading example of a post-secondary institution that is using this Aboriginal learning paradigm to achieve such key goals as revising Indigenous history and developing Indigenous theoretical and research frameworks to guide knowledge building and enhance learning.

Urban Aboriginal Peoples: A Core Demographic of the Canadian Population

For Aboriginal peoples, community is the organizing construct that underpins the formation of individual identities, communal relationships, and value systems. In its *Urban Aboriginal Peoples Study*, the Environics Institute (2010) noted the crucial importance of family and friends to urban Aboriginal residents as they build community and a sense of connection and belonging. However, the study also found that the notion of community is understood differently by First Nations, Métis, and Inuit peoples: First Nations and Inuit peoples prioritize belonging to an Aboriginal community, while Métis and non-status First Nations peoples prioritize belonging to a non-Aboriginal community. When it comes to how urban Aboriginal peoples mediate learning and other aspects of everyday life, two-thirds of residents across Canadian cities say that the intricate processes of learning and living have been variously impacted by the effects of Indian residential schools—either in a personal or family context. These schools, which existed prior to Confederation and lasted until 1996, were predicated on Euro-Canadian assimilation that erased Aboriginal languages and cultures—core essences of being and belonging—from the schooling process. As the Environics Institute (2010) study relates, "The residential school system left in its wake a tragic legacy. It is estimated that as many as 150,000 Aboriginal children attended these institutions. Many former students have reported undergoing hardship, forcible confinement, and physical and sexual abuse while attending these schools" (p. 54). In effect, residential schooling amounted to an assault on the identities, individual development, socialization, and cultural development of Aboriginal children. This erosion of Indigenous integrity continues to have effects in social, cultural, economic, and political contexts, and it has deeply impacted individual, family, and community health and wellness. In tandem with this history and its legacy of pain and disconnection, urban Aboriginal youth experience other struggles related to identity and belonging as they deal with the dissonance between Aboriginal culture and urban culture. The Environics Institute study recounts that urban Aboriginal youth are least aware of and involved in Aboriginal cultural activities and traditions in their cities. Notably, the study points to the importance of education in advancing Aboriginal culture in cities, relating that more educated urban Aboriginal peoples have greater Indigenous cultural awareness and are more likely to participate in cultural events. This highlights the importance of using the Aboriginal lifelong-learning paradigm to advance cultural learning for urban Aboriginals. Friendship centres, health centres, employment centres, and other Aboriginal service providers need to be an integral part of the development and implementation of a city's Aboriginal lifelong-learning model. Their involvement contributes to the lifewide aspect of holistic learning for Aboriginal peoples across life contexts.

The Environics Institute's urban Aboriginal peoples study locates residents as happy with their lives when they are in good health, connected to their Aboriginal heritage, and socio-economically comfortable, as indicated by home ownership or having good jobs. Those who are unhappy with their work lives include urban Aboriginal youth, part-time workers, and undereducated and low-wage earners. The top life aspiration of urban Aboriginal peoples, especially if they are young or less affluent, is to be successful in higher education. This is followed by having and caring for a family, having a worthwhile job with status and satisfaction, and owning a home. Like the Canadian public at large, urban Aboriginal people feel that the ingredients for a successful life include family, a rewarding and productive career, financial independence, and balance in life, learning, and work. When they look to the future, urban Aboriginal peoples hope for a more educated community where individuals are connected to their Aboriginal culture and experience less racism and discrimination. To enhance prospects for increased educational attainment, Aboriginal children and youth need education and learning to be (1) culturally relevant, with foci on Aboriginal history and cultural practices; (2) economically relevant, with foci on individual development and preparing for meaningful work; and (3) socially relevant, with foci on family and community as constructs important to individual identity development and socialization. These elements are essential in an Aboriginal lifelong-learning paradigm that starts with young learners and advances an ecology of learning focused on self-identity, community identity, and the ability to mediate life, learning, and work in Aboriginal and larger cultural contexts. This paradigm would counter a history of absences in learning in schooling for Aboriginal children and youth: "Relatively few [Aboriginal individuals] say they learned about Aboriginal people, history, and culture in their elementary and high schools.... Only one-third (35%) of urban Aboriginal peoples say they learned a lot or a little about their culture in elementary school; most (62%) say they learned almost nothing" (Environics Institute, 2010, p. 118). While there is a slight improvement in high school, there is inadequate attention paid to Aboriginal content during the formal schooling of many Aboriginal students. This absence is compounded by a lack of Aboriginal teachers, as well as very little instruction in Aboriginal languages in elementary and high schools.

Despite the failures of public schooling in educating Aboriginal students, urban Aboriginal peoples still value post-secondary education, with family being the primary motivator of students in their decision to participate and their main source of support while studying (Environics Institute, 2010). The *Urban Aboriginal Peoples Study* relates that higher education is primarily valued as a vehicle for individual enrichment and empowerment whereby students enjoy learning and self-actualize: "This includes making them more self confident, open-minded, mature and responsible; giving them a sense of accomplishment; and expanding their knowledge generally or about themselves as an Aboriginal person" (p. 122). This conception of empowerment is culturally based, and is one face of empowerment. The *Urban Aboriginal Peoples Study* also relates that Aboriginal students value post-secondary education as a means of obtaining quality work and improving their finances and quality of life. This aligns with the current focus on empowerment in neoliberal forms of lifelong learning that links the concept to increasing individual capacity and being a better commodity from a human capital perspective (Wildemeersch & Salling Olesen, 2012). This is the other face of empowerment, and tensions can certainly arise for Aboriginal learners at the intersection of the two conceptions.

In sum, urban Aboriginal peoples place great value on education and the ways that it assists individual and community development. While they value formal schooling and constituent forms such as post-secondary education, urban Aboriginal peoples believe that education has to be broadly construed to include and value lifelong and lifewide learning in informal and nonformal contexts as well. There is an increasing tendency for urban Aboriginal peoples to place value on mainstream and Aboriginal learning, believing that students should learn the knowledge and skills needed to mediate life and work in the larger society while learning about Aboriginal culture, language, and traditions that enhance personal identity development and community survival (Environics Institute, 2010). While this notion of education and learning as *métissage* is rife with tensions, it also broadens the idea of holistic Aboriginal learning as learning from within and without to deal with cultural problematics and the social and economic complexities of today's world, where globalization and neoliberalism are driving forces.

Lifelong Learning in the New Millennium: Who's In? Who's Out?
Locked in the Economistic

If lifelong learning existed in an ideal form, it might be as an encompassing lifewide, cohesive, meaningful, and worthwhile formation that helps citizens as learners and workers to mediate work and life successfully in a neoliberal change culture of crisis and challenge. Field and Leicester (2000) provide this description of lifelong learning approaching the ideal: "The agenda for lifelong learning encourages education for citizenship (political), seeks for wider participation (social), and emphasizes the importance of learning for economic prosperity (vocational) while recognizing the importance of individual choices and personal development (liberal)" (p. xvii). However, as Field and Leicester indicate, two key barriers exist to achieving this more holistic form of lifelong learning. First, there is the history of the concept. Lifelong learning has been a diffuse term with multiple meanings that have made the notion problematic, leaving citizens as learners to wonder about its parameters and possibilities. While lifelong learning's eclecticism does not dismiss its utility as a learning paradigm, it does confound how we deliberate its meaning and value. Second, a current narrow policy focus sets limits to lifelong learning by linking it to economistic purposes that are to be met, for example, through vocational training and prolonged schooling for youth. This positions lifelong learning as a cyclical and limited engagement that is not immersed in the spectrum of contexts and relationships that contribute to holistic learning.

From these historical and contemporary perspectives, we might ask: In what kind of shape is lifelong learning? Much of lifelong learning, especially as it has been articulated as learning for earning and for the global economy, is a neoliberal fabrication. Edwards (2000a) problematizes this economistic formation of lifelong learning as "an uncertain and troubled conceptual space" (p. 5) that is expected to deal with the complexities of contemporary social, cultural, and economic change forces. However, neoliberal lifelong-learning policies and practices seem to foreclose an emphasis on social politics and education for citizenship in an economistic turn that emphasizes privatization of and individual responsibility for learning that is primarily concerned with successfully competing in contemporary economies. As Edwards sees it, this kind of contemporary lifelong learning, which is tied to the mandated recurrent learning that neoliberalism dictates in its vocational learning agenda, "is more proscriptive and prescriptive than descriptive and analytical" (p. 5). Edwards holds that such a blinkered view of learning has the tendency to downplay social and human potential. Thus, when lifelong learning emphasizes the economistic and chooses market over social politics, it places social inclusion, cohesion, well-being, and advancement in jeopardy.

In its contemporary economistic formation, lifelong learning has been globalized in the sense that, in many nations, its discourse and policies reflect the neoliberal consensus that learning with the most worth is lifelong learning that is linked to economic advancement. Valued this way, *lifelong learning* (or *lifelong education,* as it is called in some national contexts) is a term often used positively to denote contemporary continuous learning engagements. Johnston (2000) equates its approving use with the concept's delineation as an "attractive, powerful, and politically expedient" term (p. 25). In other words, lifelong learning is a "broad, imprecise, and 'elastic'" concept with "a strategic flexibility which makes ... [it] attractive to politicians, policymakers and practitioners alike" (Johnston, 2000, p. 12). Field and Leicester (2000) contend this favourable use gives both lifelong learning and lifelong education "a normative dimension," indicating "they are mainly concerned with planned, purposeful, systematic, *worthwhile* learning—not just with any or all learning" (p. xvii, emphasis in original). Johnston adds, "The very choice of the term 'learning' also has a normative dimension.... This implies a plurality of learning approaches and learning situations, some distancing from the primacy of formal education and certainly a move away from front-end models of institutional learning" (p. 13). Using a different theoretical lens that provides a similar perspective, Edwards and Usher (2006) locate lifelong learning as a postmodern condition of education signifying ambivalence and diversity in purposes, content, processes, organization, and pedagogy. Importantly, they recognize that lifelong learning is not limited to the domain of adult education, but is "a goal to be pursued by education across the board" (p. 60). They also recognize that lifelong learning is not limited to formal education, but is located in diverse social practices outside the institutionalized educational realm. This greatly expands the meaning and parameters of *educational*. Of course, in postmodern terms, this can imply that lifelong learning contributes to the uncertainty it is intended to respond to and alleviate.

In another analysis of education "under, for, and in spite of postmodernity" (p. 123), Bauman (2001) critiques education as an uneven and less-than-substantial formation at a time when it and other orientation points, such as work, well-being, and values, are in a state of flux. He asserts, "Many games seem to be going on at the same time, and each game changes its rules while being played. These times of ours excel in dismantling frames and liquidizing patterns—all frames and all patterns, at random and without advance warning" (p. 125). As a result, many citizens feel that they are living in a volatile, fragmented, and unpredictable world in which it is difficult to move forward in some directed and assured way. In this scattered light, what are we to say about lifelong learning and how it is perceived in a liquid world that has also been variously described as postmodern, post-industrial, late capitalist, neoliberal, and disaster capitalist? In its present en vogue economistic formation, lifelong learning can be viewed as a norm, a culture, and an attitude that aids and abets neoliberalism in our contemporary change culture of crisis and challenge (Grace, 2007). Such learning is often transitory, insubstantial, and reactive in the liquid modern. It is bits-and-bites learning with short-term utility that seems made to order for Bauman's (2005) liquid life. Yet many citizens, even if they are only focused on learning for sustaining or advancing workplace performativity, want to view lifelong learning as something reliable, and as a good investment of their time, effort, and money. However, since much economistic lifelong learning takes learners into the realm of continuing and mandated learning, such learning can appear to be burdensome and invasive in relation to the whole of life. Moreover, with economistic lifelong learning modulating to the beat of neoliberalism, method, device, and technique as the historical ways used to stabilize learning become less reliable. Thus, we need to think about the limitations of lifelong learning's contemporary modus operandi based on sequencing and predictability in a change culture marked by volatility, risks, and twists at every turn. Bauman (2001) maintains that if today's citizens "expect to find a cohesive and coherent structure in the mangle of contingent events, they are in for costly errors and painful frustrations. If the habits acquired in the course of training prompt them to seek such cohesive and coherent structures and make their actions dependent on finding them—they are in real trouble" (p. 125). Lifelong learners experience this diffi-culty in neoliberal learning spaces when they view their pre-packaged learning modules as long-term solutions to their learning-and-work woes.

Lifelong Learning as Paradox and a Strategic Mainstream Cultural Production

The dynamics of contemporary lifelong learning are paradoxical. First, lifelong learning appears to be ongoing and perpetual, yet it is limited in scope. While Johnston (2000) views lifelong learning as a generally comprehensive term, he notes that the concept linked to globalization is more narrowly focused on learning for work and meeting market demands regarding employability. This shrinking of the meaning and value of lifelong learning to its economistic parameters contributes to the paradoxical nature of lifelong learning. Field (2006) describes the paradox: On the one hand, lifelong learning can be con-ceived as a loose, all-encompassing, and thus problematic term; on the other hand, it can be viewed as a concept whose meaning and value are narrowly de-termined within economistic limits. As Field sees it, this neoliberal determin-ism has become a mechanism for exclusion and control in lifelong learning. Learning is primarily about (and reduced to) more training and development for the already educated and skilled.

Second, lifelong learning is something that is apparently meant for all, yet it is undemocratic. Indeed, neoliberalized lifelong learning seems bent on con-trolling certain citizens who already have education and work experience. It engages them in learning that is demand-driven, not learner-driven. The goal is to refit citizens as learners and workers so they are made to order for today's economy. Thus the design of neoliberalized lifelong learning engenders ma-nipulation of citizens to fit economistic purposes. This manipulation is nor-malized as citizens are conditioned to accept that contemporary work culture is marked by intermittent job and skill detachment as the demands of work and the economy change. According to Bauman (2005), inherent in this cur-rent way of taking charge of workers is "tacit acceptance of an unequal, asym-metrical social relation—the split between ... the managers and the managed" (p. 53). Moreover, Bauman adds, current managerialism is "conducted surrep-titiously under the banner of 'neoliberalism': managers switching from 'nor-mative regulation' to 'seduction,' from day-to-day policing to PR, and from the stolid, overregulated, routine-based panoptical model of power to domination through diffuse, unfocused uncertainty, *précarité* and a ceaseless, haphazard disruption of routines" (p. 57).

With the ascendancy of corporatism spurred by a neoliberal public pedagogy valuing the private, the instrumental, and the individualistic in political moves to advance the global economy, lifelong learning has become a strategic mainstream cultural production that transmits neoliberalism's ambition and economistic values to citizens as learners and workers. In this neoliberal world they have little choice, as the meanings of *participatory* and *mandatory* blur in learning arenas. Since the intention of neoliberalism is to keep the economistic front and centre, lifelong learning that augments worker performativity and productivity is the desired continuous kind of learning whose development and delivery are increasingly privatized. For example, this trend is evident in Napier's (2002) description of the Singapore Learning Exchange, which he describes as a model for integrating learning into workplaces in a way "that leverages on existing systems and institutions" in the exchange of learning materials, courses, and content (p. 36). Napier relates that private management of lifelong learning focuses on producing proficient corporate citizens by creating a training administration, access, and delivery capability to support workplace learning. Asserting that the private sector is capable of managing and delivering lifelong learning to meet public-sector learning needs, he describes the Learning Exchange as a public-private venture between the Government of Singapore and his company, Accenture. The Learning Exchange consists of two major elements: "[an] 'Enterprise Learning Management System'—which provides learner administration and training administration, [and a] Learning Marketplace—which provides a training brokerage and alliances with eLearning and traditional training providers" (p. 36). Napier promotes the Learning Exchange as "an exemplar of how lateral thinking around agency or organizational learning-management and delivery opportunities can be extended to an entire country" (p. 42). Ultimately though, this set-up typifies a neoliberal pragmatic model of government-corporate control of lifelong learning in which learners engage in systematic training and development for economistic ends. The Learning Exchange emphasizes marketplace capability as the means to structure lifelong learning so participants reach the desired workplace potential: "The Marketplace is a transaction-rich electronic environment that links training providers, buyers, and users through a web-based architecture that allows for publication and registration of training courses" (p. 40). In this learning model, government-corporate needs are emphasized over learner needs in the administration of learning and training:

The learner administration component ... offers comprehensive end-to-end training services that focus on lifelong learning, and skills development and improvement for its users. The system enables an organization to track and manage the continuous learning process of its personnel.... [The system] works to benefit the organization or employer by automating the time-consuming processes in corporate training. These features promote reduction in time to on-the-job proficiency and effectiveness of administration, which in turn translates to cost savings.... [The system] has been designed with flexibility for the learner to take ownership of their personal development. The system provides a one-stop shop for the learner. (pp. 38–39)

Benefiting the system by helping learners as workers to become more efficient is the modus operandi of the Singapore Learning Exchange. However, the one-stop shopping that Napier refers to takes place in a poorly stocked lifelong-learning store. The services and supports to abet learning for social purposes or with personal intrinsic value cannot be found on the shelves.

Concluding Perspective: Whither Lifelong Learning?

Even though the notion was emphasized nearly a century ago in the 1919 Report of the British Ministry of Reconstruction, which was written after World War I (Field, 2006), the need to *learn our way out* still persists. In the *Age of Extremes*, Hobsbawm (1994) described the last part of the twentieth century as "a new era of decomposition, uncertainty and crisis—and indeed, for large parts of the world such as Africa, the former USSR and the formerly socialist parts of Europe, of catastrophe" (p. 6). Indeed, catastrophe has continued and seems exacerbated in the new millennium in the face of economic disasters and the social fragmentation, upheaval, and erosion spurred on by unchecked American imperialism, mutant neoliberalism, diverse forms of religious fundamentalism, wars, and global terrorism. All these retrograde change forces have added to the poverty, exclusion, hatred, bigotry, prejudice, and violence that get in the way of being, becoming, belonging, and behaving as human beings in the world. Amid this economic and social devolution, lifelong educators have to ask: Whither lifelong learning? This question ought to have this corollary: Is it not time to frame lifelong learning as critical action, which, in sum, can be viewed as a focus on holistic lifelong-learning policy and practice aimed at ending assaults on human integrity in life, learning, and work spaces?

Hopefully, it is not too late for lifelong learning to take us toward the good life marked by holistic growth, integrity, respect, recognition, access, accommodation, safety, security, healing, hope, and well-being. Ultimately, citizens want holistic, quality learning that contributes to quality work and a full and satisfying life. They want to be part of a proactive public that nests concerns about economic progress and quality work within social and cultural concerns about identity, difference, justice, vitality, and a meaningful life. Lifelong educators should see it as their privilege and duty to develop and implement lifelong learning as a holistic, lifewide formation that helps citizens as learners and workers to meet all these needs.

Chapter 3

Lifelong Learning Chic in the Modern Practice of Adult Education: Historical and Contemporary Perspectives

In a world deeply affected by change forces such as the knowledge economy, globalization, and information literacy and technology, lifelong learning is in vogue again. It has become a large-scale phenomenon that widely influences policy and practice across all sectors of the educational landscape. Intergovernmental organizations such as the Organisation for Economic Co-operation and Development (OECD) argue that its current renewal has revitalized the concept once more, situating lifelong learning as a lifewide and life-connected occurrence with value in today's global economy (Organisation for Economic Co-operation and Development [OECD], 2000; Organisation for Economic Co-operation and Development & Human Resources Development Canada [OECD & HRDC], 2000a, 2000b). Many national governments, notably those wed to neoliberalism in the West, have also endorsed lifelong learning, hailing it as a way out for citizens in a shifting work world. However, it has also been a way out for these governments as they manoeuvre a public-to-private shift in fiscal responsibility for lifelong learning to learners whom they cast as its prime beneficiaries (Grace, 2004a, 2004b). This shift has found increasing acceptance and accommodation, certainly in corporate circles and the attendant training industry where lifelong learning is viewed as chic and lucrative. Unfortunately, much of this lifelong learning is reductionistic, instrumental, and tied to the commodification of knowledge and economic advancement (Jarvis, 2000). It tends to sideline forms of social and cultural education.

Indeed, in contemporary times it is usually intergovernmental organizations, governments, and corporate interests that have been behind the demand for lifelong learning to be a key response to new life-and-work urgencies marking our contemporary change culture of crisis and challenge. Unfortunately, in keeping with its history as a usually marginalized educational enterprise (Grace, 2000b), North American adult education has not been an integral part of this circle with regard to setting new directions for lifelong learning. Still, this field of study has engaged in substantive critique. For example, Collins (1998) cautions that lifelong learning signifies "lifelong enculturation to a world increasingly determined ... within a nexus of unequal power relations. In such a world talk about the learning society and education for participatory democracy becomes for the majority an exercise in spinning wheels" (pp. 137–138). His perspective aligns with earlier comments made by John Ohliger (1990), a long-time critic of mandatory forms of continuing education, who provided this humanistic perspective on learning as lifelong enculturation: "We're rapidly moving in the direction of forcing everyone to lead a life spent in the never-ending pursuit of learning. But if learning never ends, does living ever begin? When would there be time for doing, feeling, just being?" (p. 29). In an interview a few years earlier, Ohliger had concluded, "Learning in society has become the sort of crippled nephew of that uncle knowledge explosion" (Brennan, 1987, p. 54).

Despite such pointed critique, lifelong learning, particularly in its economistic forms, has thrived. This actuality has left a contingent in adult education, especially in its critical practice, in a reflective mode as they query whether lifelong learning is replacing adult education, perhaps even prefiguring its demise (Wilson & Cervero, 2001). While questioning its social and cultural space and place is not a new experience for adult education, certainly in Canadian and US contexts, responses at other times when lifelong learning has been in vogue have focused less on puzzling over the field's parameters and more on enabling its survival (Grace, 1997a, 2000b). In survival mode, North American adult education has been conscious of a history of dependence on various public and private sources of funding. The field has employed responses aligning forms and functions of lifelong learning with cultural currency to adult educational projects revised for time and tides. Indeed, in the 1950s and at other times in the past, Canadian and US adult education have used lifelong learning as an integral part of a politics of promotion designed to shape adult education as a valuable economic and cultural enterprise (Grace, 2000b). Some of these responses may be viewed as compromise or even complicity with lifelong learning in its economistic forms. Nevertheless, there have been times when the field has hailed lifelong learning as a raison d'être and a cultural and economic lifeline (Grace, 1997a).

In this chapter, I turn to the history of the modern practice of adult education to speak to the versatility of lifelong learning as a fluid and indeterminate concept that some have viewed as a learner's way out and others have viewed as a learner's burden. I identify change forces that have shaped particular purposes and functions of lifelong learning over time and tides. In the wake of such forces, I discuss the need for a critical practice of lifelong learning that would engage citizens in holistic learning that attends to their instrumental, social, and cultural needs. I speak to the importance of remembering history by using the lens of the past to consider the conceptualization and parameters of contemporary lifelong learning and to critique a discernible culture of learner-worker neglect in Canada. Considering the plight of Canadian young adults as an example, I provide critical reflection on federal government policy that abets privatization of lifelong learning and aggravates the situation for learners by blaming individuals for any failure in lifelong learning. I conclude with a perspective suggesting it may well be time for a critical (re)turn in Canadian adult education to help salvage lifelong learning as a formation and project of the social.

The Historically Versatile and Contested Concept of Lifelong Learning: From the Pivotal 1919 Report to the New Millennium

In exploring the parameters and possibilities of lifelong learning, a turn to history is important. To engage the history of lifelong learning is to explore connections between past and present representations of the concept, to ponder how they differ, and to consider future possibilities for lifelong learning. Mindful that "the facts of history never come to us 'pure,' … [but] are always refracted through the mind of the recorder" (Carr, 1961, p. 24), it is vital that we discern, respect, value, and cautiously interpret the facts as we develop a historical account of lifelong learning. This engagement can help us understand the diverse and intricate formations, problems, and projects that influence and shape the concept's emergence over time. It can also help us situate lifelong learning as a versatile and contested notion as we explore its changing meanings, purposes, and desired outcomes in relation to learning for life and work. Moreover, any initiating and valuing of contemporary lifelong-learning policies and practices has its origins in past social, political, cultural, educational, and economic developments (Tuijnman, 2002). In other words, different ideologies, as well as the contextual and relational permutations at play in different decades, have helped to shape lifelong learning's present directions, priorities, and outcomes (Cruikshank, 2001, 2002; Grace, 2000b, 2004b; Rubenson, 2002).

Throughout the twentieth century a barrage of change forces, invariably tied to global socio-political, -cultural, and -economic shifts, perennially reconfigured life, learning, work, and their possibilities. In the wake of World War I, and in response to the change culture of crisis and challenge that emerged during the decades following this profoundly devastating global conflict, many envisaged learning as a lifelong process that could provide a way out and a way forward. In the modern practice of adult education in the West, the idea that learning ought to be a lifelong venture can be traced back at least to the release of the British Ministry of Reconstruction, Adult Education Committee (1919) Final Report (commonly known as "The 1919 Report"), which the committee developed to outline the kinds of learning responses and transitions needed in the aftermath of the First World War (Field, 2000b). Maintaining that learning for all citizens in adulthood should be universal and lifelong, this landmark report promoted "adult education as 'the way out' from sordid materialism, economic deprivation, and ineffectual democracy" (Cotton, 1968, p. 2). The 1919 Report affected North American adult education, with the emerging field of study and practice attempting to incorporate the necessity of lifelong learning for nation building and meeting the requirements of democratic citizenship into its principles of practice (Grace, 2000b). However, in North America and elsewhere in the West, democratic and other versions of the concept were erratically valued due to the uneven educational and larger cultural status given to forms of lifelong learning (Coffield, 2002; Grace, 2000b; Solomon, 1964; Tough, 1971); indeed, there were many conceptualizations and forms. Coffield (2002) concludes that lifelong learning has had a "bewildering number of different guises" (p. 184). It has been variously conceived as a way to cope with

- individual, organizational, and societal change;
- economic upheaval and recovery;
- unemployment and underemployment;
- social unrest and exclusion;
- professional development and the need for knowledge-and-skill building; and
- the cultural and political tides of citizenship.

These diverse reasons for engaging in lifelong learning have been variously investigated (Coffield, 2002; Field, 2000a, 2000b; Grace, 2000b), raising questions about the notion's parameters and possibilities in relation to

- policy development (with regard to individual, institutional, and societal needs and desires);
- participation (in terms of inclusive education and institutional access and accommodation); and
- the dynamics of participation (especially around issues of learner connectedness, corporate/educational and other collaborative learning models, and the culture-knowledge-language-power nexus).

Despite its potential to help learners cope and advance in instrumental, social, and cultural contexts, the idea of lifelong learning was not socially, politically, or culturally ensconced in an emphatic way in North America or anywhere else (including Britain) after the report's release. Instead, economic crisis and labour unrest in the post–World War I era, coupled with a myopic belief that the main purpose of education was to socialize the young, led to the report being shelved (Field, 2000b; Grace, 2000b).

Lifelong learning did, however, resurface with a certain new vitality in North America after World War II. In this transitional period, it was emphasized as a way out and a way forward for war veterans and other adult learners (Grace, 2000b). Collectively, three progressive notions helped position lifelong learning as a banner phrase and advantageous modus operandi in post–World War II North American adult education (Bagnall, 2001; Grace, 1997a, 2000b):

- individualism (helping individuals grow and develop for personal and public benefit)
- adaptation (using contextualized forms of education to help individuals cope with cultural change forces)
- advancing democracy (emphasizing socio-political and cultural reform through education for the public good)

These notions have left their marks on lifelong-learning philosophy, theory, and practice, and they constitute the legacy of this time of transition and rupture (Bagnall, 2001).

During the 1950s and 1960s, lifelong learning became a lifeline for Canadian and US adult education as prominent field educators such as J. Roby Kidd and Alexander N. Charters touted the value of education that extends over a learner's lifetime (Grace, 2000b). They linked lifelong learning to society's very survival and, by inference, to adult education's survival as a field of study and practice. During this period, the military-industrial complex emerged as a signifier of economic and cultural transitions that marked the beginning of what Daniel Bell (1960) called post-industrial society. In this society, the acquisition of techno-scientific skills became associated with post-industrial progress, and the power of a post-industrial state became inextricably linked to the power of science and technology (Beck, 1992; Bell, 1960, 1967; Wolin, 1996). Harbingers of neoliberalism are indicated in the trends that Bell associated with a post-industrial society marked by a coalescing of economics, science, and technology. Bell (1976) used the term *post-industrial society* as a speculative construct to think about significant changes in the nature of technology and how they were profoundly affecting the nature of the economy and work. He considered other constructs such as service society, information society, and knowledge society to be voguish, partial, and subsumed under post-industrial society as the more capacious construct. Bell offers this perspective on why he used *post-industrial* as a descriptor: "I employed the term 'post-industrial' for two reasons. First, to emphasize the interstitial and transitory nature of these changes. And second, to underline a major axial principle, that of an intellectual technology" (pp. ix–x). Bell did not wish to single out technology as the primary determinant of societal change; instead, he wanted to position it among key change forces in society, which is also shaped by history, value systems, and the way power weaves through it. Regarding the growing importance of technology, Bell stated, "A post-industrial sector is one of *processing* in which telecommunications and computers are strategic for the exchange of information and knowledge" (p. xii). He believed that information and knowledge, which had economic value, comprised the major structural components of a post-industrial society shaped by intellectual technology. Seeing societal constructs as complex and nuanced, Bell did not present post-industrial society as a discrete entity that displaced industrial society. Moreover, he declared: "A post-industrial transformation provides no 'answers.' It only establishes new promises and new powers, new constraints and new questions—with the difference that these are now on a *scale* that had never been previously imagined in world history" (p. xxii). However, Bell did highlight particular dimensions of post-industrial society, which included:

- the importance of theoretical knowledge, which is codified to inform innovations in technology;
- the emergence of a new intellectual technology that could produce models, simulations, and other means of systems analysis as vehicles to solve economic and social problems and inform policy-making;
- the growth of a knowledge class comprised of technical intellectuals and professionals;
- the change in emphasis from goods to services; and
- a change in the nature of work as a result of placing "the weight of the society … increasingly in the knowledge field" (p. 212).

As Bell saw it, these transitions made "education, and access to higher education, the condition of entry into the post-industrial society" (p. 128). Of course, education would have to be more instrumental in nature to satisfy the requirements of the new techno-scientized society.

In this transitory milieu normalizing the new, adult education (at least in its academic form) sought status not only in universities—where it often seemed marginalized in faculties of education—but also in the larger culture and society, where it was historically perceived as something remedial for society's disadvantaged and something tangential for middle-class learners who were often culturally perceived as engaging in "peripheral and ephemeral educational activities," often for leisure purposes (Grabowski in Ohliger, 1971, p. v; Grace, 1999). To counter its marginal status, many academics in the field of study, seeking to expand adult education's cultural space and place, took a stance that was divisive to the discipline of education: They maintained that proponents of the merits of schooling had overstated its value and ignored how schooling failed large segments of the populace (Field, 2000b; Grace, 2000b). Purporting that adult education could make up for the mistakes of public education for children, the mainstream field of study and practice upheld the value of techno-scientization and, concomitantly, the value of forms of instrumental education, which, of course, were needed to aid and abet post-industrial progress. This irritated adult educators such as John Ohliger (1968) who located worthwhile adult education in its long tradition as social education. Ohliger raised concerns about the commodification of lifelong learning, and cautioned colleagues to think about the concept as one in need of direction in modern practice (Grace, Rocco, & Associates, 2009). Forever the humanist, he reflected: "It seems to me that adult educators have taken the belief in 'lifelong learning' and like the little boy shot an arrow into the air, knowing not where it would fall. Perhaps it is time to stop and take a look at what we are doing to individuals before shooting off any more arrows" (Ohliger, 1968, p. 124).

While instrumental learning for adults became increasingly located as a lifelong process during the 1950s and 1960s, it was not the exclusive focus of the field. Indeed, some forms of North American lifelong learning were committed to socio-cultural reform amid the upheaval of the 1960s and 1970s that saw one disenfranchised group after another mobilize (Diggins, 1988; Marwick, 1998). Emboldened by the radical ideas of the new social movements, adult educators such as Sumner N. Rosen and David B. Rauch examined the plight of the disenfranchised, segregated, or invisible, and emphasized democratic forms of education, learner autonomy, and social justice in their research and practice (Grace, 1997a). They conceptualized lifelong learning in critical terms that paralleled the notion of lifelong education, which was in vogue in some international circles by the early 1970s. Lifelong education as learning for all across the lifespan had emerged in discussions within the United Nations Educational, Scientific, and Cultural Organization in the 1960s. The concept is historically tied to 1960s-style social activism, the political ideals of modernity (democracy, freedom, and social justice), the buttressing of civil society, and participatory and democratic forms of learning for adults (Boshier, 2000). Edgar Faure had linked lifelong education to building a learning society in his influential report *Learning to Be* in 1972 (Boshier, 2000; Coffield, 2002; Field, 2000b). The Faure Report promoted the notion as "the master concept for educational policies in the years to come" (as quoted in Coffield, 2002, p. 188). However, in a déjà vu of sorts, the Faure Report was sidelined in a manner similar to the 1919 Report. Released on the cusp of a period of global economic crisis and rising unemployment, precipitated in this case by the 1973 world oil crisis, the Faure Report was shelved and vocationalism— not lifelong education—was touted in international policy circles as the way out (Field, 2000b).

Barros (2012) relates that, in its 1960s formulation internationally, lifelong education included the instrumental goal of having adult learners keep pace with the knowledge explosion and technological changes. However, on the whole the concept of lifelong education, as promoted by UNESCO and developed by Faure and his colleagues in *Learning to Be*, emphasized state responsibility, the collective good, and social emancipation. Thus, it had a distinctly political dimension and was more concerned with locating the individual learner as part of the collective that needed social education across ages and stages to build a learning society as a conduit for social transformation (Barros, 2012). This required moving beyond the restrictions of formal education, especially as they found expression in schooling for children and youth, and engaging adults in borderless education in informal and non-formal contexts. In this move, lifelong education was touted as "a lever to change the entire understanding of the modern concept of education" (Barros, 2012, p. 121). As Barros (2012) explains, this affected the expanding field of adult education globally in the 1960s and into the 1970s: Lifelong education "went against the two structural axes that characterize the whole school model—the spatial and the temporal axis. In this way it reached beyond the public space of the school with regard to its educational practices, and stepped outside the temporal constraints of the inflexible logic of a school education by introducing the possibility of negotiating schedules and timetables with a degree of flexibility" (p. 121).

In Canadian and US contexts, by the end of the 1970s it appeared that adult education had "taken on a compulsory tinge" (Lisman & Ohliger, 1978, p. 35), and lifelong learning seemed to be a learner's burden and an unending educative process driven by "'friendly' coercion" (p. 36). During this period, the rapid expansion of the world market affected lifelong learning as the information technology revolution emerged to redefine trade and commerce (Jarvis, 2000). While this revolution in communications and information technologies had begun when the transistor was developed after World War II (Greenspan, 2008), Krugman (2009) pinpoints the acceleration of this revolution to 1971, the year that Intel introduced the microprocessor or computer chip. Personal computers became commonplace by the early 1980s, but it was not until the mid-1990s that the business world truly utilized the new technologies produced by the communications and information industries. This led to accelerated worker productivity and higher profits, and it radically changed the culture of work as new skill requirements and an increasing focus on credentialism gave work as competency priority over work as a calling or vocation: "The whole thing changed: networked PCs on every desk, e-mail and the Internet, videoconferencing and telecommuting. This was qualitative, unmistakable change, which created a sense of major progress … [that] helped bring with it a new sense of optimism about capitalism" (Krugman, 2009, p. 23).

As the revolution in communications and information technologies changed the culture of work around the world, it abetted globalization, which

Krugman (2009) defines as "the transfer of technology and capital from high-wage to low-wage countries, and the resulting growth of labor-intensive Third World exports" (p. 25). During the 1980s, the process of globalization began to influence lifelong learning in many nations, which had this main outcome: Knowledge gained priority over skill due to corporatism and new technological advances (Jarvis, 2000). Gauging the response of North American adult education to globalization, Rubenson (2000) relates that, by the mid-1980s, the mainstream field had begun to tie its fortunes to a role in advancing the knowledge economy by concentrating on the employability and productivity of learners as workers. Caught in this economic riptide, adult education grew subservient to government and corporate/post-industrial interests. These interests operated to meld the social and the economic within a politics of survival designed to advance their agendas. In this neoliberal milieu, advancing the economic became synonymous with advancing the social, so instrumental forms of learning continued to gain currency as learning with the most worth.

Since this melding of the social and the economic in the 1980s, the crisis in education has been posed as a crisis of the economic and the instrumental. To resolve this crisis, education has been held responsible and accountable for human resource and skills development that produces individuals who are techno-scientifically literate and able to compete in national and global economies. Education with the greatest worth is described as education that aids and abets these economies. Operating in this milieu, where their autonomy, control, and learning-and-work conditions have declined, educators and learners have been expected to regard teaching, learning, and work as transactions in which the preoccupations are efficiency, accountability, and performativity. Overload and the erosion of inducements and privileges mark and mar these transactions (Apple, 1988). Offering this assessment in the late 1980s, Apple (1988) concluded that education is "increasingly framed in economic terms—in the language of production, rationalization, and standardization. The voice of democracy, participation, and equality is being muted. This more democratic voice is still alive, to be sure, but it is harder to hear above the machinery of the mechanization of education" (p. 27). Apple equated this mechanization with processes of control, technicization, and intensification that he felt had resulted in "the proletarianization of ... work" (p. 45). In other words, education had been infiltrated by the vagaries of the economic and the corporatization of the social. Crises of the economic and the instrumental exacerbated a larger crisis of public life: a crisis of society and its institutions. This set a most important role for education: to resolve the growing crisis in social life (Wexler, 1992). However, instead of giving this role primacy during the 1980s, mainstream adult education made addressing unemployment its key focus in educating and training adults (Field, 2000b; Rubenson, 2000). In reality, the 1980s proved to be a wasteland for holistic lifelong learning as instrumental concerns associated with learning for work superseded social and cultural concerns. With adult education largely remaining a regulated, instrumental kind of activity, affiliated lifelong learning was reduced to another burden, another source of anxiety.

The 1990s emerged as a decade of renewed interest in lifelong learning, especially in policy circles where the foci became increasing economic productivity and competitiveness and promoting social cohesion (Edwards et al., 2002; Field, 2000b; Grace, 2004b; Tuijnman, 2002). The emergent iteration of the lifelong-learning paradigm emphasized the privatization of learning and individual responsibility and empowerment as the basis for success and a better life (Barros, 2012). As lifelong learning has continued to develop as an educational and political construct during the 1990s and into the new millennium, it has been expected to accomplish many things:

> The concept is perceived as being the best educational tool to increase flexibility and economic competitiveness; in another sense it is seen as a policy of social cohesion and for combatting exclusion through educational programs intended for adult audiences considered problematic; another interpretation presents it as a factor of employability and professional promotion; and a final one ... shows it as a strategy to develop consumer-citizen participation in the social, cultural, and political spheres of their societies. (Barros, 2012, p. 125)

The first perception has been predominant, with emphases on techno-vocationalism, consumerism, and social cohesion being corollaries. Under the heavy influences of neoliberalism and globalization, lifelong learning in policy and practice has emphasized building techno-scientific knowledge, skills, and proficiencies to advance its end goal of prioritizing the instrumental in advancing economic interests. In its current iteration, lifelong learning is about upholding neoliberal values aimed at strengthening economic output, with the social hopefully benefiting as a side effect. In inserting itself into adult education, neoliberalized lifelong learning can be construed as a force in the decline of adult education as social education. This is because this insertion has recast learning for adults as a self-directed obligation to acquire the knowledge and skills continuously needed to be a productive citizen contributing to the economic well-being of society. This positions adult education "as a management tool of the work force" and "as a tool of adaptability for the benefit of the working population," which, as Barros (2012) asserts, sidelines the potential of adult education to be a force in social emancipation and transformation (pp. 125–126). Personal well-being in the holistic context of successfully mediating learning, work, *and* life is left on the fringe of what is important to strategic learning for adults in a neoliberal context. In fact, Barros (2012) suggests that being personally happy, secure, and hopeful may be impossible as neoliberalism does its job: "The result of social options and policies of the new economy, namely the neoliberal consensus, is the systematic churning out of the unemployed, the spread of poverty, the generalization of insecure employment and a sharp drop in real wages, as well as an unprecedented creation and concentration of wealth, while at the same time there is more social inequality and a rising rate of bankruptcy" (p. 126). This sorry state of affairs requires a reinvigorated emphasis on the social, collectivism, and addressing the marginalization and disenfranchisement of many citizens as matters of equity and justice.

Looking back, with the advance of neoliberalism in the late 1970s, lifelong-learning policy development became a messy business perhaps best described as "multiple, contested and complex, … [with] no linearity in its assumptions, intentions or effects" (Edwards et al., 2002, p. 5). Despite this messiness, cyclical lifelong learning became normalized as the viability of forms of education was increasingly tied to the production of information-literate lifelong learners able to compete in and contribute to national and global economies. The OECD, UNESCO, and the Group of Eight industrial nations were among those entities that issued key policy papers on lifelong learning as "a solution to the apparent threats and opportunities of the knowledge economy, the information revolution, and far-reaching globalisation" (Field, 2000b, p. 21). These policy papers linked lifelong learning to economic output, labour-market performativity, and the pragmatic kind of social cohesion needed to enable capitalism to flourish. They placed emphasis on identifying perspectives and practices that would align contemporary forms of lifelong learning with the prevailing global economic context that saw cyber-productivity and the exchange and distribution of information increasing in value. Field (2000b) offers this assessment of lifelong learning during the 1990s: "In so far as policy developments have evolved into deliverable measures, they have almost universally focused on one single area: interventions designed to improve the skills and flexibility of the workforce" (p. 21).

Where does this longstanding predicament leave learners as subjects with other identities as persons, workers, and citizens with roles in family, community, and other social contexts? They appear to be left in a difficult place. Jackson (2011a) contends that contemporary lifelong learning values individualism, but not individual identities. Moreover, it devalues the places of equity and social justice in education and, perhaps, disconnects learning from concerns with the collective good. In the end, learners from marginalized or disenfranchised populations will not see their education and learning processes as just and inclusive if their engagement is disconnected from their personhood and from the social and cultural contexts that shape their everyday lives. And if they disengage from learning that is solely focused on forming economically productive citizens, the neoliberal tendency is to blame these learners rather than the systems and structures that limit them. In the mix, it is forgotten that whole persons need holistic learning to be productive across life and work domains. Such holistic learning requires critical pedagogies of place that complement formal lifelong learning with informal and non-formal learning, including grassroots learning and action at the community level (Jackson, 2011b). Critical pedagogies of place are shaped by the ecology—the environment with attendant learner relationships—in which they take place and "are invariably transdisciplinary, experiential, reflective, intergenerational, and potentially intercultural" (Blewitt, 2011, p. 32). They constitute a broader engagement in learning that has the potential to help learners build knowledge, skills, and capacity so they can grow as change agents who provide direction to their personal lives as well as community living (Blewitt, 2011). From this perspective, equity and social justice can be developed and sustained as goals of more holistic lifelong learning, which itself can be sustained by engaged and inclusive communities that broadly construe learning as participation across contexts and differences (Jackson, 2011c, 2011d). This provides a basis for achieving lifelong learning for all—from margins to mainstream—as learners understand themselves in relation to others, the environments they inhabit, and the ways that life, learning, and work scenarios can enable or disable their participation and progress. Within this understanding, learners can critique forms of lifelong learning, and elevate those forms that "explore lifelong learning and social justice through alternative visions for transformative action" (Jackson, 2011d, p. 289). This is at the heart of constituting lifelong learning as critical action.

Before Shooting Off Any More Arrows: Remembering History as We Confront a Discernible Culture of Neglect in Lifelong Learning in Canada

The Current Era of Privatization of Cyclical Learning for Work

In contemporary times when increasingly privatized and cyclical lifelong learning is ascendant, Field's (2000b) assessment of such learning as economistic intervention rings true for many citizens who are mediating life, learning, and work in the Canadian context. Human Resources Development Canada (HRDC) (1998), which develops and implements federal policy intended to build a skills-competent, information-literate, and flexible workforce, frames lifelong learning as a "preventative measure" (p. 2). In doing so, it places the burden of responsibility for lifelong learning on the individual, who is increasingly held accountable for cyclical participation and payment of costs. This patent public to private shift of responsibility for individual training and development sets parameters intended to keep lifelong learning focused on producing workers with the collective capacity to contribute to the growth of the Canadian and global economies. It is this shift that distinguishes the present moment in lifelong learning. While there is not adequate research to support playing up a link between individual training and development and economic productivity (Edwards et al., 2002), HRDC—in 2003 the department was split into Human Resources and Skills Development Canada (HRSDC) and Social Development Canada, with the latter now absorbed and only HRSDC existing—strongly advocates the privatization of lifelong learning. In this milieu, "neglect may be the major contribution of the new lifelong learning movement" (Thomas, 1998, p. 356). If it is understood as a neglectful movement, then contemporary lifelong learning can be construed as an active reproducer of existing inequalities and a possible creator of new sources of inequalities as the information-and-skills poor (for whom there are fewer options in the new-economy learning culture) fall further behind the information-and-skills rich (for whom cyclical lifelong learning and participation in it have been normalized) (Field, 2000b; Grace, 2004b). With the integrity of citizens as learners at stake, we have to counter discernible neglect and resist the reductionistic kind of adult education characterized by a private-business orientation that is solely concerned with linking instrumental education, strategic learning, corporatism, and global economic values (Jeria, 2001). Such education is exclusive, leaving out already disadvantaged learners.

Chapter 3

As part of this resistance, we need to revitalize lifelong learning as "both an expression and a cause of social openness and fluidity" (Field, 2000b, p. 113). This interpretation challenges us to consider the correlation between information-and-skill prowess and a new classism. We might begin these deliberations by answering a key question: How is lifelong learning as a political and economic strategy contributing to a new classism synchronized with information literacy and skills attainment? As we answer this question, we should explore the impact of privatized and cyclical lifelong learning on the political economy of adult education. We should consider how the field might assist with the social integration of the information-and-skills poor, who constitute a new struggling class in an economistic lifelong-learning world (Grace, 2004b; Jeria, 2001). Moreover, we should think about marginalized groups, such as immigrants, who are part of this emerging class. Even though they are frequently mentioned in public policy documents, immigrants regularly experience exclusion from lifelong learning (Kenny, 2004).

To meet the distinct needs of diverse lifelong learners, adult educators ought to remember the field's history as social education and focus on building a critical practice of lifelong learning. Such a practice cast as cultural work for democratic citizenship would engage citizens as learners in holistic instrumental, social, *and* cultural learning (Grace, 2002a, 2002b, 2004a). It would call on educators to engage in ethical educational and cultural work in responsive and responsible ways that help learners become not only rich in the information and skills that can help them become job-ready, but also rich in the social and cultural knowledge that is needed to be life-ready in a change culture of crisis and challenge. After all, lifelong learners need to be able to sustain themselves at home and in communities as well as in the workplace.

The Plight of Canadian Young Adults

In Canada, one group that adult educators ought to focus on in such a critical practice of lifelong learning is young adults. This group is currently a particular target of privatized and cyclical lifelong learning in federal government policy. As such, they are coming of age at a time when the Canadian Council on Social Development (1999) maintains that "the breadth and depth of public responsibility" (p. 5) has dissolved into private air. As a consequence, young adults are experiencing further alienation and disconnection as they attempt to mediate life, learning, and work. In this milieu, adult education as social education could take on a more substantial role as a life-and-work support system for young adults, challenging the federal government to reflect on what ought to be its role as a socially responsive and responsible public institution (Canadian Council on Social Development [CCSD], 1999). Such intensified field involvement could help revitalize adult education at a time when, as noted earlier, some adult educators are questioning whether lifelong learning is responsible for the current precarious position of the field (Wilson & Cervero, 2001). Moreover, it would be in keeping with the Canadian field's historical role as a critical and community-based enterprise that has emphasized democratic and just forms of education for citizens (Grace, 1998).

A turn to history also tells us that a deeper engagement in social education for young adults would constitute a different, more expanded role for Canadian adult education. The field of study and practice has been more concerned with the needs of older adults, and indeed has often blamed schools for the failures of adult learners (Grace, 1999, 2000b). This historical laying of blame is odd in that modern forms of adult education such as co-operative extension and human resource development are as representative of institutionalized education as schooling (Cunningham, 1988). Indeed, institutionalized forms of education, whether they are in the public (K–12) or adult educational spheres, can be conceived as apparatuses of social control that reproduce the socially accepted and acceptable. Regarding adult education, Cunningham (1988) asserts, "Many practitioners do not examine the darker side of adult 'schooling.' In fact, adult education is usually conceptualized and mythologized as a non-school activity having a very different agenda than schools" (p. 133). Ivan Illich, speaking at the annual convention of the American Educational Research Association (AERA) in February 1971, offered a similar critique of the adult educational establishment (Ohliger, 1971). Asserting that a pervasive certification mania and a compulsion for compulsory education drove adult education as a field of study and practice, Illich contended that adult educators were like "therapists … propos[ing] lifelong educational treatment" (as quoted in Ohliger, 1971, p. 15). Illich critiqued field research that reduced this treatment to a prescription intended to "set, specify, and evaluate the personal goals of others" (p. 16). He felt that adult education, like traditional schooling, tended to confuse process with substance, assuming this logic: "The more treatment there is the better are the results: or, escalation leads to success" (p. 9). Within this logic, Illich contended that lifelong learning had become a key part of "the world religion of a modernized proletariat" (p. 10). In this light, it is no wonder that Ohliger (1968) had asked adult educators to think about what they were doing to citizen learners before shooting off any more arrows.

As the above perspectives indicate, schooling and adult education are similar when their institutionalized forms variously set limits to life, learning, and work. By now, history should have taught us that to single out and blame any one sector of education for a failure to advance learning at some point in the lifespan is problematic. Indeed, in contemporary times when inclusive and encompassing education is threatened by neoliberalism, such divisiveness is deleterious to the discipline as a whole. These days, public (schooling for children and youth), adult, and higher education ought to see their contributions to learning as connected and interdependent. Moreover, all sectors should have a daily preoccupation with ethical educational practices that emphasize how knowledge and participation can guide just social choices (Cunningham, 1988). The need for this social focus is clear in Canada given the pervasive instrumental focus in policy from federal government agencies. For example, in its 1998 *Report on Education in Canada*, the Council of Ministers of Education, Canada (CMEC) located the knowledge-based economy and the technological reframing of modes of work as two key challenges in the transition from school to further education and employment. Describing itself as the "national voice for education in Canada" (p. 5), the CMEC suggested that learning in school ought to emphasize enhancing students' abilities to build knowledge, think critically, problem solve, and transfer skills from one area of study and practice to another. Taking a similar stance in its 1999 education-and-training report entitled *Education Indicators in Canada*, the CMEC, working jointly with Statistics Canada, emphasized the importance of cyclical lifelong learning for building a skilled and flexible workforce: "Education, at all levels, from pre-primary to postsecondary through to adult education and training, plays a crucial role in the development of individuals and society. An educated work force, capable of using knowledge to generate innovation, is vital to a strong and prosperous economy" (p. 1).

The fact that all sectors of Canadian education are seen as contributors to the creation of a productive workforce and a prosperous economy underscores the need for a daily preoccupation with ethical educational practices that situate meeting instrumental learning needs within a critical, community-based response to lifelong learning. The entire educational landscape must be involved in this contextual and relational learning project since no one sector can afford to take a separatist stance in these shaky times for education. Each educational sector must be aware of how the new lifelong-learning movement has infiltrated other sectors through policies and practices focused on building future workers for the new economy. For example, since young adults will come to them with a certain knowledge and experience of cyclical lifelong learning, adult educators ought to study how schools are embracing lifelong learning and how the federal government is implicated in the process even though public education is a provincial or territorial responsibility in Canada. They should know about school-to-work transition programs, which have emerged as a key way to address the problem of elusive or no work for underemployed or unemployed young adults. As part of learning-and-work reform in the 1990s, HRSDC and the CMEC jointly focused on developing a Canadian model of school-to-work transitions designed to provide young adults with multiple and flexible opportunities to return to school and change direction using a range of career choices (CMEC, 1998; HRDC, 2002a, 2002b). *School-to-work transitions* refer to "the various ways that young people move among and within the worlds of education, training, and work" (HRDC, 2002a, p. 1). Young adults are expected to engage in cyclical lifelong learning to adapt to these transitions: "It is possible to blend good features from both the market and institutional approaches. Indeed, many examples of school-to-work programs (such as co-operative education, young adult internships, and business-education partnerships) can be found in Canada" (HRDC, 2002a, p. 3). For over a decade, such programs have steadily permeated secondary as well as postsecondary learning (for work) settings.

Still, a significant number of Canadian young adults remain dislocated from learning and work. Why? In a real sense, the dislocated have been among the casualties of a socio-economic domino effect. During the 1990s, many sectors and firms in the Canadian economy juxtaposed increased productivity with rationalization and "downsizing and the shedding of labour" (CCSD, 1999, p. 1). The numbers of full-time jobs declined while the numbers of "low-paying, non-standard jobs" increased to the point that one in five Canadian jobs became part-time (CCSD, 1999, p. 1). Poverty escalated in this milieu, with 37 percent more children living in poverty in Canada in 1997 than in 1989 (CCSD, 1999). A new generation of disadvantaged and disaffected young adults has been left in the wake of this poverty. They lack the resources, skills, and supports needed to engage in cyclical lifelong learning for work, not to mention in other learning that is personally meaningful and life valuable. Indeed, there is a growing underclass of Canadian young adults "who will con-

tinue to have poorer educational results, and their lower educational achievements will, in turn, decrease their labour force opportunities" (CCSD, 1999,
p. 3). They constitute a significant part of the information-and-skills poor in
Canada. Of course, even if they can access and find some sort of accommodation in education and training circles, they are not guaranteed a way out. Indeed, in Canada's current economic climate, they will probably experience the
learning-and-work stalemate that materially advantaged young adults have
already been experiencing: "For many young people during the 1990s, higher
levels of education did not translate into well-paid employment. The real annual earnings of men aged 17 to 24, for instance fell 33% between 1981 and
1993, and they fell 23% for women over the same period. In 1997, half of the
employed youth in Canada were in part-time or temporary jobs, despite growing levels of education" (CCSD, 1999, p. 3).

One is left to wonder where hope and possibility lie for the current generation of Canadian young adults. One is also left to wonder about the degree to which lifelong-learning practices in Canada have been ethical in terms
of meeting the real needs of young adults. Why would young adults bother
to engage in lifelong learning at all? And when do adult educators consider
them their responsibility? The Canadian federal government includes 15- to
30-year-olds as youth (HRDC, 2002a, 2002b; HRSDC, 2004). Yet when does
young adulthood begin? How is the delineation affected by life contexts and
intense experiences, which Merriam and Caffarella (1999) discuss in relation to roles, responsibilities, agency, and learning and its motivations? If, as
Mezirow (1991) contends, perspective transformation does not seem to occur
until after the age of 30, should this be a criterion for deciding when adulthood
begins? Or is the ability to problematize and make meaning through critical
reflection on the content, processes, and premises marking particular learning-and-work experiences sufficient to indicate young adulthood (Mezirow,
1991)? Can certain situational and dispositional factors that are associated
with life in a change culture of crisis and challenge instigate perspective transformation at an earlier age? Adult education as a field of study and practice has
not grappled sufficiently with these questions.

Contemporary Lifelong Learning: No Way Out?

Reflecting a critique of instrumentalism traceable to the 1950s (Grace, 1999),
Cruikshank (2003a, 2003b) argues that lifelong learning in Canada has been

transformed from a broad-based learning paradigm with applicability to learning for life and work to an economistic process of skill acquisition disconnected from civic and social concerns. Indeed, lifelong learning may be no way out for younger or older adults because there is less quality work available. While more than half a million jobs were created in Canada in 2002, the vast majority were low-paying, service-sector jobs, and 57 percent of them were categorized as part-time and self-employment (Cruikshank, 2003b). This suggests that work in Canada's new economy is precarious in nature, with its quality in decline. In this milieu, many citizens as learners and workers constitute the entrepreneurial, the contingent, and the flexible, subsisting in an economic limbo as governments and employers manoeuvre to thrive and unions struggle to survive (Cruikshank, 2003b; Grace, 2002a, 2002b). And when things don't work out, apparently only the learner investing in lifelong learning is to blame (Boshier, 2000; Cruikshank, 2003a; Rubenson, 2002). While 1950s and 1960s individualism, especially as it appeared in a humanistic form, might have been about learner freedom (Grace, 1996), contemporary individualism appears to limit that freedom by situating learners in an information-and-skills learning culture that obligates them to participate and compete in cyclical lifelong learning. In this culture, success or failure lies with them. Rubenson (2002) sees a distinct problem with viewing lifelong learning from this perspective, arguing that the social is left behind in the rush to individualize lifelong learning:

> The obvious danger in regarding lifelong learning as fundamentally an individual project is that as the public good aspect of lifelong learning is pushed to the side, the moral imperative of social needs is being sacrificed on the altar of individual choice. Lifelong learning for active citizenship and democracy cannot be reduced to an individual project. Instead civil society refers to how and when the basic values, conduct, and competencies of democracy are developed among citizens and puts focus, not on the individual but on the relationships between individuals, as well as collective aspirations to create a better society. (p. 245)

Concluding Perspective: A (Re)Turn to Our Critical Roots

The past variously permeates the present, at least as far as the contemporary formation of lifelong learning is concerned. What began as a perceived way out in 1919 now appears to be just another stricture for many citizens as learners and workers. It seems that the individualism and instrumentalism that first took shape in Canadian and American forms in the 1950s and 1960s have metamorphosed to affect lifelong learning in new ways in its neoliberal formation. In its current representation, lifelong learning is caught up in "the abdication of the state, the celebration of the market, the glorification of profit, and the emergence of new political slogans ('there is no alternative')" (Nash, 2003, p. 188).

Contemporary lifelong learning is also a product of the influences of other change forces including the information technology revolution in the 1970s, globalization and corporatism in the 1980s, and privatization and government absconding in the 1990s. In response to these phenomena, lifelong learning has become chameleonic in nature, exacerbating the contemporary crisis of the social. In the midst of this crisis, young adults have become alienated, disinterested, and rather distrustful of government and other providers of economistic lifelong learning. In this dim light, it may indeed be time to (re)turn to our critical roots to consider what we're doing to learners, especially young adults whom the field has tended to neglect. From the perspective of Canadian adult education, Boshier (2000) offers a starting point by establishing two main tasks. First, he calls upon the field to distinguish between lifelong education (and its emancipatory focus on the learner as citizen in its 1960s and 1970s formation) and lifelong learning (and its contemporary focus on the learner as consumer). Boshier provides this distinction between lifelong education and current versions of lifelong learning:

> Contemporary notions of lifelong learning denote a seamless web of individual learners who choose from a broad array of offerings and, as such, act like consumers. The old [lifelong-education] preoccupation with active citizenship and democracy has been replaced by the imperatives of globalization and the rapid embrace of information technologies. Lifelong learning, circa 1998, bears little relationship to lifelong education, 1972, and before anyone adopts either as a slogan, theme, name of a program or a "master concept," they had better understand what lies behind their choice. (pp. 12–13)

As a second task, Boshier appeals to the field to prioritize lifelong education by working to revitalize participation, empowerment as a social construct, and education for citizenship in the educative process. Such moves would help realign learning for life and work with the ethical and political traditions that have historically undergirded Canadian adult education as a community-based and critically oriented practice (Grace, 1998; Thomas, 1998). They would challenge the economistic learning turn exemplified by contemporary lifelong learning and help rejuvenate such historical foci of learning for life and work as education for inclusive social purposes and education to strengthen individuals *and* communities. This return to our critical roots is vital, especially as we intervene in an anxious climate of fiscal uncertainty and constraint, and mediate a reconfigured crisis of the social in a change culture of crisis and challenge. In this milieu we need to find ways to reduce a learner's burden as we continue to experience demands for new kinds of work-ready learners able to meet the instrumental needs of a knowledge-and-service economy. And, in the face of new anxieties, complexities, uncertainties, and challenges linked to global tragedies such as terrorism, religious fundamentalism, American imperialism, and new forms of racism and racial profiling, we need to think deeply about the social and cultural contexts of learning for life and work in our own nations and beyond. Against these stark realities, perhaps the need for learning for life and work has never been greater.

How might we begin to make lifelong learning more critical, viable, credible, consequential, and worthwhile for citizens? First, despite the vagueness of the concept, we must contest and resist the economistic essentialization of lifelong learning so pervasive in contemporary policy development and efforts toward implementation. With the privatization of public services sweeping Canada, Cruikshank (2002) asserts that contemporary lifelong learning has been politicized in neoliberal terms with a utopian (skills for competitiveness) trend ascendant to the detriment of civil society. Such reductionism tends to fixate on learners who are already acculturated to the new economy. Indeed, with the neoliberal shift from education as a public and social good to education as an individual and private good, we have witnessed a focusing of resources on the relatively well-educated as lifelong learning is aligned with increasing investment in human resource development and intensified vocational education linked to enhancing productivity and competitiveness in work (Nesbit, 1999). By default, this focus on performance intensifies the disenfranchisement of the un-acculturated who experience learning and work as precarious ventures, and widens the gap in opportunities and income between the more and the less affluent (Cruikshank, 2002; Nesbit, 1999). From this perspective, Cruikshank (2002) claims that neoliberalized lifelong learning helps create a two-tiered job system in a new economy where there are not even enough good jobs. Moreover, she maintains that lifelong learning plays a role in increasing the polarization between the rich and the poor in Canada:

> The growing polarization of the labour market is paralleled by a similar trend in training. While a two-tiered job system is widening the gap between the rich and the poor, "lifelong learning" (HRD [human resource development]) is increasing the skills of a small number of workers in the high knowledge, high wage tier. Workers who are underemployed are ignored, and the unemployed are forced into meaningless learnfare programs. Thus, "lifelong learning" can and does serve to reinforce the creation of two classes of workers. (p. 58)

While lifelong learning is on this neoliberal path, we must not only interrogate and contest the politicization and economistic essentialization of lifelong learning, but we must also work to reactivate critical foci on democratic forms of learning and ethical and just learning-and-work practices for all citizens.

Second, in rearticulating lifelong learning as a credible and viable critical practice, we need to better understand the shifting and porous nature of the term as exemplified by its multiple meanings and uses across time and tides and across the educational spectrum (Grace, 2004b). This requires ongoing development of a lifelong-learning research agenda focused on building theory, research methodology, foundational knowledge, and longitudinal databases (Tuijnman, 2002). It also requires careful analysis of the institutional relationships between formal public education (schooling for children and youth) and "the more diffuse, heterogeneous provisions of continuing education for adults" (Tuijnman, 2002, p. 21).

Third, we need to build theories and a philosophy to guide an ethical practice of lifelong learning (Aspin & Chapman, 2001a, 2001b). Aspin and Chapman (2001b) challenge us to develop a framework to

- check congruency between principles and practices of lifelong learning;
- analyze concepts, criteria, and categories shaping any lifelong-learning project;
- consider how the development and implementation of a project aligns with the problem it is expected to address; and
- justify lifelong-learning policies and practices publicly to the people who will be affected by them.

It is this last challenge that is perhaps the most important.

Chapter 4

Lifelong Learning as a Chameleonic Concept and Versatile Practice: Recounting Y2K Perspectives and Trends

A s the year 2000 approached, the Y2K problem became a global concern. The knowledge and information society seemed at the mercy of what would happen to digitally stored data that used a two-digit abbreviation to record the year. What would happen if computers couldn't distinguish 00 as 1900 or 2000? Would they crash? What would be the impact on daily life? The Y2K problem signified fears about an uncertain future in a late-twentieth-century change culture of crisis and challenge. During this time, the field of education was dealing with its own fears and concerns as neoliberalism, which took hold beginning in the late 1970s, rearticulated notions of learning and the successful learner to align with its economistic aspirations. The advent of a new millennium continued to mix uncertainty and concern with hope and possibility as lifelong educators deliberated future forms and functions of lifelong learning. Some lifelong educators were forging ahead with lifelong learning fashioned as learning for the changing economy. Other lifelong educators critiqued this formation, arguing that lifelong learning had to be holistic so it could address the instrumental, social, and cultural needs of learners mediating life and work. These deliberations help us to understand the opposing camps and complexities marking lifelong learning into the present moment. To recapture these deliberations in this chapter, I revisit three new millennial lifelong-learning events. With the new millennium providing impetus to look back and look forward, these events provided spaces for critical reflection and assessment of the state and status of lifelong learning in many national and international contexts.

In this chapter, I focus on the conceptualization and practice of lifelong learning as it was reflected in deliberations during three Y2K lifelong-learning events held in Australia, Canada, and the United Kingdom during 2000–2001. At these events, which brought together an array of international participants, educators deliberated with policy-makers and practitioners about lifelong learning, its parameters, and its possibilities amid a range of instrumental, social, and cultural demands from government, corporate, community, and other interest groups. In reflecting on these deliberations, I discuss three life-long-learning themes that shaped the dialogic interactions at these events: (1) lifelong learning encompasses instrumental, social, and cultural education; (2) lifelong learning involves mediation of public and private responsibilities; and (3) lifelong learning occupies a precarious and paradoxical position in a world that desires to position it as a permanent global necessity. The up-shot of these deliberations is that lifelong learning remains contested terrain in terms of its multiple meanings, purposes, and desired outcomes in relation to learning for life and work. I conclude with a perspective on lifelong learning as a critical practice in a world where culture as knowledge and culture as community vie for space. I locate this practice in inclusive, holistic terms, suggesting that its key aim is to help persons become responsive and responsible citizens who are able to think, speak, and act in life, learning, and work situations.

Gauging Lifelong Learning's Parameters and Possibilities via Three Y2K Events

During 2000 and 2001, I investigated three international lifelong-learning events held in Australia, Canada, and the United Kingdom. All were broadly focused on conditions and complexities affecting contemporary learning for life and work. I variously studied event websites, participated in conferences, and analyzed background documents, keynote addresses, papers, and symposia associated with these Y2K events. In my analysis of them, I focused on how participants made meaning and sense of lifelong learning as both a concept and a practice in the face of its present location as a porous and flexible concept that broadly encompasses a fluid and indeterminate range of formal, non-formal, and informal educational practices. I considered participants' divergent opinions regarding the positioning of lifelong learning as a pervasive global phenomenon valued, at least in its economistic forms, by governments, corporate/post-industrial interests, supranational bodies such as the Organisation for Economic Co-operation and Development (OECD), and instrumentalist factions across sectors in education. I also examined how participants who were actively engaged in lifelong learning took up matters of design, content, delivery, and process. As I proceeded, my analysis became both a thematic engagement of contemporary emphases and an exploration of critical yearning. The thematic analysis explored instrumental/social/cultural, private/public, and local/global dimensions of lifelong learning as a chameleonic concept and versatile practice in a post-industrial world. The critical yearning, most pervasive in deliberations at the Y2K event in the United Kingdom, found expression both as a critique of the bounded economistic nature of contemporary lifelong learning and as a call for lifelong learning to reinvigorate critical foci such as education for citizenship and social justice. These foci have historically underpinned democratic, ethical, participatory, and public learning practices (Boshier, 2000; Grace, 2000b; Welton, 1998).

The Three New Millennial Events
The Y2K Australian Event

In July 2000, Central Queensland University (CQU), Rockhampton, Australia, hosted its inaugural international Lifelong Learning Conference (hereafter called the Y2K Australian event). This event brought together international educators, policy-makers, and practitioners to share their knowledge and understanding of lifelong learning. The participating collective also discussed pervasive life, learning, and work issues, and attempted to develop networks for education and training (Central Queensland University [CQU], 2000). While some participants raised issues about social and cultural learning in relation to community building, or examined critical perspectives in relation to developing ethical and just lifelong-learning practices, most participants focused on instrumental issues associated with knowledge-and-skill building and information literacy in an era of globalization. In attending to this array of issues, keynote addresses, workshops, and other presentations variously focused on:

- developing models for teaching lifelong learning,
- engendering creative and critical thinking,
- using lifelong-learning skills,
- using educational technology innovations,
- enhancing communication skills,
- developing models for teaching information literacy, and
- engaging in independent problem-based learning.

The Y2K Canadian Event

In December 2000, the OECD and Human Resources Development Canada (HRDC) jointly hosted an international conference in Ottawa entitled Lifelong Learning as an Affordable Investment (hereafter called the Y2K Canadian event). The conference was designed to consider the resource challenge presented in relation to changing parameters and possibilities associated with the 1996 mandate that OECD education ministers adopted with the intention of making *lifelong learning for all* a basis in fact (OECD & HRDC, 2000b). In relation to new resource issues associated with the implementation of lifelong-learning strategies, the conference specifically focused on the following:

- transformation and expansion of the existing capacities of non-public and public education
- composite resources needed to make lifelong learning for all a reality
- affordability and financing of lifelong learning for all
- role of public policy in the design and delivery of lifelong learning

Participants were invited to deliberate the contemporary public-private dialectic based on the argument that the private share of financing lifelong learning should increase due to the strain on public resources combined with the tangible private gain associated with successful and ongoing participation in lifelong learning.

The Y2K UK Event

During July 2001, the University of East London (UEL) hosted an international gathering of educational, business, and community partners to discuss lifelong learning under the auspices of the 2001 Standing Conference on University Teaching and Research in the Education of Adults (SCUTREA) (hereafter called the Y2K UK event). SCUTREA 2001 was billed as the finale to the UK Festival of Lifelong Learning, which the UEL had organized during 2000 and 2001. As part of this festival, a Global Colloquium Supporting Lifelong Learning, which was co-sponsored by the Open University and the UEL, was held from June to October 2000. The colloquium sought to have academics, policy-makers, and practitioners engage in dialogues about their work. As noted on the home page of the colloquium's website, interest groups were to discuss ways of conceptualizing and implementing lifelong learning, and to deliberate issues and possibilities related to networking in lifelong learning. However, the global colloquium was not very successful. Little electronic discussion materialized during its four-month span, even though an international invitation had been widely dispersed soliciting such participation. The website proved useful, though, as a source of background papers by Colin Griffin and others who explored critical themes that would be integral to discussions at SCUTREA 2001. This conference, as Miller and West (2001) indicated, had two key purposes: "To share perspectives on theory, policy, and practice in the education of adults and to examine the extent to which lifelong learning is emerging as an alternative route for adult education" (p. 13).

Working within this framework for the conference, Miller and West reminded participants that lifelong learning takes place in both formal and informal contexts across the lifespan, not only in schools, colleges, and universities, but also in homes, workplaces, diverse community locations, and cyberspace. Using these sweeping parameters, educational, business, and community partners dialogued about the intricacies of learning for life and work. They explored lifelong-learning patterns and expectations in light of the fact that today's governments and corporate/post-industrial interests usually articulate and situate the concept of lifelong learning in relation to learning for new economies. They also explored the term's other dimensions besides the instrumental, discussing how lifelong learning has diverse social and cultural purposes as well.

Lifelong Learning: A Vague and Contested Term

Discussing the increasing tendency to see lifelong learning as something larger than adult education, SCUTREA 2001 participants also questioned whether lifelong learning had replaced adult education. On this point, Wain (2000) has gone further, contending that lifelong learning, while still a vague and contested term, is replacing all forms of education. However, Small took a different stance in his SCUTREA 2001 presentation. He suggested that adult education, at least in the United Kingdom, had been revitalized and not replaced by lifelong learning. He contended that the installation of the Labour government in May 1997 had actually given adult education new impetus since the government gave priority to lifelong learning in the face of high unemployment. The Labour government wanted to invest in education for adults to help the United

Kingdom build a flexible, "adaptable workforce, competent when it came to re-training" (2001, pp. 368–369). Of course, such learning for work has become *de rigueur* in the face of what Aronowitz and DiFazio (1994) call the "sci-tech" revolution, which ties knowledge, not skill, to capital and technology, radically reconfiguring forms of work, skill, and occupation in the process. With information a key component of contemporary knowledge production and a major industry, Aronowitz and DiFazio maintain that government and education set policy with the express purpose of meeting the demand for the scientific and technical labour needed to move the information society forward. This, they assert, signals the "proletarianization of work" (p. 16), which assaults worker integrity and undermines worker security. From this perspective, Small might have more carefully scrutinized what flexibility and adaptability (as driving forces behind lifelong learning) cost workers. Even if he perceived some kind of revitalized adult education, it still may be nothing more than lifelong learning as transaction. Such learning is intended to serve government interests by abetting the economy, which, from a neoliberal perspective, is then construed as enhancing the social.

It was perhaps Wilson and Cervero who spent the most time focusing on the central question of the SCUTREA 2001 conference: "If lifelong learning is emerging as both an alternative route and destination for what used to be thought of as adult education, then what does the landscape through which we now journey look like and how shall we find our way?" (2001, p. 435). In taking up this question, these US adult educators wondered what the lexical substitution of *lifelong learning for adult education* means in terms of the theory and practice of adult education. They questioned how the use of the term affects adult education as a field of study and practice. Indeed, how lifelong learning is construed as a concept and a practice is a crucial, perennial concern of many critical educators mediating local/global, private/public, and individual/social concerns in their theorizing and practice. For example, Rubenson (2002) worries about the consequences now that lifelong learning has become a catch-all concept, a problematic umbrella descriptor for all and sundry kinds of formal, non-formal, and informal learning. With the contemporary conceptualization of lifelong learning so diffuse, he warns, "There is a risk of losing sight of fundamental issues like equality and justice and a temptation to move public policy concerns to the background" (p. 242). A primary focus on individuals as clients, performers, and producers, which is at the heart of the contemporary focus on economistic lifelong learning, only exacerbates this risk. For example, Boshier (2001) has discussed how the risk is manifested in New Zealand, where a contemporary version of lifelong learning merges a neoliberal commitment to privatization, the free market, and competition with a neoconservative commitment to a capitalistic morality that devalues the social and keeps marginalized groups disenfranchised. (See chapter 5 for further analysis of the New Zealand context.) He offers this perspective: "Lifelong learning tends to render invisible any obligation to address social conditions. It is nested in an ideology of vocationalism. Learning is for acquiring skills alleged to enable the learner to work harder, faster and smarter and thus enables their employer to better compete in the global economy. These days lifelong learning also denotes the savvy consumer surfing the Internet selecting from a smorgasbord of educational offerings. Learning is an individual activity" (p. 368).

In his depiction, Boshier situates contemporary lifelong learning in the private domain and describes it as a process associated with individual goals driven by free-market priorities. While his comments are made in relation to New Zealand's situation, they are more broadly relevant in an OECD context in which the notion of lifelong learning is linked to neoliberalism following this "commonsense and necessary" equation: "privatization + deregulation + open capital markets + balanced budgets + free market competition = the cult of finance" (Boshier, 2001, p. 367). As an alternative to this economistic conceptualization and practice of lifelong learning, Boshier proposes not a rerouting of the term adult education, but a revitalization of the notion of lifelong education, which he locates in the public domain and portrays as a process associated with collective goals. In describing lifelong education as accessible and accommodative learning for all across the lifespan and across educational sectors, he is inspired by Faure's conceptualization of lifelong education, which was laid out in *Learning to Be* in 1972 (Boshier, 2000). He associates lifelong education with social learning and advocacy, emancipatory ventures, and the public good. For Boshier (2001), lifelong learning, as it is presently conceived and practiced, incorporates a more oppressive set of relationships than lifelong education, which he views as the more inclusive term across the historical, social, and cultural dimensions that shape it. However, he knows that revitalizing lifelong education will be a challenging and difficult political task because "the new right gutted *lifelong education* of its emphasis on equity, civil society and participation and instead, deployed *lifelong learning* as part of the cult of finance" (p. 368).

It is perhaps in deliberations around the conceptualization and practice of both lifelong learning and lifelong education that we have a broader relational and contextual basis to consider the parameters, problems, and possibilities of learning for life and work. Importantly, such deliberations could move discussions such as those at SCUTREA 2001 beyond the narrow limit of how contemporary lifelong learning, which impacts public (schooling for children and youth), adult, *and* higher education, affects the parameters of adult education as a field of study and practice. Moreover, they could broaden the perspectives of lifelong educators and learners struggling to mediate the already contested and complex terrain of learning for life and work. They could also provide greater substance to help us answer the key question that shaped Peter Jarvis' keynote address at the Y2K Australian event: How might educators as responsible change agents constitute lifelong learning as a holistic, ethical practice? Answering this question is at the heart of building an inclusive, holistic practice of critical learning for life and work. As we answer this question, we have to focus on the diversity and locations of citizen educators and learners in life, learning, and work spaces. We also have to focus on the instrumental/social/cultural, private/public, individual/social, and local/global dimensions that complicate the purposes and meanings of learning for life and work whether we call it lifelong learning, lifelong education, adult education, or something else.

Three Pervasive Themes in Deliberations at the Y2K Events

The three Y2K events afforded important opportunities for participants to consider the parameters and complexities of lifelong learning as a popular yet problematic contemporary catchphrase used disparately to encompass different combinations of instrumental, social, and cultural education. These events demonstrated that contemporary lifelong learning has multiple intentions, porous parameters, inherent problems, and diverse possibilities. Moreover, exchanges among educational, community, and government participants at each event demonstrated the diversity of purposes, forms, quandaries, risks, and projects embodied in lifelong-learning discourse, policy-making, and educational practice. As participants discussed conceptualizations, practices, perspectives, and trends shaping lifelong learning, there was much deliberation around three pervasive themes:

- Lifelong learning encompasses instrumental, social, and cultural education.
- Lifelong learning involves mediation of public and private responsibilities.
- Lifelong learning occupies a precarious and paradoxical position in a world that desires to position it as a permanent global necessity.

Theme 1: Lifelong Learning Encompasses Instrumental, Social, and Cultural Education

At each Y2K event, educators, policy-makers, and practitioners variously supported or advanced an array of instrumental, social, and cultural interests and projects. Some linked the promise of techno-science to cultural and socio-economic advancement, and promoted instrumental forms of lifelong learning intended to intensify worker performativity and productivity. Others, emphasizing social activism and cultural work in community settings, advanced social and cultural forms of lifelong learning designed to enhance possibilities for a better life. Still others, emphasizing the need to bring together forms of instrumental, social, and cultural learning, advocated for more inclusive, holistic forms of learning for life and work.

It is the latter emphasis that I will speak to here. Work at the intersection of instrumental, social, and cultural education is necessary in a world where the commodification of knowledge, skill transience, personal dislocation, and community erosion requisition lifelong learning as a way out (Grace, 1997b, 2002a). This complementary work, which is a basis for lifelong learning as transformation, is needed to counter pervasive, reductionistic lifelong learning that has found expression mainly as instrumental learning-for-the-moment (Bauman, 1996; Grace, 1997b). With joblessness, underemployment, partial and permanent unemployment, declining wages, and the displacement of full-time work on the list of the "dystopian consequences" of the commodification of knowledge (Aronowitz & DiFazio, 1994, p. 31), citizens need lifelong learning to be something more. They require inclusive, holistic forms of lifelong learning that meet their needs as they take on multiple roles at home, at work, in learning venues, and in the community. Such learning integrates learning for work with learning for life. It places emphasis on providing and problematizing bread-and-butter instruction for workers mediating the culture of contemporary workplaces (Grace, 1997b, 1998). It also emphasizes equity, justice, participation, and education for citizenship, which, as previously noted, are embedded in Faure's notion of lifelong education (Boshier, 2000, 2001). The latter highlights how citizens are situated across life, learning, and work spaces.

Obviously, an engagement in such inclusive, complementary learning has its complexities, problems, and risks. We have to be mindful of Edwards' (2000b) caution that inclusive, holistic forms of lifelong learning may not be a cure for learner or worker dislocation. In fact, in sum, they may add to the experience of dislocation. However, a probable experience of dislocation should not be used to dismiss a possibly transformative experience of lifelong learning. Rather, it should be taken as a sign to proceed with caution, paying attention to the issues and concerns of relational learning in context. Indeed, analysis of an experience of dislocation can be used to inform an ethical and encompassing practice of lifelong learning. A learner, working with an educator as a mentor and resource, can engage in critical questioning to help clarify the purpose(s) of learning in relation to an identified problem (or problem set) and a proposed learning project that will (re)locate and hopefully benefit the learner. This modus operandi guided the educative work of a number of presenters who profiled their critical, participatory lifelong-learning projects at the three Y2K events. Examining individual, cultural, and socio-political contexts contouring learner dislocation, these presenters spoke about their initiatives to mediate learning in the intersection of instrumental, social, and cultural education. I provide three examples of these inclusive, holistic initiatives below.

Speaking at the Y2K UK event, Patricia A. Gouthro (2001) focused on the effects of gender, racial, and cultural differences on the teaching-learning interaction when a distance delivery model is used to enable lifelong learning. Engaging these differences, Gouthro thought deeply about the complementary kinds of social and cultural learning that adult learners need when they use a distance delivery model to learn about program planning, instructional methods and techniques, and other aspects of education for adults. Working from the premise that lifelong learning has gendered implications, Gouthro accentuated the fact that women's life paths include engaging in education "as part of a complex network of obligations and expectations that direct their energy and labour" (p. 133). The majority of students in her university's graduate adult-education program are women, and they use distance education to engage in lifelong learning while still fulfilling family, work, and community responsibilities. While acknowledging her program's success in addressing equity issues and removing barriers to participation, Gouthro has found that hurdles still exist. She spends considerable administrative and teaching time helping women students address issues of accommodation as they mediate the demands of life, learning, and work. It is at this point that she integrates the social and the instrumental to help create a cyber-learning culture that works for them. In addition, Gouthro advises and teaches a significant number of Jamaican students who also work in this cyber-learning context in her university's distance program. As a White Canadian feminist educator working with women and men across racial and cultural differences, she is concerned about the ethics and constitution of her practice as well as her Jamaican students' experiences of dislocation. Working collaboratively with the Jamaican students, she interweaves the cultural and the instrumental to develop coursework that reflects students' histories and the politics of their locations in the teaching-learning interaction. Gouthro considers such work at the intersection of instrumental, social, and cultural education to be vital to her mission of delivering an accommodating and meaningful educative experience. While her work incorporates key critical elements shaping Faure's notion of lifelong education, such a multi-perspective approach adds significantly to her administrative and teaching workload, which is a fact that universities, which often use such programs as cash cows, ought to acknowledge.

In another example focused on issues of equity and participation, Tara J. Fenwick (2001), also presenting at the Y2K UK event, described how the non-formal (in this case, experience gained in frontline entrepreneurial work) could inform the formal in lifelong learning. Again replicating key social elements contouring Faure's notion of lifelong education, Fenwick's project uniquely links individualism and non-formal knowledge to notions of productivity and formal knowledge that are embodied and embedded in critical understandings of justice and empowerment. Her study, with its distinctly critical edge, focuses on a diverse group of Canadian women entrepreneurs who have been successful despite the situational, dispositional, and institutional hurdles that mark their journeys in learning and work. Investigating these "workers' learning and struggles for subjectivity in the ethos of enterprise" (p. 111), Fenwick situates their learning as a mediation of instrumental, social, and cultural contexts. She emphasizes, "All conjured an enterprise, unique in product/service and structure, with little assistance and many obstacles" (p. 114). These women linked their success, which they often described in terms of personal growth and empowerment, to their contemplation and negotiation of their entrepreneurial experiences. Self-employment provided them opportunities to create a challenging and rewarding work culture in which they built self-confidence, skill sets, and their abilities to analyze and evaluate work ventures. They used their own ways of designing, planning, and developing projects in order to turn "self-crafted work" into a "self-supporting livelihood" (p. 114). Fenwick believes that educators, working in formal contexts, can use women's "field" experiences to help them construct cultural texts and inclusive, holistic practices for the classroom. She offers these helpful suggestions: First, educators can use women's stories and their analyses of mistakes and achievements in entrepreneurial ventures to show how women build presence and place in business. Second, educators can involve women as learners in teaching-learning interactions that explicitly highlight and build on women's own meanings of success.

Undergirding Faure's notion of lifelong education is a belief that learning has to be critical and encompassing in order to enable learners to be in charge of their destinies. During her presentation at the Y2K Australian event, Margaret Hornagold (2000) provided an example of such inclusive, holistic learning when she described her Indigenous practice of cultural and environmental education. Hornagold discussed her two-year involvement in an Aboriginal lifelong-learning project with the Fitzroy Basin Elders' Committee in Central Queensland, Australia. As a multi-perspective educational venture, it proved to be a complementary learning project that enabled learners to gain insights to help them address experiences of dislocation in terms of culture-knowledge-language-power issues and health-environment issues. The Elders' project had two interlocking purposes:

- to provide public education about the cultural history of Aboriginal people in Central Queensland
- to provide lessons in community building and sustainable management skills and practices, especially as they relate to attachment to the land for hunting, gathering, and spiritual purposes

In speaking to the issue of a critical public pedagogy that reflects and re-members Aboriginal history and culture, Hornagold discussed the committee's efforts to revise history and provide awareness of traditional ways of knowing, believing, and doing. This involved describing post-White settlement attempts to disperse Aboriginal persons either by murdering them or by taking them away from their traditional lands to subsist outside of family and community structures in missions and on reserves. It also involved describing how these White aggressions resulted in the destruction of Aboriginal knowledge, language, social structures, and culture, and in a loss of social control by Elders, which amounted to the demise of traditional community leadership. In speaking to the issues of sustainable management and community building, which require revitalizing Elders' leadership practices, Hornagold linked Aboriginal cultural practices and title rights to environmental education. She described how the Fitzroy Basin Elders' Committee drew on tradition and engaged in sustainable management activities within the Basin's subcatchments and river systems in order to preserve pastoral, cropping, fishing, tourism, and mining industries for the long-term future. Noting that the theme of the Elders' committee is the traditional saying of *Gumoo Wangarra—One Water One People*, she stated how it reflected everyone's collective responsibility to protect the water and land and keep them healthy. Speaking to the importance of the Elders in this holistic lifelong-learning project, Hornagold ended her presentation by depicting her relationship with the Elders: "They are teachers, instructors, innovators and mentors. They are my role models and guides in my lifelong learning experience as an Indigenous person" (p. 7).

I have discussed each of these examples in some detail to indicate how intersecting forms of instrumental, social, and cultural education provide insights to help build an inclusive, holistic practice of lifelong learning that, in critical terms, is ethical, equitable, just, and democratic. From a theoretical perspective, outlined in his colloquium contribution to the Y2K UK event, Colin Griffin (2000) contributed further insights to building such a practice as he explored the tensions and possibilities for lifelong learning variously understood as policy, strategy, and cultural practice. As policy, Griffin suggested that the meaning of lifelong learning could be partially linked to more measurable outcomes such as employability, human resource development, technological accreditation, and global competition. He sees this instrumental component of the meaning as coterminous with the advancement of public education and training. However, Griffin contends that the meaning of lifelong learning as policy is insufficient. It needs to be linked to less measurable outcomes such as social inclusion, active citizenship, and the quality of life in socio-cultural sites including educational institutions, families, communities, and workplaces. Thus, Griffin also speaks to lifelong learning as strategy and cultural practice. As strategy, Griffin locates the meaning of lifelong learning in the realm of individual responsibility and choice. In this case, the desire is to minimize state interference in individual life. Griffin believes the role of government is not to mandate education, but to provide the means and create the conditions to enable individuals to maximize their own learning across the lifespan. As cultural practice, the meaning of lifelong learning is found within daily actions that are tied to disposition (attitudes, values, and beliefs) or behaviour (lifestyle practices). Here, "the idea that learning is sited in everyday experience, and in the social relations of family, community and work, effectively distances it from public education and thus removes it from the realms of both policy and strategy" (p. 12). This sidelining of the social is a conundrum for contemporary lifelong learning that encompasses multiple forms enacted in multiple locations across formal, non-formal, and informal contexts. In underscoring this conundrum, Griffin's typology draws our attention to the tensions—instrumental-social/cultural, individual/social, private/public, and local/global—of working with contemporary lifelong learning as a chameleonic concept and versatile practice. Focusing on these tensions is central to a critical practice of lifelong learning. It is in working with these tensions that we also work with possibility so we can create more inclusive, holistic forms of lifelong learning.

Theme 2: Lifelong Learning Involves Mediation of Public and Private Responsibilities

In discussing the private/public tension as it relates to fiscal responsibility for lifelong learning, Griffin (2000) raised important questions in his background paper for the colloquium that initiated the Y2K UK event:

- Is lifelong learning part of a global trend to move responsibility for education from the public to the private sector?
- Is lifelong learning part of what is called the "crisis" of the welfare state?
- And if it is, shouldn't we reject neoconservative and market-oriented efforts to take lifelong learning out of the realm of public provision where, at least, political, policy, and programmatic issues can be debated?

These questions are at the heart of the contemporary private versus public debate regarding who is responsible for assuming the cost of lifelong learning.

This debate dominated proceedings at the Y2K Canadian event. It is a difficult debate because the issue of fiscal responsibility is so multi-faceted. First, lifelong learning takes place in diverse public and non-public settings across a host of socio-cultural spaces including the home, the workplace, leisure spaces, and formal educational spaces. Second, lifelong learning has the potential to be a significant change force affecting the parameters and future activities of the major stakeholders across the educational spectrum: early childhood education, compulsory and upper secondary education, tertiary education, and workplace and adult learning. Third, lifelong learning, especially as it pertains to adult learning, "is open-ended with respect to the timing, venue, and duration of learning, the targets of policies, and their beneficiaries" (Burke, Long, & Wurzburg, 2000, p. 6). Policy-makers and other participants from the 29 OECD member and observer countries who participated in the debate discussed these complexities. They examined the histories and existing cultures of lifelong learning in their national contexts. They shared "their experiences, insights and best practices regarding the financing of lifelong learning" (OECD & HRDC, 2000a, p. 1). They strategized around three resource questions (OECD & HRDC, 2000b, p. 1):

- What resources are likely to be required in order to make lifelong learning for all a reality?
- Under what conditions can the mandate be made more affordable to society?
- What is the role of public policy in helping to meet those conditions?

In order to accept fiscal responsibility and successfully implement lifelong-learning strategies, these deliberations led participants to consider what appears to be the contemporary bottom line: to enhance incentives for public and private investment in lifelong learning so that benefits to investors outweigh the costs. As they deliberated, the key question became an economistic one: "How does lifelong learning increase the opportunity for enhancing cost-effectiveness of provision of learning, and increasing its benefits?" (OECD & HRDC, 2000b, p. 3).

This question had been taken up in a series of background papers provided to participants in the Y2K Canadian event. In his background paper, Verry (2000) stated a position that was reiterated in background papers by the OECD (2000) and Burke, Long, and Wurzburg (2000): Since individuals, corporations, and others with vested interests in lifelong learning benefit from it, the private share of fiscal responsibility for learning for life and work ought to be bigger. Moreover, the background papers had a common theme: Lifelong learning for all will only be a reality in the face of more restricted public-sector financing and provision of lifelong learning if private funding is increased. Verry (2000) provided this summary as he outlined the complexities of strategically and resourcefully enabling lifelong learning for all:

> In contrast to other far-reaching reforms or new initiatives in education, the lifelong learning mandate changes many parameters at once. It implies quantitative expansion of learning opportunities; qualitative changes in the content of existing educational activities; qualitatively and quantitatively different learning activities and new settings, and changes in the timing of learning activities in the lifecycle of individuals. These developments imply, in turn, a strong likelihood of changes in the costs of providing and participating in education, training and learning activities, and increases in the total outlays by society for such activities. Constraints on and competition for public resources combined with the presence of substantial private returns to certain aspects of lifelong learning imply a need to increase the private share of the overall finance burden. (p. 6)

In its background paper for the event, the OECD (2000) focused on tertiary education, a most costly component of a broadly construed model of learning for life and work. The OECD noted that, during the 1990s, participation in tertiary education had increased by 50 percent in 24 countries for which the secretariat had comparative data available. Many learners came with qualifications and backgrounds that went beyond having participated in secondary education. They pointed to this growth and shift in educational participation as two key factors behind contemporary policy reflection and changes in tertiary education in relation to the procurement and use of financial, other in-kind, and human resources. The OECD analysis showed that, in nearly all member countries, student, family, and third-party financing of learner costs had been emphasized in the move from public to private financing of lifelong learning. Indeed, many countries already facilitated investment in lifelong learning through and by students. Across countries, methods of paying for tertiary education included

- student and family utilization of loans;
- deferred contributions, which are income-contingent arrangements where payments are linked to income;
- prepaid tuition plans;
- time-limited and performance-based financial aid; and
- mortgage-type loans that enable students to extend costs over a lifetime.

Of course, in a melding of the educational and the economic, such private investments were seen to demand effective and efficient education shaped through "quality assurance, indicators, [and] qualifications frameworks" (OECD, 2000, p. 5). The OECD insisted that tertiary education, as a component of lifelong learning, had to be accountable and performative.

Collectively, the review of methods of paying for tertiary education demonstrated the contemporary trend to move fiscal responsibility for lifelong learning to the private realm. Moreover, it provided impetus for participants at the Y2K Canadian event to consider how to continue to intensify the public to private shift in responsibility for assuming the costs of lifelong learning. It seemed obvious that a lifelong-learning perspective now meant that fiscal responsibility had to be located even more broadly beyond the public realm, and that responsibility for lifelong learning needed to be re-articulated around a series of options where linkages, networks, and partnerships have prime value. The OECD (2000) asked participants to examine five issues in relation to the further resourcing and financing of tertiary education:

- mobilising the resources;
- facilitating investment through and by students;
- limiting expenditure growth and improving effectiveness;
- financing for equity; [and]
- fostering a lifelong pattern of participation. (p. 5)

The upshot of these deliberations was that they showed that private financing and provision of tertiary education had to continue to increase, supplanting public (taxpayer) financing of personal lifelong-learning plans. However, in this displacement process, financing for equity is often reduced to means-tested financial aid and supplemented (instead of no) tuition fees. Thus, critical questions need to be raised here: To what extent do new ways of resourcing and financing lifelong learning encourage and enable learner participation (access, accommodation, and choice), particularly by those groups traditionally under-represented in tertiary education? To what extent does this shift in the financing of education help to reinscribe instrumental performativity as the raison d'être of learning for life and work? If it is perceived that instrumental forms of learning provide the most useful knowledge and skills worth the educational investment, then how does this impinge on possibilities for more inclusive, holistic lifelong learning? After all, the benefits of social and cultural forms of lifelong learning cannot always be measured in dollars and cents.

In considering these questions, we need to reflect critically on what constitutes an ethical practice of lifelong learning. Peter Jarvis offered a starting point in his Y2K Australian keynote address, during which he analyzed new-economy pressures on learning for life and work. He suggested that we begin by conceptualizing learning spaces such as classrooms as global spaces where we embed instrumental and economistic concerns within inclusive, holistic forms of education that also address social and cultural concerns. He stated his belief that this requires us to locate lifelong learning in moral and political terms, which situates it as a matter of context: "We are imprisoned in a global classroom—we cannot escape from it as long as we live—but it is what we use our learning for that is the moral question that confronts us, recognizing that others are constantly seeking to control the context within which that learning takes place for other ends" (2000, p. 26).

Situating lifelong learning in context in order to consider *learning for whom and learning for what* is crucial to developing inclusive, holistic forms of lifelong learning. Speaking at the Y2K UK gathering, Aspin and Chapman (2001a) highlighted the need to rearticulate lifelong learning as inherently good learning that is prerequisite to holistic life and work. In other words, in a perspective that aligns with the more critical positions of Jarvis (2000) and Griffin (2000), they propose that lifelong learning has to be located fundamentally as "a public good, for the benefit and welfare of everyone in society" (p. 39). This requires bringing together instrumental, social, and cultural learning to provide learners with broader knowledge and skill sets that advance work and life. Aspin and Chapman believe this is possible within what they call "the triadic nature of lifelong learning: for economic progress and development, for personal development and fulfilment, [and] for social inclusiveness and democratic understanding and activity" (pp. 39–40). Working with such multiple purposes for lifelong learning, we can work against essentialization of the concept's meaning in instrumental or other singular terms as we focus on desired learning outcomes. We can begin this process by surveying how others describe the term *lifelong learning* as a concept and a practice, and by surveying how others use it in theories and in policies (Aspin & Chapman, 2000). In this process, it becomes important to define lifelong learning relationally and contextually in critical terms. Failing to do so would indeed be problematic. As Griffin (2000) argues, "If it is philosophically impossible to define lifelong learning, then it may be impossible to define equal opportunities, social justice, social inclusion and exclusion, and all other supposed objects of social policy discourse" (p. 2). Thus, we must locate lifelong learning in relations and contexts so we can fully explore the parameters and possibilities of private and public responsibility for lifelong learning. As citizen educators, this is our responsibility to citizen learners.

Theme 3: The Precarious and Paradoxical Position of Lifelong Learning and the Desire to Position Lifelong Learning as a Permanent Global Necessity

While lifelong learning has historically occupied a precarious position in education and culture (see chapter 3), it has adapted by assuming a chameleonic nature that, over time and circumstance, has tied the concept to diverse instrumental, social, and cultural ventures and forms of education (Grace, 2000b, 2002b). Indeed, the tides of individualism, corporatism, post-industrialism, globalism, and other shape shifters continue to modulate the meaning of lifelong learning into the present moment. Its discursive meaning, coupled with its conditional space and place, contribute to the paradoxical position of lifelong learning in education and culture. In his Y2K Australian keynote address, Peter Jarvis (2000) described this paradox:

> The lifelong learning society has become part of the current economic and political discourse of global capitalism, which positions people as human resources to be developed through lifelong learning, or discarded and retrained if their job is redundant. Education has, therefore, become the "cause" of the inability of corporations to recruit employees who have the necessary knowledge and skill to perform in the competitive knowledge-based labour market and, paradoxically, the "hope" that these corporations have that they can produce new commodities in a more efficient manner. (p. 23)

How does this paradox affect education and culture's desire to position lifelong learning as a permanent global necessity? Since many academics, policymakers, practitioners, and students still cling to the hope that lifelong learning will be a way out and a way forward, the other side of the paradox, education as a cause of post-industrial malaise, is often shunted aside in the rush to focus on cyclical lifelong learning for purportedly better living and working. Burke, Long, and Wurzburg (2000) outlined some of the many reasons offered to accent the need and extol the value of lifelong learning in contemporary times:

- an aging workforce
- techno-scientific change forces
- globalization of the market
- the changing nature of work and new work patterns
- underemployment or unemployment due to mismatches between supply and demand in terms of skilling the workforce

In addition, Burke, Long, and Wurzburg pointed to the fact that the face of the workforce is also changing, as better-educated, white-collar workers are now more prevalent than blue-collar workers in the global economy: "The strongest growth in employment [in OECD member countries] has been in producer and social services. From the mid-1980s through the late 1990s, the fastest growing sub-sectors of these have been business and professional services and health services with educational services the next fastest" (2000, p. 8). Not only are these workers expected to engage in cyclical lifelong learning for periodic updating of their knowledge-and-skill sets, but they are also told they need to participate to shield themselves from a range of risk factors, including

- reduced standards of living,
- a decline in social cohesion,
- increased *fiscal drag* due to increased economic dependency, and
- constraints on the potential of economies to grow (Burke, Long, & Wurzburg, 2000).

These risks add to the blurring of the social and the economic in contemporary times, where learning that is valued in an economic context is often construed as synonymous with learning that is valued in a social context.

In the midst of these transitions, vocationalization of education has flourished, providing another means to regulate lifelong learning and enhance its necessity. Wain (2000) provides this understanding of the context that enables vocationalist discourse to advance:

The "myth" of the learning society about today connects the utopian dreams of the present and future with the interests of employers and of advanced capitalism, and the attainment of increasing levels of performativity. It emphasizes the optimal development of human capital through an investment in lifelong learning strategies, working with the assumption that a learning society that articulates these strategies will stay competitive in the global economy. In short it generates a vocationalist discourse which occurs within an ambit of labour and market concerns, and this discourse wins ready support and collaboration from governments within agendas focused on creating increasing prosperity and getting as many of the unemployed as possible back into the labour market. (pp. 39–40)

This tendency to vocationalize education has been quite pronounced in tertiary education, where the discourse of lifelong learning has gained ground by intersecting traditional higher educational foci with vocational foci (Aronowitz, 2000; Candy, 2000). Indeed, there has been an international trend to combine vocational training and academic studies in an attempt to produce graduates with more extensive qualifications (Doughney, 2000; Verry, 2000). However, such a merger can be more controversial than seamless, and it does not always lead to the kind of cross-sectoral movement that is intended. Leesa Doughney (2000), in her presentation at the Y2K Australian event, emphasized that supporting and implementing cross-sectoral lifelong learning has conditions for success. Reviewing the Australian experience with composite education, in itself a contentious term, she concluded that cross-sectoral lifelong learning requires particular policies that enable the systemic and institutional frameworks needed to aid and abet such learning. For Doughney, such policy development involves deliberations about competing conceptions and philosophies of lifelong learning. It also involves interrogation of the hegemonic utilitarian and economistic models of lifelong learning that have had currency in government and policy communities of Western nations during the last few decades.

In his keynote address at the Y2K Australian event, Philip C. Candy (2000) also examined the vocationalization of tertiary education as he spoke about graduate skills for an unpredictable future. He began his presentation by situating Western universities as historically adaptable and enduring institutions. He then related that, in contemporary times, adaptation and endurance mean negotiating tensions arising from the debate over conflicting roles. Key questions undergird this debate: Should universities maintain a traditional role focused on offering social critique and building social awareness? Or should they assume a more utilitarian, contemporary role focused on advancing national and global economies? Candy related that those who would answer "yes!" to the latter question constitute a collective of new-economy interest groups that include governments, businesses, the professions, and many learners. They want universities to offer more vocationalistic education that produces "work-ready" graduates. However, universities that respond to this demand may, as a consequence, experience dislocation as their institutional roles change. Aronowitz (2000) suggests that if universities do experience dislocation, they have only themselves to blame. As he sees it, this is because they are implicated in their own conundrum as they condition students to engage in cyclical lifelong learning that muddles the differences among education, learning, and training. Indeed, the logic of cyclical learning is instilled early, when those just starting tertiary education move into vocationalist mode. In their efforts to survive in the face of a future of cultural and economic incertitude, beginning students are asked to subscribe to "a market logic that demands students be job-ready upon graduation. Under these imperatives, colleges and universities are unable to implement an educational program that prepares students for a world of great complexity" (Aronowitz, 2000, p. 158). In the process, students as learners may also experience dislocation as the parameters of getting a university education change. As noted earlier, we increasingly see forms of lifelong learning being mandated to help citizens cope with the changing nature of work. In this scenario, learning appears incessant. It becomes burdensome for students, and just another reason that they have little time to spare.

Deliberations at the Y2K Australian event also indicated that, in the rush to cyclical lifelong learning, the vocationalization of tertiary education has been coupled with an emphasis on information literacy. Various presenters made it clear that literacy today encompasses more than the ability to read and write. To be literate in the knowledge economy, Jan Partridge (2000) declared that one must be information-literate and have "the capacity to seek, retrieve, organise, analyse, synthesise, and present information using a variety of sources and formats" (p. 209). In her Y2K Australian keynote address, Patricia Senn Breivik (2000) investigated the link between information literacy (as an enabler) and lifelong learning (as a goal). She asserted that learners need to be able to access, evaluate, and use information productively so they can address issues and solve problems in their personal, civic, and work lives. She located information literacy as an encompassing concept and process that can include building computer, library, media, network, and visual literacies. Taking a vocationalist stance, Senn Breivik challenged institutions of formal learning to assume responsibility for preparing graduates who are information-literate and able to function in the many informal and non-formal learning situations where adults need to be able to discover, analyze, and problem solve. She asserted that helping graduates to build information literacy skills is a way to respond to calls from government, employers, professions, and students themselves for learners and workers who can "communicate well, think critically, work well in teams, be flexible, or be lifelong learners" (p. 3).

However, if information literacy functions only as an enabler of lifelong learning in instrumental, pragmatic terms, then limits are placed on its utility. While enabling learning for work is important and necessary, information literacy also needs to be more broadly concerned with enabling learning for life so at-risk youth and adults have the skills not only to be employed, but also to be active, discerning citizens who have quality of life. When information literacy is merely an enabler of the instrumental, it provokes a techno-induced classism that continues social inequalities and economic inequities. Senn Breivik provided an example of this in relation to the growing digital divide in the United States: "Technology is broadening the gap between the haves and have-nots. The gap is so great that Silicon Valley company employees, who are not among the company owners and investors, increasingly cannot afford to live within commuting distance; so in order to be able to stay in business, the companies are now being forced to consider relocation" (p. 3). In this light, information literacy as an enabler should also be relocated: in this case, to the intersection where instrumental, social, and cultural forms of education meet. Senn Breivik did suggest that the Silicon Valley debacle demanded an expedient policy emphasizing people empowerment that is focused on an information-literate citizenry, universal access, and quality information. However, such a policy would have little utility in practice if it did not move beyond a vocationalist stance. Aligned with the status quo that government, employers, and the professions desire, information literacy can be used as a device to help maintain social hierarchies and the mainstream culture-knowledge-language-power nexus. Of course, information literacy can also be a tool for transformation if it is used to enable social activism and cultural work that helps people transgress the ties that bind them. Like many educative means, it can be used to support transaction or transformation.

Concluding Perspective: Lifelong Learning as a Critical Practice

Building and sustaining a critical practice of lifelong learning are indeed chal-

lenges in contemporary times, when education for "critical citizenship has become an unprofitable, if not subversive category" (Giroux, 1993, p. 15). A key
aim of such an inclusive, holistic practice is to help persons become responsive
and responsible citizens who are able to think, speak, and act in life, learning,
and work situations. Working to achieve this aim amounts to locating a critical practice of lifelong learning as a form of cultural production and cultural
work (Giroux, 1993). A critical practice of lifelong learning places issues of
democracy, equity, justice, and citizenship at the heart of learning for life and
work. It promotes contextualized learning in the intersection of the ethical and
the political, bringing history to bear on economics and culture as it exposes
the impotency of non-relational and decontextualized learning that is boxed
in by the supposed neutrality of expertise and the myopic controls of special-
ism (Grace, 2000a). This is not to say that a critical practice of lifelong learning
downplays or ignores the acquisition of specialized knowledge or technical
skills, which are at the core of food-on-the-table instruction and education
for survival. Rather, an inclusive, holistic critical practice embeds such instrumental learning within a broader learning paradigm that includes social and
cultural learning as well. It recognizes that matters of context, relationship, and
disposition play out in learning and other socio-cultural spaces.

As educators, a critical practice of lifelong learning challenges us to construct learning communities that empower citizen learners as "co-responsible
subjects" (Apple, 1993, p. 3) in building and sustaining practices that enable
lifelong learning for all amid the interplay of culture, knowledge, language,
and power. Thus, a critical practice of lifelong learning incorporates the following tasks:

- building instrumental, social, and cultural knowledge and skills
- making knowledge and skills work in terms of access, accommodation, and
  choices for citizens as learners and workers
- interrogating language, meaning, and action in lifelong-learning discourses
- addressing equity, justice, civil rights, and multicultural issues in relation to
  life, learning, and work
- emphasizing the historical context and writing revisionist history
- enhancing education for active and full citizenship

As they work to accomplish these tasks, citizens as educators and learners assume diverse roles as instrumental learners, social activists, political strate-

gists, and cultural workers as they engage questions of purpose, policy, and practice in lifelong learning.

In fulfilling these roles, educators and learners are effectively working to build and sustain an encompassing lifelong-learning community. One way to engage in this multi-tasked assignment is to use the typology that Raymond Williams developed in his work in cultural studies as part of his search for a lived and knowable community. His typology is built around two ideas: culture as knowledge (where, with the advent of post-industrial society, valued knowledge has been cast as techno-scientific knowledge) and culture as community (where, from social and cultural perspectives, valued knowledge remains associated with work, popular culture, class, and community relationships) (Grossberg, 1997). Building an inclusive pedagogy of lifelong-learning community requires that we struggle over and understand these two conceptualizations of culture, which expand both the spaces that culture can occupy and the bases constituting knowledge. By taking up culture as community we can build popular knowledge associated with differences including work culture, customs, and community attachments. This helps us to investigate how social relationships are formed, lived out, and represented in cultural spaces such as workplaces and community settings. By taking up culture as knowledge we can come to terms with formalized knowledge with worth in the intersection of the economic and the cultural. This helps us as we reflect on what is valued and what ought to be valued in building information literacy. From Williams' perspective, juxtaposing these knowledges amounts to navigating learning spaces as cultural border zones where we can expose the problem of living between culture as knowledge and culture as community. This juxtaposition demonstrates the inextricable link between culture and power, and it indicates that culture is a site of struggle where the relationships among culture, language, media, and power are always changing.

If culture as knowledge and culture as community were synchronous entities impacting lifelong learning as a concept and a practice, then a dynamic equilibrium between learning for the marketplace and learning for life might be possible. In this inclusive, holistic milieu, instrumentality would be situated as part of a multi-focal array that includes foci on equity, justice, work-life balance, and an assortment of other social and cultural concerns. Addressing issues framing these foci is at the heart of critical education as a discourse and a practice. For example, such foci inspired recommendations and commitments contained in the Hamburg Declaration, which was a critical document adopted by the Fifth International Conference on Adult Education (CONFIN-TEA V) held in Hamburg, Germany, from July 14 to 18, 1997. In a mid-term review of conference goals and the implementation process held in Bangkok, Thailand, from September 6 to 11, 2003, over 300 participants from more than 90 countries reflected on the purpose and enactment of the Hamburg Declaration. The review recounted how the declaration had supported a broad-based agenda for adult education and learning focused on themes including democracy, justice, gender equity, disability, poverty, literacy, xenophobia, racial profiling, social exclusion, peace, work, higher education, health, and the environment (CONFINTEA V, 2003a, 2003b). These concerns remain aligned with adult education's historical focus on community and the political ideals of modernity—democracy, freedom, and social justice. Such concerns can also define an inclusive and holistic critical practice of lifelong learning in our contemporary global change culture of crisis and challenge.

Chapter 5

International Educational Policy-Making in a Neoliberal Change Culture of Crisis and Challenge

Since making *lifelong learning for all* its mantra in the mid-1990s, the Organisation for Economic Co-operation and Development has spearheaded various educational policy initiatives focused on lifelong and lifewide learning that expect the involvement of all sectors of public (schooling for children and youth), adult, and higher education. However, these initiatives, predominantly driven by a neoliberal, economistic mindset, are not confined to institutionalized forms of education. They have infiltrated other learning spheres as well, criss-crossing the domains of formal, informal, and non-formal learning. Despite this prevalence across a range of learning domains, contemporary lifelong learning does not adequately focus on the holistic life needs of citizens. For example, education for citizenship is, at best, a secondary focus of contemporary lifelong learning, which, in sum, has been frequently and variously reactive, instrumental, specialized, fragmented, and sporadic in its everyday practices. In this reductionistic learning culture, lifelong learning is viewed as an individual responsibility, learners and workers are considered commodities, and learning is packaged as a consumer product. Field (2006) sums up how many learners experience this conscripting culture:

> There are many for whom participation is a story of coercion, boredom, and repeated failure. For many, participation is not a matter of personal choice and identity; it is a matter of following instructions.... As the discourse of permanent lifelong learning has spread, and worked itself through into the language and practices of continuing professional development and constant updating, so a degree of coercion has also emerged, often gaining widespread acceptance as people come to see lifelong learning as a basic survival mechanism. Internalised

expectations mean that a significant number of adults—perhaps a majority—regard learning as something they have to do if they are to survive and thrive.... For most people, the learning imperative is implicit and largely unspoken. (pp. 130–131)

Perhaps Field's most important argument is that lifelong learning itself has emerged as a key contributor to social exclusion and inequality in life, learning, work, consumption, well-being, health, and citizenship. This is a serious indictment in an era when government and corporations extol the virtues of lifelong learning in unison.

Is this standing reflected in educational circles? Certainly, economistic lifelong learning has significantly affected higher education across many nations in recent years (Candy, 2000; Catts, 2004; Newman, Couturier, & Scurry, 2004). It has also had a moderate effect on public education, at least in some countries such as Canada (Grace, 2007). When it comes to permeating adult education in some national contexts (like the United Kingdom), there is suspicion of lifelong learning as a usurper or replacement for the field of study and practice (Jarvis, 2008). Perhaps this is because adult education appears diminished in the face of more broad-based lifelong learning today. Field (2006) sees lifelong learning's threat to adult education this way: "The lifelong learning debate appears to threaten the existing adult education structures, not only because it is so clearly dominated by economic and vocational concerns, but also because it celebrates and promotes a fragmented and distributed view of learning" (p. 22). This situation is exacerbated by the reality that contemporary adult education is not prominent as social and cultural education. Moreover, the field seems poorly equipped to handle the incursion of the vocational and the economistic into its terrain.

Against this backdrop, in this chapter I focus on Canada's lifelong-learning policy culture. I consider how matters of policy articulation and exclusion, responsibility and citizenship, and access and accommodation locate individuals in this culture. I use the example of youth in the province of Newfoundland and Labrador to show how a neoliberal mindset that casts economic progress as the basis for social progress can work against social cohesion, aggravate a politics of dislocation, and intensify a politics of blame. I then compare Canada's lifelong-learning policy culture to those found in Australia, New Zealand, the Republic of Ireland, and South Africa. Here I consider how lifelong learning has emerged in these nations in the face of a pervasive, global neoliberal policy consensus. I examine the institutionalization of lifelong learning in Australia and the required adaptability of universities in a neoliberal lifelong-learning milieu. I look at tensions in universities between holding on to liberal tradition and advancing learning for the knowledge economy. Next, I consider how the emergence of lifelong learning has followed a somewhat different trajectory in New Zealand. I discuss the severe effect that neoliberalism has had on social inclusion and cohesion in that country, and I consider its aberrant turn away from lifelong-learning policy throughout the 1990s when other nations were rushing to generate it. I then explore the lifelong-learning culture in the Republic of Ireland where, of necessity, there has been a major focus on adult learning. Here I consider the many challenges to social cohesion that the Irish Republic faces in the wake of the impact of neoliberalism. In a final comparison, I examine the lifelong-learning policy culture in South Africa. I speak to the power of globalization and neoliberalism, as I question why there wasn't a post-apartheid turn to a critical and holistic form of lifelong learning in that country. I look at the work of South African scholars who have focused on bringing the critical to bear on lifelong-learning policy development and implementation. I end the chapter with a consideration of what ought to constitute lifelong learning as critical action so nations can move beyond the current neoliberal policy consensus and make lifelong learning something more, something whole, that revitalizes the social.

When Lifelong Learning Goes Awry: Critical Perspectives from Canada

And you never let the hard times
Take away your soul
And you stopped the tears from falling
As you watched the young ones go …
And home I'll be
Home I'll be
Banish thoughts of leaving
Home I'll be

—Rita MacNeil, Atlantic Canadian singer, "Home I'll Be"

Trends in government policy development and interventions in Canada are similar to those outlined by Field (2006) in reference to the British context. Canadian youth are one group that has been deeply affected by neoliberal trends in lifelong learning. Collectively, they, with their specific learning needs, can be construed as making up a system of regional learning communities across the country. These needs are defined by

- a region's "have" or "have-not" economic status within the nation,
- federal government policy intended to promote privatization and learning for the contemporary global economy, and
- neoliberal learning that frames performativity and responsibility in individualistic terms.

In this milieu, youth often get caught up in a politics that blames them when they do not succeed in lifelong learning. Youth participation in learning comes down to this reality: Taking responsibility for one's performance (or failure to perform) affects the degree to which youth find acceptance and accommodation in communities, work, and the learning cultures that shape them. However, there is a more systemic issue: Governments advancing a neoliberal agenda are failing youth. One Canadian government response to its failure to meet the socio-economic needs of youth has been to expand the definition of youth so that 15- to 30-year-olds are broadly construed as youth in the current federal context. In doing so, the federal government is not only situating the problem of youth dislocation in learning and work as a long-term phenomenon, but it is also perpetuating and perhaps normalizing the state of younger learner exclusion in these arenas as it blurs the boundary between youth and adulthood. This exclusion has ramifications for full citizenship. Not to participate in whatever forms of learning and work are offered, regardless of their quality and worth, can, in a real sense, be interpreted as contributing to an erosion of citizenship (Grace, 2007). This is because being a full and contributing citizen of a nation is usually considered synonymous with being employed, paid, and productive. In a neoliberal politics exalting individualism, youth are blamed when they do not participate and when they do not succeed.

For some time, Canada's economy and culture have been affected by a pervasive and invasive neoliberal policy consensus that stresses the value of a knowledge-based economy, technology and skill development, and a learning society in which cyclical lifelong learning is not only a norm, but also a culture and an attitude (Grace, 2007). In this neoliberal milieu, which prioritizes the economistic, Canadian youth are expected to move into cyclical lifelong-learning mode during formal schooling. Moreover, they are expected, if not mandated, to stay in this mode throughout their work lives in today's change culture of crisis and challenge. In this stress-filled learning culture, what does lifelong learning mean for Canadian youth? What is its value to them? For a growing contingent, it appears that lifelong learning has little meaning and little value. A current Canadian phenomenon indicates that increasing numbers of youth are disengaging from participation in what might be perceived as cyclical lifelong learning for control, which requires learners to jump periodically on a learning treadmill so they can update skill sets or acquire new skills necessary to meet changing job demands (Grace, 2007). The 2008 report of the Canadian Council on Learning on the nation's composite learning index (CLI) provides evidence that this troubling trend to forgo learning is noticeable in high school (CCL, 2008). The CLI, which was created in 2006 to be an annual statistical assessment of the country's progress in lifelong learning, indicates that high-school dropout rates for male youth (aged 20 to 24) in small towns and rural areas have been excessive, with dropouts noting they were not satisfied with their schooling and just wanted to work.

Cyclical lifelong learning for control reflects the current federal learning-and-work policy that focuses on individual development of learners and workers. This policy concentration gives primacy to instrumental and economistic concerns, and presumes a trickle-down effect in which learning that abets a prosperous economy is also expected to enhance society. This decentring of the social is problematic for such reasons as it conflates simply being technically skilled with competency, and it isolates training and development for workers from broader social, cultural, and political considerations (Grace, 2007). In this milieu, many youth are experiencing dislocation in life and work. For them, neoliberalism means that everyone is making youth responsible, while no one seems to be taking responsibility for them.

When neoconservatives cast government as unwieldy and interfering too much in the private domain, they set the scene to enable government to abrogate its public responsibility, especially for dislocated youth and other disenfranchised citizens who are seen as dependent and dysfunctional. Neoliberals have exacerbated this situation by subsuming the social within the economic and suggesting that a functional citizen is a working citizen who contributes to national and global economies. While neoliberals have paid lip service to social cohesion as somehow begotten from economic progress, the social is usually an afterthought in setting economistic corporate, government, and educational agendas. According to Giroux (2004), we are witnessing a war against the welfare state, which "is a war against the notion that everyone should have access to decent education, health care, employment, and other public services" (p. 82). Ultimately, this is a war against social democracy and disenfranchised groups within civil society that are considered drains on the economy. Those who are variously uneducated, undereducated, unemployed, or targeted due to racial, ethnocultural, sexual, and other differences comprise what Giroux calls "disposable populations" (p. 84) that apparently must be contained. They are not nurtured as agents within a politics and pedagogy of hope and possibility that value integrity and imagination, dreams and desires, justice and joy. In this milieu, youth have been particularly affected. Giroux describes what is disturbing about the neoliberal present and contrasts it with the political project that guided democracy invested in the welfare state:

> What is so troubling about the current historical moment is that youth no longer even symbolize the future.... [For much of the twentieth century,] youth not only registered symbolically the importance of modernity's claim to progress; they also affirmed the centrality of the liberal, democratic tradition of the social contract in which adult responsibility was mediated through a willingness to fight for the rights of children, enact reforms that invested in their future, and provide the educational conditions necessary for them to make use of the freedoms they possessed while learning to be critical citizens. (p. 85)

As Giroux sees it, we are now witnessing "the abdication of adult responsibility to children" (p. 86). Freedom, justice, and possibilities for democratic choices and mediation are at stake for youth:

> Youth have become one of the primary sights onto which class and racial anxieties are projected. Their very presence represents both the broken promises of capitalism in the age of deregulation and downsizing *and* a collective fear of the consequences wrought by systemic class inequalities and a culture of rapacious greed that has produced a generation of unskilled and displaced youth expelled from shrinking markets, blue-collar jobs, and any viable hope for the future. (pp. 90–91)

Social Erosion and an Inadequate Culture of Lifelong Learning: A Personal Viewpoint

I was born and raised in a small rural fishing village on the island portion of the Canadian province of Newfoundland and Labrador. As someone who became well educated, I had choices, including the choice to move elsewhere. Many Newfoundlanders, notably many youth, are not so lucky. These youth experience instability in learning and work and consequential out-migration as engrained cultural norms. They find it difficult and frequently impossible to obtain quality work close to home. The majority of working youth have been engaged in lesser-quality work in retail sales (34 percent), restaurant and fast-food services (20 percent), the service industry (12 percent), and general labour (11 percent) (Government of Newfoundland, 2003). In addition to the difficulty of finding quality work at home, many youth have had little input into the form, function, and cultural sensibility of their learning (Grace, 2007). For them, out-migration, especially if they are less educated, is often perceived as the only escape from the social misery that accompanies unemployment, underemployment, and the lack of educational opportunities that come with average or below-average achievement in formal schooling. Indeed, the population of youth in Newfoundland and Labrador is anticipated to decline by 25 percent between 2003 and 2016 (Grace, 2007). This out-migration is a dilemma. It amounts to a greying of the province at a time when there is a Canada-wide increase in aging baby boomers and retirees (Tutton, 2008). Still, there may be hope for a reversal of this trend. Now that the province is benefiting from the discovery of offshore oil and natural gas, it is in the process of developing a Youth Retention and Attraction Strategy (Canadian Policy Research Networks [CPRN], 2008). The strategy will be informed by what has been learned from dialogues conducted in 2008 with youth living in the province or elsewhere in Canada. The goal of the strategy is to have youth aged 18 to 30 choose to live and work in their home province.

In the following vignette, I consider the dislocation of youth in Newfoundland and Labrador from a personal perspective:

I grew up in the fishing village of Flatrock, which lies about 20 kilometres northeast of the provincial capital, St. John's. When you drive along Wind Gap, the back road leading into the community, you come to a hilltop that overlooks a harbour bound on one side by the Beamer, a neck of sedimentary rock that juts about a kilometre out into the Atlantic Ocean. A huge sea cliff called Red Head pinpoints the harbour's other side. In the summertime when I was growing up, many boats used in a then thriving cod fishery were anchored in the inner harbour. There were many fishers in my village whose mode of survival for self and family involved seasonal employment in the fishing industry, coupled with government social assistance for the huge chunk of the year remaining. In this lower socio-economic milieu, many families struggled to survive. However, while the effects of material poverty were apparent, many villagers experienced the benefits of a cohesive social in their everyday lives. Indeed, many of us were raised knowing the strength and support of extended family and the community collective. People came together to assist others who were experiencing hardship. I knew the comfort of connectedness growing up. It is perhaps best captured in my memories of my grandparents, Nan and Pop Grace, who were as influential in my upbringing as my parents. I remember fondly going to sleep to the sound of waves rolling onto the beach that lay just a few hundred metres from their saltbox house.

I have other memories though, memories that speak to dislocation and separation.

There was always someone young from the community moving away. Out-migration seems to have marked every generation born in our economically deprived, yet socially rich fishing village. As a child, I remember going to the post office on my birthday and at Christmas to get the presents that my Aunt Mary always sent me. As a young woman, she had obtained employment with the US military, which had a number of bases in the province during the post–World War II period. She eventually married a soldier and moved to the United States. I remember her trips home and my grandparents' deep sadness when she would leave to go back. It seemed that everyone in the community knew this experience. We all talked about relatives who lived "on the mainland" in other parts of Canada or in the United States.

Fast-forward to the present moment, and little has changed. Indeed, since the early 1990s the problem of out-migration, as contemporary Canadian Census data verify, is worse, exacerbated by the decline of the cod fishery and a dearth of other work opportunities. My own family continues to be affected. One of my brothers and two of my sisters now have grown children who have left behind dismal prospects at home and moved to Alberta, a resource-rich and wealthy province that many youth see as their land of opportunity. My three nephews all finished high school; each was an average student. To date, only one has opted for post-secondary education. When I asked the others why they didn't go to college in Newfoundland, all felt that more education provided no guarantee of getting a job on the island. Furthermore, access to education beyond high school is an issue in Newfoundland. It's easy to be excluded from further education when you're pigeonholed as an average secondary-school student.

The nephew who went to college had his name on a waiting list for a few years before gaining entry to a competitive technology program at the College of the North Atlantic in St. John's. After finishing high school, he found himself caught in the dead end of minimum-wage work in the retail sector, so he moved to Alberta where there are many low-level jobs in various oil-related industries that pay very well. The lure westward is the dollar, but bottom-feeder jobs in a high-tech economy take a toll. When he finally was accepted into college, he went back home. However, after he graduated he returned to Alberta to find employment.

For a second nephew, joining the Canadian military seemed to be the way out. However, a stint in Afghanistan, where every day meant seeing a people ravaged and his own life put in constant danger, withered that perspective. After returning from Afghanistan, he finished his commitment to the military on a base in Edmonton. Wanting to experience what Canadians call the "Alberta advantage," he made his home in this "have" province upon his release from the military. He is currently employed in the oil industry, using skills he learned as an explosives technician in the military.

A third nephew, who was the last to finish high school, joined his cousins in Edmonton and quickly found low-level, but high-paying employment as a roughneck on an oil rig. Education holds little interest for him at this point.

My nephews share a house and all are adjusting to life "away," where they now find the connectedness and community they knew at home with one another and other migrant youth from back home. For now, they live life in the moment and do not seem to worry about the future of the oil industry. Banished by the lack of opportunities at home, they seem destined to remain part of the Newfoundland diaspora. In a twist on Rita MacNeil's lyrics, perhaps their reality is: "Home they'll never be."

My story about my nephews is a story about the ways that geography and undereducation or undervaluing of education play out across life, learning, and work contexts. There are other stories though, such as gender narratives that also impact access and accommodation in relation to work. Gouthro (2009) situates gender differences in work contexts as a political and philosophical concern for lifelong educators as they deal with the decontextualized learner in neoliberalized lifelong learning. Similarly, Fenwick (2004) points to the gendering of skilling and work as structural imbalances that treat females unfairly. She notes the persistence of gender inequity in terms of access and accommodation in lifelong learning framed in neoliberal terms. She also uses the example of the cod moratorium in the early 1990s in Newfoundland and Labrador to discuss how a depleted resource base brought about out-migration and the concomitant erosion of communities and their social fabrics. In exploring the cod moratorium as a change force, Fenwick indicates that there has been an unexplored gender subtext embedded in attempts to retrain workers and associated with changes in family and community structures, social conditions, and the rush to find jobs outside the province. Her point is apropos. For example, out-migrant males, not females, are more likely to find employment in low-level jobs such as engaging in hard manual labour as a roughneck in the dangerous working environment of Alberta's oil rigs. As Fenwick recounts, women have traditionally struggled to find employment in such better-paying industrial jobs in a masculinist work culture. However, employed males are hardly winners as they deal with the high-risk work environment of oil rigs. They remain on the periphery of the idealized entrepreneurial economy of oil-rich Alberta. They are weighed down by under-education and the class location it induces, which are also at the heart of power relationships at play here.

We might also consider the struggles of workers who live and try to function outside the parameters of the male/female binary. What about a transmale worker born biologically female, but living in his affirmed male gender? How would he fare as a roughneck? With sex and gender traditionally expected to function within the parameters of the male/female binary, this worker would likely have problems adjusting to boundaries and expectations guiding workplace behaviours and performance, which has implications for the worker's social acceptability, success in employment and career opportunities, economic security, and, most importantly, personal safety (Chief Public Health Officer, 2012).

Still the Status Quo: Canada as a Case in Point

In Canada, as in many developed nations, much of the talk about lifelong learning in policy circles is framed within neoliberal terms that link citizen participation in learning to the ability to contribute to economic growth and development (Saunders, 2007). Mentioning community development or raising demographic concerns such as Canada's aging workforce, its unemployed or underemployed youth, and its significant undereducated population always seems to be done in the context of equating full citizenship with being more functionally employable and contributing to national productivity and global competitiveness (Grace, 2009b). Paradoxically, while there is national aware- ness of the need for second-chance education for so many needing literacy and life skills, Canada's neoliberal lifelong-learning paradigm is predominantly constructed in economistic terms that emphasize more knowledge-and-skill building for those who are already educated and employed. This paradigm undermines the notion of an inclusive society, and it does little to shrink the ranks of the undereducated, the functionally unemployable, and other citizens who become invisible and even disappear in national unemployment statistics (Grace, 2007).

The predicament of disenfranchised citizens is substantiated in the report *Too Many Left Behind*, which Myers and de Broucker (2006) prepared for the Canadian Policy Research Networks (CPRN). These researchers related that 5.8 million Canadians aged 25 years and over lack a high-school diploma or higher credentials, and 9 million Canadians aged 16 to 65 years lack functional literacy skills. They found that Canada's less-educated adults had poor access to learning opportunities, whether as government-funded community educa- tion, employer-sponsored training, or second chances in a formal educational context. Moreover, they concluded that Canada's adult education and training system is a complex, fragmented, and incomplete entity in which employers remain focused on higher-skilled workers. They noted that the needs of the less educated go largely unmet because there are few lifelong-learning poli- cies and programs to support less-educated adults to become more educated. Moreover, they stated, "While most adults who return to school will enjoy sig- nificant economic benefits and improved labour market prospects, these ben- efits are not guaranteed up front. In most cases, returning to school requires great sacrifice and a profound leap of faith" (p. vi). Myers and de Broucker provided this explanation of a specific problem that workers face in accessing learning:

How to encourage employers to provide more training, especially to the less- skilled employees, is a complex issue.... One of the most troubling aspects of Canada's economy is that the competitive human resource strategy of too many Canadian firms is based on a low-cost/low-added-value approach. This approach perpetuates a low-skill/low-wage equilibrium in which neither employees nor employers demand higher levels of skills. Firms that gain their competitive edge from low-cost, low-skilled work have little incentive to invest in labour force development. (p. v)

   The 2008 Canadian CLI indicated that this is certainly the case in Canada. With regard to the availability of workplace training, Canada lags behind many nations, with slightly more than half (56 percent in 2003) of workplaces providing some kind of workplace training (CCL, 2008). Most of this training centres around new staff orientation and health-and-safety training, and not managerial, supervisory, or literacy and numeracy training. Only about one-third of workplaces reimburse employees for training engaged in outside of work hours. In sum, only one-quarter of working-age adults participated in some form of job-related training, and the majority of them are more educated, having participated in some form of post-secondary education.

   While Myers and de Broucker point out the wide gap between the more educated who have most access to learning opportunities and the less educated who perennially experience access problems, their vision of learning for Canadian adults remains a pervasively economistic, neoliberal vision. While one might expect the title *Too Many Left Behind* to forecast some sort of social analysis and a call for radical change, the vision that these researchers present seems to be just another neoliberal mantra upholding learning for earning: "The social and economic importance of encouraging adults to engage in continuous learning throughout their working lives is undisputed. Better-educated individuals earn higher wages, have greater earnings growth over their lifetimes, and experience less unemployment. Better-educated nations have higher long run economic growth and higher standards of living" (p. iii). Specifically, two economistic notions are central to this vision: As graduates of formal schooling, youth should leave with a minimum skill set to abet employment, and adults should have ongoing access to learning opportunities to hone literacy skills, life skills, and workplace skills. In a CPRN response to *Too Many Left Behind* entitled *Towards an Effective Adult Learning System*, Saunders (2007) interestingly (and perhaps predictably) relates that government officials, educators, and researchers participating in a series of regional roundtables to discuss Myers and de Broucker's report validated their vision. He indicates that there was no serious contestation of the economistic, neoliberal focus of the learning envisioned in the report.

   Too Many Left Behind did not problematize the conceptualization of lifelong learning. It did not provide sufficient analysis of what is embodied and embedded in the notion of the right of adults to learn and how this connects to who gets to learn and who is left behind. It did not create a framework for deconstructing—from critical or other social perspectives—the meanings that subsequent CPRN roundtables produced for such notions as learner-centred, coordinated/seamless, aligned, articulated, collaborative, equitable, relevant, sustainable, visible, available in community, attractive to adult learners, and respectful of adult circumstances. Indeed, the key characteristics of an effective adult-learning system that the roundtable participants identified were so aligned with Myers and de Broucker's vision that the hegemony of neoliberal thinking about lifelong learning in Canada would seem secure.

Too Many Left Behind did call for increased state involvement in lifelong learning, a position that, as I've noted, goes against the grain of neoliberalism's advocacy of more privatization of learning and increased individual responsibility for the costs and success of learning engagements. However, the suggested increase in state involvement was not in the context of the old welfare-state focus on the social. Instead, state assistance was ultimately intended to be a controlling measure, ensuring that lifelong learning benefits the national economy and Canada's position in the global economy. State assistance would take such forms as increased government financial support of appropriate (read economy-enhancing) programs, incentives for employers to support training programs for less-educated and less-skilled employees, and increased government investment in literacy and life-skills training. These policy guidelines once again suggested a new millennial, neoliberalized kind of lifelong learning in which both Big Government and Big Business would invest in learning for adults with a primary economistic focus. More state involvement would mean more control in setting the parameters, expectations, and modes of surveillance for lifelong learning, which would help Big Business to accomplish its neoliberal agenda.

All this amounts to what appears to be government's continuing abrogation of social responsibility in Canadian lifelong learning. Still, there is some hint of critical social critique in *Too Many Left Behind*, even though it is not labelled as such. For example, Saunders (2007) notes that there is acknowledgement and discussion of the difficulties learners can have in mediating Canada's current adult-learning system; the inadequacy of simply investing in workplace-based training; and the social benefits of lifelong learning including "personal empowerment, family well-being, participation in voting, civic engagement, and social cohesion" (p. 11). The need for involvement of multiple interest groups is also considered:

> Some of the proposed actions [for improving Canada's adult-learning system] are directed to governments (e.g., development of a policy framework, provide sustained funding to community-based initiatives); some to schools, colleges, and universities (increase the flexibility of course offerings); some to community groups (bring key stakeholders together at the community level); some to employers and employer associations (identify champions and share promising practices); some to unions (put workplace training on bargaining agendas); and many would require partnerships among two or more of these (develop common assessment tools and a referral protocol). (p. 11)

There is enough breadth of focus here to indicate that contemporary lifelong learning ought to make space to address the instrumental, social, *and* cultural learning needs of citizens. This requires those with vested interests in lifelong learning to think about holistic lifelong learning that focuses on more than creating learning opportunities for workers. A focus on economistic lifelong learning has to be juxtaposed with foci on social and cultural learning. No interest group should assume that individual, family, and community development will result from the domino effect of economic development, especially since there is no evidence that neoliberalism can guarantee these social outcomes. After all, the disenfranchised are still with us in Canada and elsewhere, even after decades of coping with the ambition of neoliberalism.

Citizens with Disabilities: Another Troubled Canadian Demographic in Troubled Economic Times

People with disabilities are another disenfranchised group in Canadian lifelong-learning culture. Out of concern for their happiness and well-being, lifelong learning needs to address disability issues and matters of access and accommodation contextually and relationally in learning and work across the lifespan. There is much work to do. For example, in their investigation of the professional knowledge base of learning disabilities of Canadian teachers and psychologists in training, Philpott and Cahill (2008) found the basic emphases to be on assessment and what constitutes reasonable accommodation. As these researchers note, Canadian pre-service professionals need to know more: They need to know that provinces and territories control policy-making, definitions of disabilities, and assessment and accommodation practices, although, ultimately, the rights of individuals with disabilities are protected by the Canadian Charter of Rights and Freedoms and, to some degree, by common case law. Thus, readiness to practice and meet the holistic needs of individuals with disabilities is affected by law and policy.

How might we frame learning practices across the lifespan for individuals with disabilities? Certainly, lifelong learning should not be segregationist. In attending to disability issues in childhood, it is important to educate children with disabilities in mainstream school environments, just as it is important to train and include adults with disabilities in mainstream workplace environments later in life. In Canada, 64.7 percent of children with disabilities attend regular school, with an additional 24.9 percent attending regular school with special education classes (HRSDC, 2010). Like their school peers, children with disabilities have hopes and dreams tied to career aspirations and success in the future. They benefit from the support of significant adults such as parents, guardians, and teachers. As they get older and move along in their schooling, they benefit from such supports as counselling and therapy, life-skills training, and speech and language therapy (HRSDC, 2010). These children variously enjoy or resist aspects of life in schools just like their peers. Like other children, they need to be respected, recognized, motivated, and accommodated as they meet expectations, achieve goals, and become more confident in their abilities. This inclusive approach, aided by human and technical supports, can place them on a positive lifelong-learning trajectory. As they move into adolescence with increased ability and capacity to mediate the challenges and barriers they face in life and learning, they can use assets built and enhanced through learning to grow into confident, resilient individuals. Human Resources and Skills Development Canada (HRSDC, 2010) recognizes this, noting that youth with disabilities transition more successfully into adulthood when they are supported in their quest to reach their career goals. Despite difficulties performing academically and completing education on time, 56.3 percent of youth with disabilities attend school, college, or university, with 89.8 percent of them participating full-time (HRSDC, 2010). As they move into adulthood, working-age individuals with disabilities variously participate in workplace training and other forms of adult learning to increase their employability and workplace productivity. As HRSDC relates, this is particularly important for adults who acquire disabilities during their work lives so they can remain employed and satisfied with their work accomplishments. Adult learning for workers with disabilities contributes to positive outcomes in the workplace. In sum, from childhood to adulthood, educators need to think about lifelong learning and the methods, devices, and techniques that learners with disabilities need to support learning success that can be translated into success in life, education, and work.

Difficult Times for Workers with Health Problems or Disabilities

In Canada in 2006, the disability rate was 14.3 percent (4,471,870 people), up nearly 2 percent from 2001 (HRSDC, 2012). Kim, Gomes, and Prinz (2010) relate that the employment rate of Canadian workers with health problems or disabilities was about 47 percent in 2006. This low rate is affected by this group's lower level of education—the high-school completion rate for individuals with disabilities is 75 percent compared to 86 percent for the Canadian population without disabilities. About 17.6 percent of unemployed Canadian workers with disabilities do not look for work for fear of losing part or all of their current social transfer income if they find employment, and 11.5 percent fear losing subsidized housing or prescription drugs coverage (HRSDC, 2010).

Following Canada's *Employment Equity Act*, lifelong learning for work for individuals with health problems or disabilities must not only address the learner's concerns with access, accommodation, and full inclusion, but it must also situate these concerns within the contexts, relationships, and dispositions that engender systemic barriers and hinder employment equity. In Canada individuals with disabilities are particularly under-represented in the private sector including banking and communications (radio and television broadcasting) (HRSDC, 2010). Against the grain of the neoliberal emphasis on performativity, employers need to be educated about what it means for workers with disabilities to participate and be integrated into the labour force and to use their education, skills, and experience to achieve job satisfaction. These workers may require reduced workloads, alterations in job design, physical modifications to the workplace, or flexible work schedules (HRSDC, 2010). Employers also need to be aware of the ways in which their actions may be discriminatory and exclusionary as they relate to working-age adults with disabilities, whose overall labour force participation rate is 59.6 percent (HRSDC, 2010). Employers also need to consider how they may be maintaining or creating barriers that contribute to the significantly lower employment rate for this marginalized population.

Employers can learn to develop new mindsets and approaches in employ-
ing workers with disabilities. In a study of employers' perspectives on super-
vising youth aged 16 to 19 with disabilities in employee training programs,
Lindsay and colleagues (2012) focused on employer disposition, noting that
employers' perceptions of these youth affect whether they are hired and accommodated, and have access to opportunities in the workplace. During the
investigation, employers' initial concerns focused on work compatibility (content and quality), physical accommodation, and the time and effort required
to meet needs and integrate youth into the workplace. Some employers experienced a favourable change in disposition prompted by their observation
of positive youth attitudes, their own successes as mentors, and their learning about the abilities and capacities that youth with disabilities contributed
to the work environment. As Lindsay and associates relate, "Some employers
conveyed being positively surprised by the skill level of these youth. The un-
derestimation of their skills may have been a result of employers' stereotyping
them or recognizing they might not have as many skill building opportunities
compared to their peers" (p. 2). Employers' experiences working with youth
were key in changing their mindsets. Employers' informal learning by engaging with youth with disabilities needs to be complemented by workshops and
other opportunities to learn about disability stereotypes and myths, as well
as strategies for communicating with and accommodating these youth in organizational settings. Just as it is important to support youth with disabilities
to enable them to prepare for and have positive work experiences, it is also
important to support employers.

Like their counterparts in other OECD countries, Canadian workers with
health problems or disabilities have a lesser chance of being employed, even in
good economic times, and have a high risk of being poor and dependent on
disability or other social welfare payments. Moreover, they experience inequi-
table treatment in terms of services and supports because policy is set at the
provincial or territorial level without concern for a national standard. In these
times of persistent global economic crisis, with an accompanying decline in
labour demand, it is even more difficult for these workers to find long-term,
quality work. This difficulty is compounded by the contemporary medical-
ization of labour market problems, described by Kim, Gomes, and Prinz as
follows: "This is about benefit systems using medical problems (or conditions
labeled as such) to determine entry into long-term disability schemes. This
has the effect of categorising and managing workers in terms of their disability

or incapacity rather than what work they are able to do" (2010, p. 3). As Kim, Gomes, and Prinz relate, this phenomenon, while less evident in Canada than in most other OECD countries, puts the focus of operational policy-making on enabling the system rather than enabling the worker who finds it difficult and time-consuming to access and utilize the menagerie of benefits and employment services. For workers with health problems or disabilities, the crux of the problem is the system's failure to identify and intervene early on to "prevent the labour market detachment that often precedes long-term benefit dependency" (p. 7). This effectively removes the worker with health problems or disabilities from the job market by setting aside any concern with worker capacity and readiness while offering them basic, though often inadequate, social protection. While Kim, Gomes, and Prinz rightly suggest placing emphasis on the capacity rather than the disability of workers, they nevertheless seem more focused on worker productivity than on the positionality and needs of marginalized workers. In keeping with the neoliberal tendency to blame workers for not succeeding and not contributing to economic advancement, they circuitously blame workers with health problems or disabilities by suggesting they are unaccountable in the Canadian context because, generally, the system does not obligate them to seek employment or participate in programs geared toward finding or preparing for work. And in keeping with another neoliberal tendency to shore up the economic as a way to shore up the social, these policy analysts suggest providing these marginalized workers with open access to employment support services, with the goal of increasing their work capacity and enabling their employment or improving their employment status. This would supposedly improve their social situation by default; however, making any social improvement has to be seen as a complex contextual, relational, and dispositional process. In addition, the focus on capacity does not erase the disability, thus there is also the matter of worker accommodation post-employment. While Kim, Gomes, and Prinz recognize the need to develop a workplace support system to enable the long-term employability of workers with health problems or disabilities, any concern for worker productivity needs to be balanced with a concern for the workers themselves. This requires considering what it means for marginalized workers with health problems or disabilities to (1) participate fully as learners and workers, and (2) be treated as persons and citizens by government departments, policy-makers, employers, trainers, and co-workers. In this regard, lifelong learning must not only focus on marginalized learners and their needs and inclusion, but it must also focus on employers and the larger citizenry and increasing people's knowledge and awareness of worker health or disability and what constitutes worker access and accommodation.

Working within a neoliberal paradigm, OECD countries including Canada have prioritized the reform of sickness and disability policy, with the goal of increasing its efficiency and effectiveness in improving employment and social outcomes for marginalized workers with health problems or disabilities (Kim, Gomes, & Prinz, 2010). In speaking to the inadequacy of disability policies in Canada, August (2009) notes that many adults with disabilities remain outside the socio-economic mainstream, which limits their full citizenship and participation in life, learning, and work ventures. From a neoliberal perspective, he is particularly critical of passive income support strategies as a convention in everyday disability policy. He describes "passive benefits" as "benefits that are intended to contribute to general living expenses rather than specific needs, and that are paid either without behavioural conditions or expectations, or through delivery models like welfare that do not effectively enforce conditionality" (p. 25). August argues that these benefits for individuals with disabilities and low-income earners generally result in workers choosing short-term support over employment, maintaining a cycle of dependency and poverty. With a focus on performativity that gives primacy to efficiency over equity, August suggests moving from a passive to an active social policy perspective by utilizing "individualized, income-tested supports and services intended to minimize disability impacts on work and daily living" (p. 1). As August sees it, such a strategy would help adults with disabilities to be more economically independent, reducing their levels of dependency and poverty and increasing their value as human resources. He provides the following proposal—steeped in a neoliberal modus operandi—to bring adults with disabilities into the workforce, reducing benefit dependency and recovering sidelined human resources through economic participation: "Instead of our current system of state charity, consider the possibilities of an income support system that expects and requires an input of socially constructive self-interest from each individual, and in return offers a form of social wage substitution as part of a form of non-entitlement social contract.... [It is time to regain] the wasted human potential currently warehoused in passive income support programs" (pp. 24–25).

Would this neoliberal proposal simply reduce these human beings to some lesser form of human capital? Would it acknowledge their subjectivities and realities as citizens with health problems or disabilities? What would be the social cost and how might it assault the human integrity of adults with disabilities? For example, this approach takes the focus off disabilities and ignores the 43.8 percent of working-age Canadian adults with disabilities for whom the disabilities themselves constitute barriers to labour force participation (HRSDC, 2010). Moreover, it implies that *adults with disabilities* constitute a particular and undifferentiated group of people who can work, instead of seeing them as a spectral community of individuals with varying abilities and capacities to work. Interestingly, August contends that "any attempt to target programs to adults with disabilities as a group is likely to produce poor results" (p. 5). However, his reasoning here is based on the idea that disability is a norm—we are all disabled to some degree—so it is difficult to decide who gets into the group. It is also based on his belief, couched in neoliberal terms, that "discrete programs create strong incentives to demonstrate incapacity rather than ability or potential" (p. 5). Indeed, particular groups and discrete programs go against the grain of neoliberalism's intention to produce workers who are functionally employable and able to contribute to economic output. This places limits on what it means to be a responsible and contributing citizen. Policy-making for adults with health problems or disabilities needs to take the complexity of this community as a multivariate population into account; this has real ramifications for the ways that matters of equity and efficiency are taken up so that concerns for human integrity sit alongside concerns about worker productivity. Policy-making should also consider the competitive disadvantage of adults with health problems or disabilities as a systemic problem where barriers deter integration of workers and give them little choice. Here we might start by asking a basic question: What constitutes the good life for adults with disabilities? An answer that pays attention to contexts, relationships, and dispositional factors would certainly point to the need to address systemic barriers in the quest for the good life.

Models of Disability: Biomedical versus Social

Harpur (2012) relates that two governing disability models have guided public policy-making: the biomedical model, which focuses on repairing "defective" persons with disabilities, and the social model, which focuses on removing structural, dispositional, and environmental barriers and building the capacity of those with disabilities to live satisfying lives with the proper supports. In a nuanced analysis of the models, Tossebro (2004) maintains that, conceptually, disability is more complex than a biomedical explanation that says it is about a body with functional limits due to health problems. Yet he notes that, although it has been contested since the late 1960s, this understanding permeates political and professional discourses on disability. Tossebro describes the biomedical model as one that focuses on prevention and/or medical, psychological, or educational treatment of individuals while promoting the creation of special environments when all else fails. He relates that those who resist the biomedical perspective place an emphasis on changing the environment, instead of just focusing on changing persons with disabilities. However, as he concludes, this "environmental turn" has had little impact on everyday conceptualizations of disability and attendant communication. In part, this is due to the fact that there are competing understandings of the environmental turn. Tossebro describes what he calls weak human-ecology-like models that position disability within the person-environment interaction whereby personal dysfunction is associated with physical and other environmental demands. Here, disability is seen as relational and relative to the environment and its constitution. Tossebro also discusses what he refers to as the stronger social model of disability that emerged in the United Kingdom. This model had its origins in the perspectives of Vic Finkelstein and Paul Hunt, leaders of the British Union of the Physically Impaired Against Segregation (Thomas, 2004). They argued that human impairments were embedded in disability imposed by society and the environment (ibid.). This model accepts that some people have personal impairments, but holds that both the non-impaired social majority and the environment cause disability (Thomas, 2004; Tossebro, 2004). In fact, in its emergence in the UK context, the social model of disability has consistently made the trademark point that "it breaks the causal link between impairment (significant bodily differences culturally marked as 'abnormal') and disability (restrictions imposed by social barriers)" (Thomas, 2004, p. 25). Harpur (2012) relates that the social model distinguishes impairment from disability by showing "how it is not a person's impairment that makes them disabled, but the way in which society is structured, which means the impairment becomes disabling" (p. 3).

From this perspective, it is society that needs to change by removing the barriers that disable individuals with impairments. The focus can then be on providing the resources and supports necessary to mediate life with impairments: "Disability advocacy needs to support individuals to deal with the impact of their impairment while also fighting to stop society from creating barriers" (Harpur, 2012, p. 4). This basic principle that social barriers, and not human impairments, cause disability is of great significance to active disability politics in countering the biomedical model (Thomas, 2004). It keeps the focus on the failure of society and the environment to adapt, which creates barriers that interfere with individuals' abilities and capacities to engage in quality life, learning, and work. Thus the political task "is to change the environment in order to create equal opportunities for larger portions of the human variation— to recreate the environment to 'fit' more people" (Tossebro, 2004, p. 4). Still, as Tossebro relates, while the social model of disability is amenable to addressing accessibility and anti-discrimination issues, its sidelining of an individual body's functional limitations is still problematic: "One argument would be that the social model overestimates what can be accomplished by environmental changes, for instance for people with severe cognitive disabilities.... Another more formal argument is that in the social model, disabled people are by definition discriminated against. Disability does not *lead to* fewer opportunities, it *is* fewer opportunities" (p. 5, emphases in original).

The nihilism permeating this latter argument suggests a lasting hegemony without agency and hope for people with disabilities. To counter this, Thomas (2004) suggests returning to the origins of the social model of disability and revitalizing its social relational aspects. This would create dynamics and possibilities for societal and environmental change and enhanced citizenship. Here it becomes important to (1) consider the impact of human impairment itself and its contribution to disability (issues of being), and (2) engage in social analysis to tease apart the relationship between the impaired minority and the non-impaired majority (issues of belonging). As Thomas relates, "Whether in the name of care or welfare, or in the name of social hygiene and eugenics, the outcome has been the systematic social exclusion of people with impairment in all arenas of social life" (pp. 23–24). In this light, it is important to complicate disability as a biopsychosocial, cultural, and political construct affected by environment, human impairment, and societal dynamics. This places people with disabilities in a spectral community where they need to create unity across differences and mobilize to enable their rights in life, learning, and work domains. This keeps the social relational dimension of disability at the forefront of social action and social change. Thomas asserts that restrictions or limits on activity are a product of both human impairment *and* disability defined as forms of oppressive social behaviour directed at people with impairments: "The social relational perspective understands disability to be those restrictions of activity that result from the exercise of power to exclude: disability only comes into being when restrictions of activity are socially imposed, that is, when they are wholly social in origin. It can then be accepted as self-evident that other restrictions of activity in the lives of people with impairment do arise directly from their impairments" (p. 29).

The rights of people with disabilities and possibilities for their inclusion are advancing worldwide. Harpur (2012) asserts that the United Nations Convention on the Rights of Persons with Disabilities (CRPD), which came into force in 2008, is based on and extends the social model of disability, heralding a contemporary disability rights paradigm focused on the right to health and rehabilitation, as well as the right to work in an inclusive and accessible environment. The CRPD is the first human rights convention specifically focused on protecting the rights of individuals with disabilities (Harpur, 2012). Harpur provides a range of reasons that it is necessary, including: (1) individuals with disabilities constitute 20 percent of people in developed countries; (2) in relation to non-disabled persons, individuals with disabilities are four to five times more likely to be denied their right to work; and (3) individuals with disabilities in developing nations experience unemployment rates that reach 80 percent. The CRPD does not position disability as defectiveness, but locates it as a facet of social diversity. With regard to work, the CRPD focuses on prohibiting discrimination on the basis of disability from recruitment to hiring to continuing employment in a safe and healthy environment where one is appropriately remunerated, has grievances remedied, and can advance in a career (Harpur, 2012). With regard to education, the CRPD states that workers with disabilities need to be able to participate in continuing education and vocational and technical training that abet job performance and career advancement. This is anti-segregationist. It is what people with disabilities want. It should be what the non-impaired social majority supports.

Comparing the Lifelong-Learning Policy Cultures of Canada and Other Late Capitalist Economies

For at least a decade, Canada and a host of other late capitalist economies have experienced a pervasive neoliberal policy consensus that promotes cyclical lifelong learning as a key dynamic (Grace, 2006b, 2007). These nations—Australia, New Zealand, the Republic of Ireland, and South Africa are compared to Canada here—have advanced lifelong-learning policy cultures based on an ethic that aligns learning with performativity, productivity, flexibility, and innovation. While this ethic nurtures lifelong learning as an economistic formation, it is not encompassing enough. This is because pronounced demographic, social, cultural, and political changes sit alongside economic changes in impacting the lives, work, and security of citizens who take on multiple and varied roles at home, at work, and in their communities. Field (2006) argues that these profound changes suggest "that the learning society is already here: we live in it, here and now" (p. 47). However, the dynamics associated with contemporary change forces intimate that what we are experiencing across countries is perhaps better described as national iterations of a lifelong-learning culture. These iterations encompass ways of "doing" learning in late capitalist times whereby policy privileges learning for economic over social/public purposes. In this restrictive ecology of lifelong learning, instructors usually work with learners who mirror themselves; that is, they interact with already educated, middle-class clients. If ever there was a learning society, it is now in decline as social dysphoria intensifies concerns with disenfranchisement and exclusion, individual health and well-being, safety and security, environmental problems, and the contingent and precarious nature of work in the global economy.

Is there a way forward for lifelong learning? Olssen (2006) thinks so, as he questions whether lifelong learning, now "a specifically neoliberal form of state reason in terms of its conception, emergence and development" (p. 214), can be revitalized. He believes that a form of lifelong learning as critical action is possible: Its structures would be mobilized in the service of "a progressive emancipatory project based upon egalitarian politics and social justice" (ibid.). Such democratic social learning would endeavour to protect "learning from neoliberal appropriation ... [while] link[ing] it to a conception of social justice and development" (p. 225). With critical thought and Foucault's theorizing both central in his analysis, Olssen's multi-perspective approach can be described as critical postmodern. Olssen wants to rearticulate a view of security that shifts the political exercise of power, moving it away from regulating and managing learners and toward freeing citizens within a lifewide social-learning paradigm that emphasizes equity and social justice. His model requires revising lifelong learning to take it beyond its status as an economistic technology of control abetting a neoliberal governmentality that intensifies a competitive market formation that positions workers as commodities.

Governmentality, as conceptualized by Foucault (1984/1997), incorporates diverse practices that comprise, delineate, arrange, and direct the strategies that individuals use in relating to others. From this perspective, neoliberals seek to control other individuals within the strategic confines of privatization, corporatism, instrumentalism, and individual empowerment linked to economic output, all in the interests of improving learner and worker performance and productivity. Thus, neoliberalism as governmentality is what Foucault (1982/1997) would categorize as a technology of power aimed at directing learners and workers to meet economistic ends. Still, Foucault sees learners and workers as having a choice, using technologies of the self either to align and act within neoliberal parameters set out for them, or to contest and counteract neoliberal strategies in the interests of their happiness and well-being. For Foucault, technologies of power and technologies of the self are inextricably linked. The encounter between them is governmentality. When learners and workers resist neoliberal strategies, the interplay involves struggles over what constitutes quality learning and work, and individual growth and development not only in the sense of skill building, but also in the sense of developing attitudes.

Within neoliberal governmentality, "neoliberals theorise the role and importance of labour in terms of a model of human capital. In essence their theory starts with the human individual in terms of a classification of skills, knowledge, and ability. Although, unlike other forms of capital, it cannot be separated from the individual who owns these resources, they nevertheless constitute resources which can be sold in the market" (Olssen, 2006, p. 219). In this regard, as Olssen points out, neoliberals support state interventionism when it nurtures and maintains economic liberty. For education to enable this liberty, it focuses on individuals who are held responsible for their ongoing learning. In this milieu, Olssen states that learners have to become "the entrepreneurs of their own development" (p. 224). Here, the social and the political lose importance and distinctiveness as they fade into what Olssen calls "a marketisation of the state" (p. 219). This has resulted in a state abrogation of its social responsibility for the welfare of its citizens.

Olssen's model suggests that lifelong learning can be something more: It can be rejuvenated as a democratic social project by focusing on individual and societal security and well-being through dialogic encounters focused on human rights and needs, active citizenship, the provision of resources, and freedom for all. Paradoxically, Olssen feels this project can be enabled by many of the skills and opportunities for development that are associated with lifelong learning shaped by the discourse of neoliberal governmentality:

> If learning is now represented as social and political engagement in a global community, it constitutes a form of political participation.… In a social view of selfhood, participation is coterminous with any form of agency—whether in language, or communication or institutional engagement. Given the exclusionary and disequalising tendencies of power, participation theory strives to enumerate more or better quality inclusion. As well as permit inclusion, any adequate conception must promote a specific conception of involvement, pertaining to the uptake of skills and knowledge in order to empower their lives and others. In this sense participation involves learning in a mutually reciprocal process as the basis of survival in a constantly changing global society. (p. 227)

Olssen's conception of learning positions the learner as an agent whose individual survival abets community survival in a change culture of crisis and challenge.

The Australian Lifelong-Learning Policy Culture: Liberal and Neoliberal Tensions

In describing the emergence of lifelong learning in Australia since the 1990s, Chapman and colleagues (2005) conceptualize lifelong learning from three standpoints. The first standpoint is instrumental: lifelong learning is equated with the training and skill development needed to enhance workplace performance. This narrowly focused perspective was pervasive in lifelong-learning policy development in the country in the mid-1990s. The second standpoint, which gained currency in the late 1990s, is much broader, positioning lifelong learning as a concept that could have intrinsic as well as extrinsic value. It maintained that lifelong learners could pursue intellectual, vocational, and personal learning, which could prove transformative. The third and most recent standpoint is integrative, as it builds on the first two. It asserts that lifelong learning must "continue throughout life, as a necessary part of growth and development as a human being, as a citizen in a participative democracy, and as a productive agent in a process of economic change and advance" (p. 100). This multifocal viewpoint parallels those that propose broader parameters for lifelong learning in Canada (Grace, 2007). Learning is meant to be both lifelong and lifewide. It begins with preschool and never stops, and involves formal, informal, and non-formal learning in an array of institutional and other community settings. Paralleling the contemporary Canadian case though (Grace, 2007), Chapman and her associates acknowledge that the third standpoint is not a dominant acted-upon stance in government and corporate arenas. Nevertheless, they maintain that it is the standpoint that comes closest to defining what is meant by lifelong and lifewide learning for all.

Chapman and colleagues (2005) also explore the institutionalization of lifelong learning in Australia, relating that the Australian Commonwealth Government, like many other national governments, has positioned lifelong learning as a strategic priority in efforts to improve the country's status in the global economy. They note that this strategizing seemed to be a logical response to the economic upheaval and growing unemployment in Australia in the 1990s. In an earlier status report on lifelong learning in the country, Aspin, Collard, and Chapman (2000) recount that instrumentalized, skills-focused lifelong learning was predominant during this decade, with youth being particularly targeted. Overall, they observe that lifelong learning remained both conceptually diffuse and poorly implemented.

Even still, lifelong learning, albeit in a more privatized form, was seen as a way out and a way forward in efforts to increase the functional literacy and numeracy of Australians. Moreover, lifelong learning, rearticulated within a more integrated system of vocational education and training, was also seen as a way to make learning more adaptable to meeting workplace needs. Teachers, trainers, researchers, and learners were expected to commit and contribute to fulfilling these purposes of lifelong learning. The encompassing scale of this learning nationally demanded extensive work and collaboration across educational sectors that included universities and colleges as well as adult and community education. As Chapman and colleagues (2005) relate, this work required a new national disposition toward lifelong learning as exemplified, for example, in the 1999 report from the state of Victoria's Department of Education on seamless education and training: Everyone would have to subscribe to the learning dynamic "of a flexible and seamless system of post-compulsory education and training that provides multiple pathways and entry points into and out of study and work at varying stages throughout the lives of individuals, thereby maximizing educational mobility for Victorians. Seamlessness refers to the openness of sectors of education and training to individuals from a range of educational backgrounds" (p. 116).

Higher Education's Investment in Lifelong Learning

While all educational sectors in Australia have been expected to work together to develop a lifelong-learning culture, it seems that higher education has been most invested in situating lifelong learning as a national educational modus operandi. Candy (2000) speaks to the utility of universities in a neoliberal milieu: "By focusing on developing lifelong learners in undergraduate programs, by broadening the scope of community outreach, and by forming strategic partnerships, universities are simultaneously reaffirming their historic commitment to providing support for learning in its many forms, contexts, and manifestations throughout life, as well as recognising the imperative to produce employable and vocationally prepared graduates" (p. 17). As Candy relates, Australian universities, following the general trend in Western universities, have become more focused on developing work-ready graduates who possess technical knowledge and skills, communication competence, time-management and organizational skills, computer skills, and the capacity to work collaboratively. They have been undergoing a process of "massification" in response to current economic pressures and the incursion of a larger public into academe. Moreover, universities are reconstituting themselves "more directly and unambiguously as training grounds for people to join the economy" (p. 7). With governments, employers, professionals, and many students pressuring universities to assist in advancing the economic, Candy relates that "the historic role of higher education as a social critic and conscience" is less valued (pp. 7–8). More value is now given to producing graduates who can make a smooth transition to today's work world where they can become expert practitioners in their professional fields.

All this indicates that universities are responding in earnest to the imperatives of neoliberal pragmatism. As Jarvis (2000) sees it, this locates them as vulnerable institutions that appear to be adapting and enduring, in the sense Candy describes above, only because they have succumbed to serving the ends of late capitalism. Indeed, universities appear to have little choice. They have to fulfill the role of servant to corporations that demand specific kinds of workers who can contribute to economic efficiency:

> Higher education ... has had to change at a phenomenal rate, providing continuing professional education ... for the knowledge workers. Indeed, universities are being forced into becoming institutions of lifelong learning, and developing

all their delivery systems and procedures accordingly—which might be no bad thing in itself! However, the program of courses offered, and much of the research undertaken by the universities, shows that they have been subordinated to the demands of the market, and especially to those of the large corporations. (p. 23)

As an indication of the pressure on universities to acclimatize to neoliberalism, Jarvis observes a contemporary phenomenon: When traditional universities have failed to keep up, corporations have responded by setting up corporate universities that develop their own systems of instrumental education and training. In the face of such corporate dominance, Jarvis concludes that universities have been reduced to conduits for conveying what the knowledge society values. In this milieu, citizens are reduced to "human resources to be developed through lifelong learning," which is expressed as credentialism (p. 23). As learners increase their instrumental value, they are expected to perform outside any critically intelligent design. They are not to question corporations and governments, their collective quest for economic returns, or the mistakes they make in this quest. Moreover, they are not to question whether there is more to life than work. In a neoliberal milieu, work is life, or at least that is what ideal neoliberalized citizens should think as notions such as learner freedom are shunted aside in the quest to deliver what has value in the marketplace. As Jarvis concludes, in this milieu "all the education and learning that relates to our humanity—but not to the economy—is relegated to the margins of corporate and sociopolitical society" (p. 25).

Catts (2004) takes a stance similar to Jarvis, asserting that the perceived adaptability of universities is something forced within a survivalist response. He describes higher education's involvement in cultivating lifelong learning in terms of required adaptability that amounts to mediation of corporate and political change forces that have diminished the traditional, more liberal educational purposes of higher education. As Catts sees it, the role of universities today is twofold: to help students develop skills to sustain prowess in the practice of lifelong learning and to help them attain disciplinary or professional knowledge. Candy lists analogous roles: *"the development of lifelong learners,* and the broader *provision of lifelong learning opportunities"* (p. 14, emphasis in original). However, the emphasis on instrumental, economistic lifelong learning has tended to reduce both options for higher education and choices for students. Catts acknowledges higher education's dilemma: the creation of new, exploitable, economistic knowledge has become the domain of corporations, which has weakened the ability of higher education to influence what knowledge has most worth. Furthermore, juxtaposing the development of competent lifelong learners with creating opportunities to build professional knowledge suggests a dichotomy in roles that can produce tensions. A more historical concern with liberal education and molding insightful, proactive, well-rounded graduates could be pitted against a more neoliberal pragmatic concern with vocational education and producing graduates with specific knowledge. Somehow there must be mediation of both concerns since, as Candy (2000) observes, even specialist expertise is not enough: "Employers have increasingly emphasised that graduates also need to be adaptable and flexible; and that they need to be able to: manage themselves and others, communicate well orally and in writing, keep up to date in their chosen field, be technologically literate, and generally to manifest a range of more generic or transferable attributes in addition to their subject-matter skills and knowledge" (p. 8). Circuitously, Candy makes a case for more attention to be given to liberal education as a shaper of critical thinkers and flexible problem solvers.

How might we understand the historical adaptability of universities that Candy describes or the required adaptability that Catts discusses? We might turn to Bauman (2001), who asserts that both the autonomy and centrality of universities and scholarship are under scrutiny. As he sees it, one factor exacerbating the crisis in university education is "the rapid weakening of the orthodox institutional bases/guarantees of the universities' authority" (p. 129). Bauman declares that today's universities cannot claim to be exclusive producers and disseminators of knowledge; they have to compete with other agencies that are arguably "much more in tune with the cravings and fears of contemporary consumers" (p. 130). These consumers see the acquisition of knowledge and skills as enabling, increasing their capacities as workers. Bauman provides this summary of the wane in the influence of universities at a time when employers, not universities, seem better able to address the learning dynamics required to adjust to the professional needs of flexible occupations:

The permanent and continuing technological revolution transforms the acquired know-how and learned habits [of citizens] from assets into a handicap, and sharply shortens the lifespan of useful skills, which often lose their utility and "enabling power" in less time than it takes to acquire them and certify them through a university diploma. Under such circumstances, the ad hoc, short-term professional training administered by employers and oriented directly to prospective jobs, or flexible courses and (quickly updated) teach-yourself kits offered through the market by the extra-university media become more attractive (and, indeed, more reasonable a choice) than a fully fledged university education which is no longer capable of promising, let alone guaranteeing, a life career. (p. 131)

Bauman indicates a key repercussion of this apparent decline in the authority and utility of universities and scholarship: There is an increase of tensions between those academics who still value the liberal tradition of universities and other academics who are buying into neoliberal values in their new work to orient university education to the values of the marketplace. Bauman states the main consequence of neoliberalizing university education: "Spiritual leadership is a mirage; the task of the intellectuals is to follow the world out there, not to legislate for standards of propriety, truth and good taste" (p. 135). In this milieu, university education is reduced to preparing for work; it is no longer more broadly about critically preparing for life and mediating the contexts, dispositions, and relationships that shape being, becoming, belonging, and acting in the world today. Still, in a world in a state of flux, the latter kind of open-ended and encompassing critical education is crucial. It can address instrumental, social, *and* cultural concerns by attending to learning for work within the larger context of enabling learning for life.

Seemingly unable to mediate liberal and neoliberal interests in education, universities appear to be caught in a quagmire regarding whether to place value on liberal tradition or buy into neoliberal lifelong learning as a survivalist strategy. Aspin, Collard, and Chapman (2000) provide this Australian perspective, which reflects the favoured neoliberal stance. They believe that universities have a key role to play in creating a culture of lifelong learning to which citizens subscribe; universities have to enable and encourage students to engage in learning as a continuous lifelong process. To advance higher education, they add that vocational education and training (VET) institutions have to play a similar role in increasing strategic partnerships with universities that elevate lifelong learning "as a concept, a value and a set of opportunities" (p. 180). Of course, this rigid and apparently rigorous culture of lifelong learning endorses instrumental/professional knowledge as the kind of knowledge with most worth. This culture also abets privatization of higher education and pushes for deregulation of fees so students will absorb more of the cost of their engagement in lifelong learning. This accentuates the need to remember liberal concerns with the social context. As Aspin, Collard, and Chapman state,

"In Australia there is an increasing awareness of the obligation for educators and policy-makers to take into account the social dimension of the need for learning across the lifespan" (p. 188). In this light, they call for more research on disenfranchised groups—including unemployed youth, aging workers, Indigenous students, immigrants, and the homeless—to inform lifelong-learning policy-making focused on social inclusion and cohesion. Notions of civic responsibility and community engagement may not have completely dissolved into neoliberal air.

Beddie (2004), who was appointed executive director of Adult Learning Australia in 2002, advocates for socially democratic forms of learning that meet the needs of the disenfranchised. Valuing learning communities as a catalyst for promoting collective responsibility, she calls on educators and administrators to take responsibility for engaging all citizens in holistic lifelong learning that attends to ethical, contextual, and relational matters. As she sees it, such learning can work against unevenness and advance intrinsic and social as well as economic values in critical learning for life and work. In surveying her work with Adult Learning Australia, Beddie describes the task of engaging citizens in critical forms of lifelong learning as quite challenging. She feels that the large majority of working-age Australians participating in lifelong learning are extrinsically motivated: they engage in vocational training and workplace learning for economistic purposes. She offers this explanation: The Australian lifelong-learning policy culture has sidelined learning for democratic citizenship that would address inclusion or other civic concerns. It caters instead to the already educated, helping them to become more information literate and savvy about technology. Beddie notes that this instrumental focus has marginalized many Australians. She quotes 2002 statistics indicating that 45 percent of Australian adults lack sufficient levels of numeracy and literacy to cope with the everyday demands of life and work, and that one in five Australians is not functionally literate. Sadly, these statistics mirror Canadian statistics (Myers & de Broucker, 2006), leaving me to wonder why two advanced late capitalist economies have such unhealthy social underbellies belying their economic prosperity and "developed" status as nations.

When governments abrogate their public responsibilities and sideline the social, disenfranchisement of certain citizens is exacerbated. Beddie declares that social problems multiply in such situations, as the uneducated and undereducated are more likely to experience poor health, make bad consumer choices, engage in crime, and have a negative attitude toward participation in lifelong learning. In solving these social ills, she insists that lifelong learning as critical action has to prioritize meeting local, organic needs as part of a civic responsibility to help individuals and communities build social and cultural capital. In the Australian context, Beddie maintains that governments and universities have ignored this responsibility in the rush to vocationalize university education as a form of mass education that favours multinational corporations, rather than local communities. Who matters when the private and the global are valued more than the public and the local? It would seem that uneducated, undereducated, older, and poor adults don't matter much at all. This certainly is the case when, for example, the disenfranchised encounter lifelong learning as unavailable, inappropriate, coercive, or expensive training (Grace, 2007). And this is too often the case.

The New Zealand Lifelong-Learning Policy Culture: A Different State of Affairs

The lifelong-learning policy culture in New Zealand since the 1970s significantly contrasts with lifelong-learning policy development and implementation in Canada and Australia. Most notably, Tobias relates that in New Zealand "lifelong learning barely featured in policy formulation in the 1990s" (2004, p. 585). Indeed, the National governments of the early and mid-1990s stayed distant from the concept in their policy-making. This absence contrasted with the emphasis placed on lifelong-learning policy-making in many OECD nations during this period. It also contrasted with previous emphases on lifelong learning within New Zealand. As Tobias recounts, the 1970s and 1980s variously constituted a period of considerable public-policy development in relation to lifelong learning. During the 1970s, lifelong learning benefited from some practical implementation and success in areas including community education and adult literacy. Tobias relates that this progress waned in the late 1970s in the face of global change forces and the compromising of the welfare state.

Lifelong learning was once again on the radar in public-policy discourse in the mid-1980s, and expectations were high following the election of a Labour government in 1984. Indeed, as Boshier (2001) points out, it was a Labour government that had created a welfare state in New Zealand in 1935. However, from 1984 to 1999 neoliberalism was ascendant, and New Zealand became immersed in "a radical experiment in free market economics" (Boshier, 2001, p. 361).

Boshier reports that living standards declined during this period. Parallel-ing the negative effects of neoliberal economics on Canadian and Australian youth, this decline had a particularly dire impact on 15- to 25-year-old New Zealanders, with Maori youth among the most affected. Boshier provides this conspectus of the social turmoil that youth and others experienced during a time when lifelong learning declined as a vehicle for social reform in the face of economistic change forces: After 1984 there was a "precipitous decline in literacy and numeracy rates, escalating expulsions from schools, a deepening problem of Maori underachievement, confusion of demoralized and under-paid teachers, dismissal (through restructuring) of large numbers of skilled educators, [and] 78% cuts (in a single year) to adult education and [the] emer-gence of an underclass" (p. 362).

Boshier describes the limited formation of lifelong learning in this new economy as "a troubled, contested and sometimes mean-spirited programme that didn't deliver the goods to an increasingly impoverished and cantanker-ous underclass" (p. 361). Indeed, learning as a lifelong and lifewide endeavour that might address access, accommodation, and equity issues was sidelined in policy formulation during this period in which neoliberalism was ascendant. This ideology worked to shift educational and other social responsibilities from the public to the private sector, as it located the market as the driver of public policy direction. Tobias notes that New Zealand, like many other nations un-der neoliberalism, witnessed the growth of instrumentalism, vocationalism, credentialism, and a new managerialism that set more limited parameters to what comprised valuable learning. This technocratic mindset was evident in the *Education Act* (1990), which merged tertiary or vocational and university education under a learning-for-life theme, undermining traditional university concerns with liberal humanism and social advancement (Boshier, 2001). To-bias concludes, "Within these frameworks, the long-established linkages be-tween education, citizenship, and the state were largely severed and replaced by linkages between education, the consumer and the labour market" (p. 573). These new linkages found expression, for example, in the *Education Amend-ment Act* (1990). Tobias notes that the New Zealand government positioned the act as its legislative centerpiece in restructuring post-compulsory educa-tion, endorsing a narrower economistic, instrumentalized, and commodified discourse of lifelong learning. The act situated universities as markets driven by student enrolments and economic interests, and it reduced post-compul-sory education to its more formal context, downplaying the needs of voluntary organizations involved in informal and non-formal adult and community education. Progressive, liberal, and critical perspectives on lifelong learning were not valued in this context.

As neoliberalism gained a solid grip on governance in New Zealand under the National or National coalition governments throughout the 1990s, there was further abrogation of public responsibility for lifelong learning. In a synopsis of the sorry situation that learners faced during this time of declining support in the early 1990s, Tobias writes, "little reference in public policy discourses was made to lifelong learning and little recognition was given to the potential significance of a range of lifelong learning initiatives" (p. 577). In reference to the 1994 strategic report entitled *Education for the 21st Century*, which emphasized a front-end model of initial and preparatory education over lifelong learning, Tobias reiterates the state's limited perspective: "The report provided little evidence of understanding or sympathy for those wider lifelong learning goals, which focus on the integration of personal, social, and democratic ends" (p. 578). Scourged by neoliberal ideology, lifelong learning as a lifewide endeavour appeared to be moving off the public-policy radar in New Zealand, with the notion of holistic, democratic, ethical, and just forms of learning not even constituting a blip. By the late 1990s, mention of lifelong learning in public-policy discourse was limited to a focus on the commodification of lifelong learning for employment: "This employment focus was … [to be accomplished] by opening tertiary education up to the competitive demands of the marketplace. The tertiary system was to be made more responsive to the demands of individual learners and potential learners" (Tobias, 2004, p. 579).

There was a public-policy shift in 2000 after the election of a Labour/Alliance government in November 1999 that gave prominence to lifelong learning in its terms of reference for the newly established Tertiary Education Advisory Commission (TEAC). However, Tobias asserts that TEAC failed to link lifelong learning overtly with broader social, economic, and cultural goals that would affirm citizenship as a central focus. Nevertheless, as Tobias points out, TEAC did broadly define tertiary education to include diverse forms of formal and non-formal education and training, and it stressed the importance of lifelong learning in discussing the role of tertiary education in a knowledge society that has a range of localized effects on individuals and communities. Tobias concludes, "Where it was less successful was in its failure to link its philosophies of education and lifelong learning with 'a critical theory of society'" (p. 584). This failure to emphasize lifelong learning as critical action breaks with what Tobias describes as a national history of lifelong learning that situated the notion within the social democratic tradition, as it did in the 1970s, for example. From this historical perspective, Tobias argues that lifelong learning in New Zealand has been more complex than any recent neo-liberal expression of it would suggest.

The Irish Lifelong-Learning Policy Culture: It's More about the Adults

In deliberating the nature and meaning of lifelong learning and matters of purpose, provision, and participation in the Republic of Ireland, Kenny (2004) observes that social cohesion is commonly mentioned in the rhetoric used in lifelong-learning policy circles. However, she feels that the notion is not taken very seriously. She states that if social cohesion had contemporary clout and value, then it would bring participants in lifelong learning—educators and learners alike—face to face with the history of marginalization and exclusion in Irish national and local contexts. It would show them how much of their participation is predetermined within a neoliberal politicization of lifelong learning. Kenny suggests that a failure to emphasize social action and advancement helps to explain why there is a pronounced poor attitude toward participation in lifelong learning among adults in the Irish Republic. She relates that only 20 percent of the population takes courses of any kind, and most of these learners are already educationally advantaged. Changing Irish demographics such as an increasing immigrant population are also having an impact. Increased immigration has intensified concerns with access, accommodation, and equity in learning and work. In gauging reaction to immigration in Ireland, Kenny notes the Irish tendency to see cultural difference as a deficit associated with difficulty. She points out that individual citizens and churches, hanging on to tradition and historical notions of dominance, have contributed to the exclusion experienced by new immigrants. She also discusses three other cultural phenomena with ramifications for lifelong learning in the Republic of Ireland. First, there is a significant marginalization of older women, most of whom are undereducated and do not work outside the home. Similarly, education and employment are precarious ventures for older women in Canada, especially immigrant women and women of colour. Second, in another example paralleling the Canadian experience, Kenny notes that increasing socio-economic inequalities and geographic remoteness have limited access to information and communications technology for many Irish citizens. Third, there is a high unemployment rate—15 percent or nearly four times the national average— among early school leavers (15- to 29-year-olds). This bleak picture is replicated in Canada, Australia, and New Zealand, for example, where high youth unemployment and underemployment and the lack of quality work are problems (Boshier, 2001; Grace, 2007). In Canada, these negative outcomes are exacerbated by the tendency among youth (broadly defined by the federal government as 15- to 30-year-olds) not to participate in lifelong learning (Grace, 2007). Possibilities for holistic lifelong learning are also hampered by the fact that, since at least the 1960s, there has been inadequate provision of education for citizenship in Canada, resulting in youth having declining political knowledge and diminished civic engagement (Grace, 2009b).

Focusing on the needs of excluded and vulnerable youth who have experienced schooling as a psychically and biographically damaging engagement, and have left school early, we need to develop social and cultural education models that help all youth develop as learners and citizens who can mediate the complexities of change, institutional and community cultures, and civil society in order to learn and live in contemporary times (Grace, 2009b). Using the example of a second-chance education and training intervention in the Republic of Ireland called Youthreach, McGrath (2006) provides one such model. He asserts that education and training beyond formal schooling need to focus on broader social inclusion in addition to the usual emphasis on labour market integration if youth are to develop as full citizens. He argues that this requires social policy intervention that emphasizes developing the individual capabilities of youth as agents who are able to build individual relationships and allegiances so they can have interactions that they find meaningful and significant. It is McGrath's contention that "in order to activate educational inclusion for the most vulnerable, support for interventions that respond to the 'individualized' needs and capabilities of young people is critical for the realization of authentic social inclusion policy" (p. 596). In developing such policy, McGrath asks us to consider a key question: "How might we characterize 'inclusion' at the interface between personal lives and social policy interventions?" (p. 596). In his answer to this question, McGrath speaks to the importance of creating an active learning culture in which youth experience support, security, and self-comfort that gives them courage to try as individuals who know that when they choose to speak, they will be heard. He discusses inclusion in the context of the Youthreach learning process:

Analysis of young people's narratives suggests that what unanimously appeals to young people, irrespective of their attraction to the program on the basis of the training allowance, are the structures of communication between tutors and participants, which can be interpreted as psychosocial processes of group inclusion, fostering relations of trust and promoting a sense of ontological (psychic) security. (p. 602)

For struggling youth, these processes promote exploratory learning and thinking outside the box. These outcomes contribute to more encompassing lifelong learning that helps them grow as persons, workers, and full citizens. It provides them with knowledge that feeds the will to power necessary to overcome life risks including poverty, physical and emotional abuse, family dysfunction, and poor parenting or other deficient relationships with adults. This is inclusive lifelong learning as critical action that remembers its commitment to social and cultural education as part of the holistic development of learners.

The Republic of Ireland and the United Kingdom: A Brief Comparison

In a comparison of lifelong learning in the Republic of Ireland and the United Kingdom, Field (2000a) relates that both countries, in keeping with a Western European trend, have emphasized lifelong-learning policy-making and demonstrated at least the desire to translate policy into practice. Indeed, he asserts that the idea and language of lifelong learning have been politicized in both countries to the point that the term has "become a convenient political shorthand for the modernizing of education and training systems" (p. 218). Scott (2000) is less certain about the prominence and longevity of lifelong learning, at least in the UK context. While the concept seems to have supplanted adult and higher education in the United Kingdom, he questions "how long even this diffuse but discrete category can survive in a society in which 'learning' is just one element within wider patterns of individual identification, social realization, economic actualization and cultural consumption (all, of course, intertwined)" (p. 29). Still, he admits that lifelong learning as a transgressive, generally privatized contemporary concept has given rise to a new paradigm in the conceptual and policy remapping of British post-secondary education.

Field (2000a) notes that both the Republic of Ireland and the United Kingdom have focused on adults, even though the Irish Republic has a younger population. This is in contrast with the more pronounced focus on youth in countries such as Canada, Australia, and New Zealand, as previously noted. In the case of the United Kingdom, in the national *Inquiry into the Future for Lifelong Learning*, Schuller and Watson (2009) recognized the cultural dilemma for UK youth that is exacerbated by educational unfairness:

> For young people and those who cater for them, the transition to adulthood is marked by multiple arbitrary and often conflicting dividing lines. Instead of helping young people to move consciously into adulthood, the current system is a confusing tangle. In many respects, it serves only to prolong dependency and child status, whilst apparently allowing adulthood. Educationally, it is also deeply unfair. It gives some groups far more access, not just to more education on some meritocratic basis, but to more opportunities to develop and grow. (p. 89)

From this perspective, it is understandable why some UK youth drop out of school early, resulting in the United Kingdom having a very poor record on early school leaving. Schuller and Watson add that those who go on to higher education have their own problems, including increasing student debt. Sadly, they note "many young people disappear from sight, being neither in education nor employment" (p. 90). Too many of these youth can be found in prison or among the homeless.

So what has been the primary focus of lifelong learning in the United Kingdom? It has been building workplace knowledge and skills through vocationally oriented education and training. Field (2000a) provides the logic for this emphasis: vocational training has cultural legitimacy and is considered politically safe to promote; it lends itself to non-regulatory types of intervention at the local level; and, it has been easier to access government funding for vocational training (something that is changing with increased privatization of learning).

While the Republic of Ireland has also focused on vocational education and training, it has balanced this with an emphasis on advancing the country's general adult-education infrastructure. This is reflected in the landmark White Paper entitled *Learning for Life 2000*, which is the Irish national policy statement on lifelong learning. With respect to identifying priorities for adult education along the lifelong learning continuum, the Irish government broadly focused on such components as consciousness raising, citizenship, cohesion, competitiveness, cultural development, and community building (Jarvis, 2007). While political and economic forces have impacted developments in lifelong learning in the Republic of Ireland, this array of components aligns with Maunsell's (2010) assertion that social forces remain a key influence on lifelong-learning objectives, as they have historically. Indeed, Maunsell contends that government policy, as presented in the 2000 White Paper, has situated lifelong learning as a mainstream educational force shaped within the interdependence of aims to advance social inclusion and have the economy prosper. However, despite the rhetoric advocating social advancement, lifelong learning is still considered to have a crucial role in labour market policy in the Republic of Ireland (Jarvis, 2007). Moreover, Field (2000a) notes the novice policy-making status of the Irish Republic, which is in reactive mode as it tries to deal with an inferior adult-education system. Field describes the basis of the cultural crisis: "Internally, rapid economic growth has outstripped the supply of indigenous labour: the working population in Ireland rose by almost 50 percent in the 1990s alone, for example, so that policy-makers are increasingly looking towards new types of labour market entrants (primarily women, but also a small number of officially-encouraged immigrants) and continuous upskilling for existing workers" (p. 218).

In both the Republic of Ireland and the United Kingdom, as Field relates, policy implementation lags behind policy development. Moreover, he points out that despite recognition of the lifewide possibilities for lifelong learning in both countries, "policy has advanced across a relatively narrow and conventional front" (p. 219). This raises issues regarding how we should transfer lifelong-learning policy into practice as a mediation of institutional and individual interests. It also raises issues regarding access and equity, and highlights a need to advocate for lifelong learning as critical action.

The South African Lifelong-Learning Policy Culture: The Power of Neoliberalism and the Global Economy

Currently, South Africa, in affiliation with its neighbours in the South African Development Community, is posing questions similar to the ones raised above in Canadian and other national contexts. Indeed, as Aitchison (2004) notes, any nation might ask these questions since, to date, no nation has truly come to grips with holistic lifelong learning and its meaning and value in policy-making and practice. These questions begin with a focus on the designation "lifelong learning" and include the following: "Is lifelong education the same as lifelong learning?" (Aitchison, 2004, p. 539) Is the former more public and a state responsibility? Is the latter more individualistic and a personal responsibility? "Do the massive financial implications of establishing a system of lifelong education, with no necessary economic benefit in return, … inevitably lead to talk about lifelong learning for rhetorical, inspirational and propagandist purposes but a continuation of the old educational order more or less unchanged?" (ibid.).

During apartheid, lifelong learning was not a possibility for many South Africans: It was "a dream in a land where so many [had] no education at all" (Aitchison, 2004, p. 518). In this bleak period in South Africa's history, Pendlebury and Enslin (2000) recount that there was systematic abandonment and obstruction of lifelong learning. Apartheid meant separate and unequal education, poor working conditions, and limited opportunities for most of the country's citizens. In the anti-apartheid climate of 1990, things started to change. Aitchison relates that the National Education Policy Investigation (NEPI), which issued its adult education report in 1993 and used the term lifelong education, emphasized the notion and construed it more broadly in communal, co-operative, lifelong, and lifewide terms as "a more comprehensive and visionary concept … [that] includes formal, nonformal, and informal learning extended throughout the lifespan of an individual" (p. 518). Although this all-encompassing goal of lifelong learning was extremely important for the new South Africa, it would not be achieved in the emerging post-apartheid nation. Despite the obvious need to accent the social, lifelong learning went awry. Aitchison recounts how "narrower interests related to training, competency and the world of work" prevailed in early educational policy formulation (p. 519). For example, the Education Department of the African National Congress developed a policy framework for education and training that placed lifelong learning at the core of a focus on education for economic development; continuous skill upgrading had to be aligned "with the rapidly changing and dynamic nature of the world economy and universal knowledge base" (p. 520). While there was some social focus on equity and redress, learning for work and credentialism were given more weight in policy development. As Aitchison notes, in the post-1994 policy-making period, which was also marred by huge implementation failures, "'lifelong learning' was rapidly adopted in government communications as a rhetorical shorthand term for all that was desirable in a system of education" (p. 521). By 1995, the Ministry of Education seemed to have forgotten pre-apartheid radicalism, shifting its focus and language to the rhetoric of education and training for human resource development. As the 1990s passed, policy-making continued to put the economic before the social to meet market needs and, concomitantly, the needs of workers seeking credentials to mediate the market. While there was some emphasis on the undereducated, as indicated by the focus on adult basic education and training (ABET) in a 1997 policy document, Aitchison questions the degree to which document principles such as learner-centredness and the provision of learner support were realized. As he saw it, adding a T to ABE reduced ABET to "education for economic skills" (p. 529). Aitchison concludes, "Generally, the implementation of ABET was impressive at the level of policy, systematization, standardization and regulations but weak to disastrous on the ground in practice and growth" (p. 532).

As the foregoing overview indicates, South Africa, emerging as a democracy during the 1990s, took the same neoliberal turn in lifelong learning that nations such as Canada and Australia did. This common turn speaks to the power of neoliberalism and the global economy in shaping lifelong learning. Certainly, in the early post-apartheid period in the new South Africa, we might have expected a pronounced, even dominant emphasis on "the social" in lifelong-learning policy development and intervention. Why wasn't the social more predominant in post-apartheid lifelong-learning discourse? Is it still possible to engender lifelong learning as critical action in South Africa?

In her work to establish a sustainable lifelong-learning institution in higher education in the South Africa, Walters (2006) provides a useful conspectus of steps for taking a critical turn in lifelong-learning policy development and intervention. Emphasizing the conditional and the contextual, she begins with two questions: "What are the regulatory, financial, cultural, historical, [and] legislative frameworks, which encourage or discourage the implementation of lifelong learning practices? Is there consensus on a working definition of lifelong learning?" (p. 74). Walters sees the trend in lifelong-learning policy formulation to intersperse concerns with social cohesion and equity amid predominant neoliberal concerns with the economy and employment as an opportunity: It is a structured way to complicate lifelong learning in terms of the concept's concerns with "vocationalism and performativity, social control and incorporation, pluralistic complexity within a post-modern framework, personal development and growth, and radical social purpose and community development" (p. 73). Walters maintains that putting lifelong learning into institutional practice entails significant pedagogical, organizational, and social changes that take into account regulatory, financial, historical, legislative, and social/cultural frameworks; strategic partnerships and linkages; research, teaching, and learning; administrative policies and ways of operating; and student support systems and services. She points out that these characteristic elements make up the Cape Town Statement for realizing a higher education institution that enacts lifelong learning as a flexible, convenient, and relevant everyday practice. This statement, building on work started at CONFINTEA V, was intended to provide a framework to explore relationships among lifelong learning, higher education, and active citizenship (UNESCO, 2001). The framework could then be developed further in national and local contexts. Applying it to South Africa, Walters insists it is important to consider non-traditional students and non-traditional ways of learning that now impact the social/cultural fabric of the country's higher education institutions. To round out the emphasis on situating lifelong learning within an economistic narrative that promotes performativity and productivity, Walters calls on educators to emphasize lifelong learning within an emancipatory narrative that raises concerns with social justice, equity, and active democratic citizenship, especially for those whom the first narrative leaves out. She declares, "Lifelong learning within an emancipatory narrative is concerned with social justice and active citizenship amongst groups who are 'marginalized' within particular societies" (p. 81).

In their discussion of such an emancipatory narrative, Pendlebury and Enslin (2000) suggest a need to combine redistributive justice with a holistic lifelong-learning paradigm in South Africa. This melding is a prerequisite to accomplish the country's "most urgent project, which is to achieve a democratic polity, a just, equitable and inclusive society, and a strong, globally competitive economy" (p. 149). Since many youth and adults "sacrificed their already limited educational opportunities as a consequence of apartheid" (p. 150), Pendlebury and Enslin suggest that the emergence of lifelong learning in South Africa has to be different: The international focus on lifelong learning in post-compulsory education will have to be translated into a post-primary rather than post-secondary emphasis. Furthermore, they insist: "In countries hitherto ravaged by war and poverty or, in South Africa's case, protean policies of exclusion, disempowerment and inequality, the moral and political imperative is to ensure that educational provision does not further disempower the already disempowered. Uncritical policy borrowing runs the risk of ignoring this imperative" (pp. 150–151).

In this regard, taking a neoliberal turn and emphasizing education for economistic purposes (human resource development) simply won't do in South Africa. Such education excludes the uneducated and undereducated who are living remnants of apartheid. Thus Pendlebury and Enslin stress both the crucial need to attend to adult basic education and the profound need to redress the losses suffered under apartheid by "homeless and imprisoned youth and those militarized at a young age through the struggle against apartheid" (p. 153). South Africa is not singling out adults like the Republic of Ireland or youth like Canada, Australia, and New Zealand. All age groups are in dire straits. Meeting their diverse needs is an ultimate challenge for lifelong learning that will test its mettle and substance in a post-apartheid ecology of learning. However, lifelong learning in South Africa seems far from able to meet this challenge. This is because the country is emphasizing economistic lifelong learning to the detriment of the basic education and social learning needed to alleviate the plight of so many disenfranchised citizens. Arguing that adult basic education is crucial to the successful development and implementation of lifelong-learning policy and practice in South Africa, Pendlebury and Enslin provide this synopsis, which does not bode well for lifelong learning in the developing nation:

> The dominance of the economic arm of lifelong learning policy and doubts about the efficacy of the *Skills Act* in improving the lot of the most disenfranchised groups are confirmed by controversy concerning progress in adult basic education and training (ABET) since 1994…. There are grounds for believing that little if any progress has been made to provide inclusive and readily available adult basic education and training to South Africa's large population of illiterate adults, who according to one estimate comprise 11 percent of the adult population. What is more, 45 percent of the adult population have not received a full general education. (p. 154)

To redress this social injustice in education, lifelong learning ought to take a pronounced critical turn in its emergence in South Africa and advance ethical and equitable treatment for all citizens still trying to recover from the history of apartheid.

Concluding Perspective: Moving Beyond the Current Neoliberal Orientation toward Lifelong Learning

Since neoliberalism has permeated lifelong-learning policy formulation for some time now, Sutherland and Crowther (2006) suggest that holistic lifelong learning is more likely to blossom "on the margins of dominant institutions and in contexts less constrained by the dominant policy discourse" (p. 10). This suggestion should worry us, since it implies a binary situation. On the one hand, instrumental and economistic forms of lifelong learning could be the predominant focus of institutions in which the promise of lifelong learning has apparent limits. On the other hand, social and cultural forms of lifelong learning could be more the domains of local communities and social movements where hope and possibility are often energizers of learning. To the degree that this is already the case, "lifelong learning is actively reproducing inequality. It may even be creating new sources of inequality, as well as providing a new legitimacy for power and privilege" (Field, 2006, p. 114). In this scenario, the promise of lifelong learning is mired in fatalism, in the inevitability of the dominance of neoliberal forms of lifelong learning, and in the further erosion of the social.

Critical educators such as Field (2006) refuse this fate; he makes a case to see lifelong learning beyond the reductionism that marks the current neoliberal policy consensus: "Because the policy case for lifelong learning is so closely bound up with skills and competitiveness, it is easy to lose sight of the profound transformation of individual biographies, in respect not just of work, but also of home, leisure, consumption, or even intimate relationships" (p. 69). As Field implies, lifelong learning ought to be a complex conditional, contextual, and relational phenomenon similar to what Walters describes in the South African case. It ought to evolve in the intersection of the economic, the cultural, the social, and the political as individuals learn to deal with unpredictability in life, transitions in learning, precariousness in work, and worker mobility. This situates lifelong learning as critical action. It involves humanizing lifelong learning and including the economic within a broader contextual focus. As Field sees it, our goal should be to engender lifelong learning in forms and projects that are "economically efficient, socially equitable, ecologically sustainable, and politically democratic" (p. 175). Sutherland and Crowther (2006) agree in their call for a broader construction of lifelong learning that connects everyday life to broader public issues. Such an engagement in lifelong learning would encompass learning the diverse knowledge and skills needed to be productive at work, build healthy relationships, and live "in families, communities and societies in ways that are mutually caring, beneficial, and supportive" (p. 3). However, a caution is warranted. In spelling out the promise of lifelong learning to build knowledge and understanding of the self and others, Sutherland and Crowther slip back into the neoliberal stance of equating useful learning with continuous learning. This slippage begs two perennial questions: How far is continuous learning from mandatory learning? What does the neoliberal promise of lifelong learning do to learner freedom? These questions must be addressed in emphasizing the agency of learners in shaping lifelong learning as critical action.

Chapter 6

Transnational Travesties for Sexual Minorities as Subaltern Learners: An Exchange with Robert J. Hill

Lifelong learning should be about learning for all of life, which positions it as "inherently untidy" (Schuller & Watson, 2009, p. 23). It ought to include historical, social, cultural, political, and economic contexts, so lifelong learning is ultimately understood as encompassing educational and cultural work for social transformation (Allman, 1999; Grace, 2007). Still, as I have indicated throughout this book, lifelong learning as critical action remains enigmatic in many quarters. Burke and Jackson (2007) provide this contemporary description of mainstream lifelong learning as a narrow and inadequately contextualized field of study and practice that is not broadly committed to inclusion and justice for all learners across relationships of power: "In the main 'the field' is described as though it is neutral, ahistorical and uncontestable, with little account given of a wide range of different histories and competing 'fields,' including those of adult and continuing education, community based learning, and the personal and political learning that takes place in, for example, trade unions, women's groups, or groups for other marginalized people, such as gay and lesbian groups, Black and minority ethnic groups and so forth" (p. 9).

Within the politics and culture of neoliberalism, such sidelining of the social has been widespread. Much of the Global North has experienced a pervasive neoliberal policy consensus that stresses the value of a knowledge-based economy, technology and skill development, and a learning society in which participation in cyclical lifelong learning is an expectation (Grace, 2006b, 2007). Drawing on Foucault to frame this consensus within a politics of control, Fejes (2008) asserts that neoliberal lifelong-learning policy aims not only to construct learners (technologies of control), but also to have learners construct themselves (technologies of the learner). Social learning for cultural transformation goes against the grain of this politics of control that not only conflates being a competent worker with simply being a skilled worker, but also isolates training and development for workers from broader social and other contextual considerations (Forrester, 2005; Grace, 2006b). This decentring of the social is worrisome, especially in relation to those whom mainstream lifelong learning fails. Schuller and Watson (2009) speak to this in positioning learning in relation to improved well-being in the UK report, *Inquiry into the Future for Lifelong Learning*: "Sometimes it has little or no effect; sometimes it can even have negative effects, overall or for some groups" (p. 23).

As it is framed within neoliberal pragmatism, lifelong learning in its contemporary cyclical iteration aims to produce an information literate citizenry, generate quality information, and provide universal access, all in the name of presenting itself as a medium and infrastructure for knowledge-and-skill building that aims to sustain and enhance the economic sector (Grace, 2006b). The upshot of this neoliberal bolstering of the economic is purportedly a bolstering of the social. However, while advancing the economic is important for creating jobs and relative stability for workers, advancing the social has not been obvious or guaranteed under neoliberalism as a contemporary kind of pragmatism. Indeed, social cohesion has been of little or, at best, secondary concern. "It is in this sense, among others," Freire (2004) asserted, "that radical pedagogy must never make any concessions to the trickeries of neoliberal 'pragmatism,' which reduces the educational practice to the technical-scientific training of learners, *training* rather than *educating*" (p. 19).

This remark should not be taken out of context as a Freirean dismissal of the technical and the scientific. Indeed, Freire valued them, but he did so by intersecting instrumental and economic issues with social, historical, cultural, and political concerns. He was troubled that neoliberal pragmatists tended to avoid this complex intersection. For example, consider the case of a homeless contingent of urban, gay, male youth who subsist through sex work that makes them vulnerable to possible brutality at the hands of police or the johns who solicit their services. Neoliberal pragmatists would tend to react to their plight in a "fatalistic manner, always in favor of the powerful—'It is sad, but what can be done? That is what reality is'" (Freire, 2004, p. 58). Even worse, neoliberal pragmatists would likely place sole blame on these youth, these walking wounded, for their predicament, suggesting that they had brought it upon themselves. They would ignore or downplay how systemic issues and destructive cultural forces such as heterosexism—the presumption and privileging of heterosexuality—and homophobia have socially ostracized and damaged these youth, making their recovery and moves toward resilience most challenging processes (Grace, 2009a).

Blaming sexual minorities for the troubles in our lives and miring us in helplessness and hopelessness have been commonplace in heteronormative culture and society. A poignant expression of this retrograde politics of blame is hauntingly captured in the late Jerry Falwell's post–9-11 remarks, which express the homophobia and xenophobia that have long permeated rightist politico-religious views in US culture: "I really believe that the pagans, and the abortionists, and the feminists, and the gays and the lesbians who are actively trying to make that an alternative lifestyle, the ACLU [American Civil Liberties Union], People for the American Way, all of them who have tried to secularize America, … I point the finger in their face and say, 'You helped this [—the terrorist attacks on New York and Washington, September 11, 2001—] happen'" (CNN, 2001, p. 1).

When Falwell, a US televangelist who founded the Moral Majority and used it to mobilize and politicize the United States' religious right in the 1980s, made these unconscionable comments during a broadcast of the conservative Christian television program *The 700 Club* on September 13, 2001, he basically issued a hate message that constituted an immoral maligning of a contingent of the US population whom he saw as a secular menagerie of social outlaws. As an expression of his politics of blame and debasement, Falwell's words did damage that his apology later that day could not rectify. In presenting his list of those he presumed to be despicable, he threw his brands of Christian fundamentalism and xenophobia into an unholy and uncivil new-millennial mix with other regressive cultural change forces, including American imperialism, Islamic fundamentalism, and global terrorism. These dark forces weigh heavily on ordinary people, spawning paranoia, deadly violence, and an inhumanity that normalizes suffering and loss on a global scale. Collectively, they are the latter-day global signifiers of the devolution of culture. These unrelenting forces are daily deterrents in the quests of so many global citizens to live full, happy, and satisfying lives.

For those citizens who had previously known relative safety and security in many Western nations, September 11, 2001, is remembered as the day that ushered in the unthinkable—terrorism any time, any place. In the wake of the terrorist attacks on New York and Washington, and the interminable global wave of terrorism that has been pervasive since, many global citizens live in fear of evildoers capable of infiltrating the socio-cultural spaces where ordinary citizens live their everyday lives. Now everybody knows what it is like to be afraid and to be watched. Of course, feeling fearful and sensing that you are being watched are hardly new experiences for sexual-minority persons. They are part of our long history of coping with the miseries of heterosexism and homophobia. We have long lived with gay bashing as our ongoing terrorist encounter; it has left many in our spectral community maimed and many dead. Violence—sometimes premeditated and calculated, and sometimes reckless and rash—has been the homophobe's perennial answer to ignorance and fear of sexual-minority differences. As a result, sexual-minority people—consciously or unconsciously—are preoccupied with safety and security all the time, in every place.

The sting of cultural homophobia and the violence it begets are evident in the everyday experiences and frequent tragedies that mark the lives and work of sexual-minority persons (Grace & Benson, 2000; Grace, 2006c; Janoff, 2005). Instances of physical violence against sexual minorities, which include a spectrum of criminal acts such as assault and battery, rape, and murder, are well documented (see, for example, a Canadian account in Janoff, 2005). We also commonly encounter incidents of symbolic violence, which include shaming, harassment, name-calling, and rightist politico-religious denunciation. Perhaps the most common representation of symbolic violence in our everyday lives is the homophobic graffiti—for example, gay pornographic images and words like "faggot" and "cocksucker"—scrawled on ordinary and visible surfaces like locker doors or public washroom stalls. This graffiti is a poignant and constant reminder that debasement and defilement are norms in our everyday.

Replicating this sad state of affairs, sexual minorities regularly, albeit more subtly, experience ignorance, fear, violence, silence, and exclusion in lifelong learning and adult education (Hill & Grace, 2009). This reality of lesbian, gay, bisexual, trans-identified, queer, and other persons across the spectra of sexual orientations and gender identities is testament to the fiction of lifelong learning as globally inclusive education. While many mainstream advocates of lifelong learning have made social inclusion and cohesion thematic in their rhetorical framing of its contemporary discourse and practice, they only seem concerned with making neoliberalism look like something more encompassing and palatable (Grace, 2006b, 2007). Their construction of the social is limited, as they frequently marginalize or avoid power relationships, particularly those related to sexual orientation and gender identity, in framing learning for life and work. Even variously critical, feminist, radical, and liberal lifelong educators who link lifelong learning to issues of social learning and social justice tend to be silent on sexual-minority issues. Why would any lifelong educator do this and contribute to lifelong learning as a travesty for sexual minorities? It may be an oversight tied to heterosexual privilege, or worse, a deliberate omission linked to heterosexism, homophobia, biphobia, and transphobia. Or maybe a silent educator views an engagement with sexual-minority issues as risky business that could damage a career. Nevertheless, educator silence speaks to the hegemony of heteronormativity in lifelong-learning discourse and practice. A trek through the literature shows that there has been little focus in contemporary lifelong learning and adult and higher education on sexual orientation and gender identity, and their variations and expressions (Hill & Grace, 2009). This is another example of an assault on the social in framing and engaging in lifelong learning in neoliberal times.

Despite this exclusion in mainstream spaces, sexual minorities do engage in learning. In both developed and emerging nations, they have always created spaces within the heteronormative lifeworld. Production, exchange, and distribution of knowledge of same-sex rituals and traditions, cross-gender role expressions, and non-heteronormative sexualities have historically contributed to a process of subaltern lifelong learning that is actually more common than is often recognized (Grace & Wells, 2007b; Hill, 1995). In many locations, such lifelong learning has been minimized or erased within repressive heteronormative and queer-phobic narratives—both secular and religious—that the purportedly righteous tell one another and use to indoctrinate others. To counter this exclusion in the future, international organizations dedicated to lifelong learning have to engage in vital educational and cultural work for social transformation so sexual minorities are recognized, accommodated, and respected. This work has to be learner-driven so those on the margins can set the terms of their own self-definition to counter the dismissal and defilement that have historically accompanied their disenfranchisement. Such engagement requires inclusive lifelong educators to take up a key role as public intellectuals on the international scene. In this role they can help to establish the conditions that enable sexual-minority learners everywhere to "see themselves" and self-articulate their identities and how they wish to represent themselves. As this cultural work proceeds, those marginalized because of sexual orientation and gender identity and expression will be able to claim a history, a spectral community, and a self that is free to be, become, belong, and act. However, for now, the hegemony of heteronormativity as a hidden yet assumed conceptual framework in lifelong learning and adult education has restricted sexual-minority inclusion in these educational domains. Moreover, it has limited possibilities for social learning in the knowledge-culture-language-power nexus where learners could engage sexual orientation and gender identity as relationships of power (Grace, 2001; Grace & Hill, 2004).

An Exchange with Robert J. Hill: Internationalizing Sexual-Minority Inclusion

In the exchange with Robert J. Hill that is the focus of this chapter, we can see the power of heteronormativity at play in international adult education as a representative site in which heterosexual privilege is institutionalized. Hill locates international adult education as a structurally exclusive, loosely configured, and problematic learning society that is prone to systemic degradation of, and violence toward, sexual minorities. Hill's stories from the field expose the longstanding exclusion of sex, sexual, and gender differences from policy-making, knowledge building, and setting the parameters of practice in this educational arena. Focused politically and pedagogically on transformation, these stories highlight the need to reform lifelong learning and adult education so they can become inclusive educational formations that accommodate sexual minorities as historically marginalized and misunderstood global citizens who have a right to learn, know, and be safe, secure, visible, and involved. Such reformation is in keeping with Burke and Jackson's (2007) belief that educational research, discourse, policy, and practice should be reflexive engagements that "always lead to the development of new knowledges, with the potential to lead to transformative action" (p. 3). This stance connects knowledge building to lifelong learning as critical action for social justice and cultural transformation. To take up this stance, social educators and learners have to muster the courage to engage in lifelong learning as an act of resistance.

Resistances are political and strategic acts aimed at making life better for those marginalized in diverse life, learning, and work spaces. As dynamic lifelong-learning practices, Burke and Jackson conceptualize resistances as "counter-hegemonic practices that operate at the micro-level of everyday experience and attempt either consciously or unconsciously to challenge and subvert hegemonic regimes of truth and privileged discourses and identities" (p. 140).

These resistances as contestation of coercive or non-consensual participation in lifelong learning "often take place despite fear of reprisals. Resistances take place within unequal power relations, where some identities carry power, authority and privilege, whilst others are despised, ridiculed, and subject to derision" (pp. 140–141). Ultimately, as Burke and Jackson assert, resistances "are about the negotiation, politics and contestation of representation, recognition, marginalisation, authority, silencing and legitimization" (p. 142).

Burke and Jackson's description of resistances can inform lifelong learning about and for sexual minorities, shaping it as a political process intended to transform both the learning process itself and the learning community as a site where just and sustained action can begin. Within lifelong learning as critical action to assist sexual minorities, resistances need to be global in scope. They have to take place in nations where sexual minorities already have some rights, freedoms, and protections, but where social and cultural homophobia are still deterrents to everyday inclusion. And, perhaps most importantly, they have to occur in nations where visible and active members of sexual minorities are imprisoned or executed. The first step is increasing global awareness by using queer public pedagogy and creating international forums to draw attention to this global persecution and genocide. Exposing oppression of and brutality against sexual minorities is vital since safety and security and, in too many instances, lives hang in the balance. In this work, lifelong learning as critical action has to be a living process that is focused on protecting and enabling sexual minorities to live lives in which integrity is maintained by respecting and accommodating a spectrum of sex, sexual, and gender differences.

As a prelude to the following exchange with Robert J. Hill, I present key aspects of his biography as a segue to exploring his resistances to contest and counter heteronormativity in international adult education. In a real way, these resistances constitute a counter-hegemonic practice in which Bob lives out lifelong learning as critical action. They expose what Burke and Jackson call "structural inequalities and discursive misrecognitions" (2007, p. 141) in mainstream lifelong learning. As Hill engages in lifelong learning as critical action, his resistances offer challenges to lifelong educators to unlearn, rethink, and change as they engage in new knowledge building and in praxis that has a twofold intention: to interrogate not only how educators understand sexual minorities as lifelong learners, but also how they understand themselves. As an engagement in counter-hegemonic lifelong learning, Hill's resistances are about reflexivity, social and cultural subversions, engendering change, and "developing political awareness, regaining criticality, and acting as an active trigger for sites of struggle" (Burke & Jackson, 2007, pp. 161–162). They may be small steps in particular moments, but they are important steps politically and pedagogically in the incremental work to make a better world for sexual minorities. They inform the concluding section of this chapter, which is a discussion about moving beyond a contemporary paralysis of the social in lifelong-learning culture. Here I discuss the politics and pedagogy that could drive lifelong learning as critical action so it might advance sexual-minority inclusion and accommodation globally. These politics and pedagogy would engage participants in critical learning focused on being, becoming, belonging, and acting as constituents of an inclusive critical global citizenship.

Getting to Know Robert J. "Bob" Hill

I have known Bob Hill since 1994 when we met as doctoral students at the Adult Education Research Conference (AERC) held at the University of Tennessee, Knoxville. The previous year during the AERC conference held at Pennsylvania State University, State College, Bob had worked strategically and successfully to set up a lesbian, gay, bisexual, transgender, queer, and allies (LGBTQ&A) caucus (Grace & Hill, 2004). Despite detractors, Bob was instrumental in creating a communicative space and a site to resist heterosexism and homophobia at AERC. Over time, he inspired a number of us to become involved. The caucus still exists and there has been an annual LGBTQ&A preconference since the first one was held at San Francisco State University during AERC 2003. In the spirit of Myles Horton and Paulo Freire (1990), Bob and those of us who have worked with him over the years have made the road by walking. It has often been a difficult journey where we have been subjected to the homophobia of certain colleagues and their abrasive efforts to deter a queer presence in North American adult education (Grace & Hill, 2004). Encouragingly though, it has also been a journey that a contingent of adult education scholar-allies have supported in word and action.

Bob traces his drive to engage in work for human and civil rights to influences that include "growing up gay in a homophobic society, [and being] a son of a working-class railroader father and a poor but proud Appalachian mother" (Hill, 2007, p. 158). Now, as an academic, Bob is deeply aware of his privilege. He, along with Phyllis Cunningham (1991), believes that academics should make their privilege visible as they create an ideological space to engage in work for social justice in academe. This is vital so they and their students can do intellectual work that keeps ethics at the heart of what they do. However, Bob is deeply aware of the limits of his privilege as an academic and the ways his queer visibility has been problematic for him. He thinks about the complexities of his positionality, and his need to be politically strategic and culturally savvy as he relates to the people and cultures that he encounters in his everyday. Bob knows that particular people and cultural sites within his university, the academy at large, the political system, and the wider community present barriers to his social activism and cultural work. However, he also knows that there are many people and sites that enable and fortify him in his quest to create an ethical, better world for sexual minorities. Weighing the odds amid the "proclivities, interests, actions, and happenstances" (Hill, 2007, p. 155) that have marked his life both inside and outside academe, Bob is always willing to take risks to be vocal and to engage in cultural work for the social transformation of the life circumstances of sexual minorities and other disenfranchised groups (Hill, 2005a, 2005b). In his autoethnography, in which he explores himself in relation to others and his cultural surroundings, he relates:

> As a queer anti-oppression researcher and educator, risk is central to my life. It appears in my writings when I advocate for activism as the practice of adult education; public policy; international adult education; environmental adult education; lesbian, gay, bisexual, transgender, and queer (LGBTQ) issues in education; and queer theory. Embracing risk opens up the possibility to engage with marginalized and oppressed populations, like sex-workers, sexual minorities, self-identified radical environmentalists, people of color, activist women, and other troublemakers.... My teaching, research, and practice—tightly defined around social policy in several distinct areas, such as sexual orientation and gender identity rights; the impacts of globalization, new social movements, and democracy on lifelong learning; environmental adult education; and learning for social transformation and sustainable development—stem from a pedagogy of risk and possibility. A little outrage goes a long way! (Hill, 2007, p. 155)

Bob describes his research agenda as multifocal and transdisciplinary, with the unifying feature of using lifelong learning to facilitate positive change and personal and social transformation. Epistemologically, he frames his cultural work using the premise that knowledge is socially constructed. He undertakes this work in national (regional) and international contexts, believing in the value of diversity and promoting social justice in his commitment to make life better for marginalized and oppressed populations. Bob's research focuses on fully developing the human personality (the right to be, become, belong, and act); enhancing quality of life; and strengthening fundamental human freedoms. Central in his cultural work within problem-solving contexts is his work with sexual minorities (lesbian, gay, bisexual, trans-identified, and self-identified queers, including both adults and youth). As a gay man and critical lifelong educator who works mainly in group and community contexts, Bob focuses on knowledge acquisition to enhance the human capacity to challenge inequalities through situated learning (Lave & Wenger, 1991). This paradigm suggests that activities, culture, context, and content are key elements of successful educational endeavours. In other words, learning is a socio-cultural experience and social interaction is a primary means through which learning occurs. Moreover, learning fundamentally involves association with, and within, a community of theory, practice, and identity in which activities are often significantly more important than knowledge and skills in the learning process.

This view of learning contests and confronts lifelong learning as travesty for sexual minorities. It was evident in a critical incident that Bob experienced during the Sixth World Assembly of the International Council for Adult Education (ICAE), which was held in 2001 in Ocho Rios, Jamaica. While the focus of this World Assembly was global citizenship, gender justice, and understanding the hierarchy of gender relations and the construction of gender identities, Bob's experience of intolerance and discrimination clearly indicated that some ICAE member organizations from culturally conservative countries still had much work to do to address pervasive homophobia and unaddressed sexuality and gender issues in their midst (Hill, 2001a, 2002). As an adult educator who is also a visible and engaged gay activist, Bob was told by the leadership of the Caribbean Adult Education Association, the ICAE member organization hosting the World Assembly, that his safety could not be guaranteed because his public stance supporting sexual-minority rights put him in direct jeopardy. Bob was advised to leave. Part of the controversy focused on an act of resistance whereby he had added gay themes and the phrase "Difference is a fundamental human right!" to an artistic mural. Bob's resistance and the concomitant threat to his safety became a critical incident, garnering the support of the ICAE leadership and providing ICAE participants with an opportunity to raise the issue of organizational intolerance of same-sex orientation at a workshop on global citizenship and gender justice. Workshop participants recognized that the right to be different is a human right, and they agreed to propose the inclusion of this phrase in the final declaration of the World Assembly. They articulated that at future World Assemblies of the ICAE, the security of everyone facing discrimination and intolerance must be guaranteed. This move would lead popular educator Larry Olds (n.d.) to write in his memoir that Bob's art attack had caused an "uproar [that produced] sharp conversations ... in the corridors and rooms of the conference.... The mural turned out to be an outstanding example of art as education doing its job" (p. 127).

This was a pivotal moment in the ICAE's history. Until the Sixth World Assembly of the ICAE—where sexual orientation or personal preferences were recognized for the first time in the World Assembly's final declaration—silence about sexual minorities was a cultural reality in the international adult-education community. While using the term *personal preferences* is problematic for sexual minorities, it nevertheless had import. As Bob noted, by including the term with sexual orientation, gender non-conformity is also guaranteed equal rights. This is because the term *personal preferences* draws attention to the fact that many trans-identified individuals, whether homosexual or heterosexual, are targets for discrimination based on how they dress, look, and behave—for example, gender-crossing clothing, use of body ornamentation, use of cosmetics, and effeminacy in males or masculinity in females. By including personal preferences, Bob concluded that the World Assembly had expressed sensitivity to the diverse array of culturally constructed sexual-minority identities and differences around the world. He also concluded that the term's language, whether used wittingly or unwittingly, is a critique of the hegemony of how Western nations conceptualize the limited sociological categories "gay" and "lesbian" (e.g., see Murray, 1995). Most importantly though, as Bob pointed out, the upshot of this World Assembly outcome is a universal positioning of the fundamental human right to be different.

The Exchange: A Global Queer Exposition

APG: As much as globalization can be construed as encompassing, it has also been exclusionary from social and political perspectives. It has affected a huge portion of the world's population, including sexual minorities. Could you discuss this impact on us?

RJH: Globalization has had a tremendous impact on societies and cultures, many of which have been the subject of investigations and research in the academy. The hegemony of the technologically developed nations—the so-called "First World" or Global North—over the less technologically developed ones—"Second- and Third-Worlds," often from the Global South—dominates the discourse on globalization. With respect to us, little research has examined (1) how human rights for sexual minorities, espoused by activists/educators from both the Global North and Global South, have impacted places where rights are limited or totally absent—places where being, becoming, belonging, and acting relative to sexual orientation and gender-variant expression are taboo; and (2) how indigenous, local customs and cultural expressions of non-normative sexualities have been homogenized and flattened by the export of Western "gay-and-lesbian" culture that is highly commercialized. The latter has erased local particularities in favour of identities constructed on imported (mostly American and European) expressions, resulting in cultural (homo)genization and commodified identities. This is "McPinking," a term coined because the phenomenon parallels the "McDonaldization" of the globe, and the colour pink is often associated with sexual minorities. A few articles or texts present this McPinking of the world with the spread of Western lesbian, gay, bisexual, transgender, and queer constructions, including such tools of cultural hegemony as techno-beat music, the bar and nightclub scene, and the commercial paraphernalia that constitute "the material queer" (Chasin, 2000; Morton, 1996). The tensions and adaptations occurring when processes of globalization bring one system of gay or lesbian language into contact with another has also received some attention (Leap & Boellstorff, 2003).

I'd also like to add that globalization is a "bottom-up" phenomenon. By this I mean the processes and functions described by Albrow (1996)—active dissemination of practices, values, technology, and other human products and constructions—that originate in local contexts can have global consequences. For instance, sexual minorities in global diaspora, displaced from homeland to Empire, speak from both bondage and freedom perspectives. Diaspora is thus "not a political or geospatial location, but [rather] a critical lens" (Alexander, 2008, p. 103) that allows people in the "Queer diaspora" (see Gopinath, 2005) to accentuate "becoming" for all of us to see. This is a process from which we can all learn.

APG: While it can be argued that globalization has certainly promoted a particular (Western) material formation of sexualities, is there another side to the narrative? How are lifelong learning and adult education implicated in constructing this narrative?

RJH: Discussions on globalization in lifelong learning and adult education present several assumptions (Holst, 2006; Mayo, 2005). One is that, in the age of globalization, nations are overrun by vastly more powerful transnational actors. A corollary from human sexuality discourse is that local expressions of sexualities are overtaken by hegemonic, monolithic forms from imperialist Western cultures. Thus it can be surmised that the emergence of organized movements that resist hegemonic oppression of sexual minorities—regardless of whether the sexual minorities are local and indigenous, or those adapted from the West—are also a result of globalization. Still there are those who contest the sole description of globalization toward homogeneity of values and norms, and who "see an opportunity to rescue local identities" in globalizing processes (Stromquist & Monkman, 2000, p. 7). As Deacon, Hulse, and Stubbs (1997) have reported, with globalization comes a significant shift in social policy, sometimes resulting in actors pressuring states in favour of social justice. This often opens new opportunities for local sexual-minority communities.

Two dynamics—how human-rights education for sexual minorities has impacted unjust places and how indigenous, local customs and cultural expressions of non-normative sexualities have been impacted on the global scene—are related here. For instance, some nations resisting outside human-rights models have characterized them as another form of Western cultural hegemony and ideological imperialism. They have built their argument on the false presumption that same-sex desires and gender-altering behaviours are not local, indigenous, or regional phenomena, but indicators of Euro-American corruption of their society. Thus, for example, many African and Islamic discourses are either unaware of or intentionally deny historical forms of same gender and transgender behaviour, although various forms of homosexuality have historically existed, and sometimes thrived, within African and Islamic worlds (Murray & Roscoe, 1997, 1998; Murray & Viljoen, 2007; Schmitt & Sofer, 1992). Consequently, when queer expressions are imported from the West, they often replace or displace, rather than place, non-conforming practices on host countries. Additionally, they can offer hope for human-rights struggles, specifically constructed from *métissage* of local and global cultures. The result is queer cultural cross-fertilization and the potential for transnational encounters and alliances, which are inspiring and filled with opportunities, but also present challenges and dilemmas. The formation and growing success of the organization Queer Peace International (2009) is illustrative. This consortium of sexual minorities and straight allies from 40 countries engages in networking and outreach to build peace and reconciliation in queer communities globally.

APG: Heterosexual privilege, heteronormativity, homophobia, and transphobia have collectively created an environment of hostility and an invitation to violence against sexual minorities. Can you speak to this harsh reality from a global perspective?

RJH: Historically, violence directed toward sexual minorities has had its perpetrators in diverse institutional, societal, and cultural contexts. The state and civil society have often oppressed, silenced, marginalized, and committed crimes of aggression against lesbian, gay, bisexual, trans-identified, and queer peoples and communities. In countries where various sexual orientations and gender identities are granted governmental permission (Sanders, 2007), local traditions and cultural norms may still place sexual-minority individuals in harm's way. Even when a country's laws "tolerate" homosexualities, sexual-minority citizens may live under a death sentence imposed by self-appointed guardians of social and cultural norms.

Members of sexual minorities often exist in culturally imposed solitary confinement because of fear that links survival to silence (Hill, 2003a, 2003b). Across the world, because of our non-heteronormative sexual orientations and gender identities, sexual-minority women and men (and those who select ambiguity) are maltreated: we are often mercilessly bullied as youth, shunned or victimized as adults, committed to psychiatric hospitals as punitive measures to correct alleged deviances, and imprisoned (Hill, 2003c). In the absence of safeguards on human rights, we are a distinct subpopulation of the world's refugees and asylum seekers. Transgressive gender- or sex-role "violations" by us are consequential. Additionally, in some countries, we are deprived of our right to lifelong learning about ourselves, our communities, our histories, and our cultures—deprived of full opportunities to learn to be, become, belong, and act. Without queer history, there are only limited ways to construct our identities, and limited identities produce greatly impoverished people.

Amnesty International's worldwide campaign against torture calls attention to the global fate of many sexual minorities. The special report, *Crimes of Hate, Conspiracy of Silence: Torture and Ill-Treatment Based on Sexual Identity* (Amnesty International [AI], 2001) reminds us of a horrid global reality:

> Torture and other cruel, inhuman or degrading treatment are prohibited under international human rights law. Yet in countries all over the world, lesbians, gay men, and bisexual and transgender people are being tortured or ill-treated by state officials, or with their acquiescence, because of their sexual identity.... Lesbians, gay men, and bisexual and transgender people all over the world suffer persecution and violence simply for being who they are. They are tortured or ill-treated by state officials to extract confessions of "deviance," and raped to "cure" them of it. They are attacked in their homes and communities to punish and intimidate them because of their sexual orientation or gender identity. (p. 1)

APG: Given this dreadful reality, how has the international community working in lifelong learning and adult education responded to this persecution?

RJH: Let me speak to two examples: CONFINTEA V (an acronym for the French title), which was the Fifth International Conference on Adult Education held in Hamburg, Germany, in 1997, and the CONFINTEA V Midterm Review, held in Bangkok, Thailand, in 2003.

By way of background, CONFINTEAs or International Conferences on Adult Education have been held every 12 years since 1949; the last two occurred in 1997 and 2009. In 1997, there was no mention of sexual orientation or gender expression. I knew that missing the opportunity to address these issues at the 2009 conference would mean the next chance would not come until 2021. Thus it was imperative to capitalize on the window of opportunity in 2009 to avoid the silence on sexual-minority issues that marked the 1997 conference.

At the invitation of the United Nations Educational, Scientific, and Cultural Organization, more than 1,500 representatives of governments and non-governmental organizations attended CONFINTEA V. Conference participants spoke of shattering an institutional learning monopoly by recognizing that non-formal and informal education have vital roles to play together with formal education taking place in schools, colleges, and universities. This was significant for sexual-minority communities, where much informal and non-formal adult education occurs, even though it goes unrecognized and unrepresented in much adult education (Hill, 1995; Hill & Grace, 2009). CONFINTEA V participants developed various themes to promote their assertion that adult education is the key to the twenty-first century. Socially focused themes included: (1) Adult Learning, Democracy, Peace, and Critical Citizenship; (2) Improving Conditions and Quality of Adult Learning; (3) Adult Learning, Environment, Health, and Population; (4) Adult Learning for Aging Populations, Migrants, Prisoners, Persons with Disabilities, Indigenous Communities, and Cultural Minorities; and (5) Enhancing International Co-operation, Solidarity, and Networking for and through Adult Learning (CONFINTEA V, 2003b).

These thematic emphases have direct relevance to sexual minorities as global citizens. Yet more than a decade later, most government policy-makers, as well as educators working in lifelong learning and adult education, have not interpreted and applied any of these themes in a consideration of the rights and needs of sexual minorities. For example, under the theme of Adult Learning, Democracy, Peace, and Critical Citizenship, sexual minorities are clearly ranked as second-class citizens in most countries of the world. All too often, sexual-minority individuals and communities are denied full and equal rights, justice and equality, free will, and the right to organize. In many jurisdictions, we are also denied opportunities to participate in civil society and open economic development in formal and informal economies. This composite exclusion deeply impacts the well-being and public and personal health of sexual-minority citizens who are disenfranchised from the kinds of access and accommodation that go hand in hand with the rights and privileges of full citizenship in democratic cultures and societies.

In Hamburg, there was a call for governments to adapt to the realities of a host of marginalized peoples. Civil society, too, was challenged to help individuals express their aspirations and create learning opportunities throughout life. However, sexual minorities were NOT included in the mix. There was no envisioning of our dreams to experience justice and live full lives. For example, many of the articles of the Hamburg Declaration promoted gender equality, and articles 25b, 28, 29, 37b, 38b, and 49d of the Agenda for the Future, adopted by CONFINTEA V to provide a framework to advance adult education and lifelong learning globally (UNESCO, 2001), directly addressed the status of women. Still, the unique characteristics and needs of lesbians continued to be overlooked, and gender identity was avoided altogether. While CONFINTEA V adopted the perspective of learning throughout life, it failed to live out the notion of *lifelong learning for all*, as sexual minorities were once again denied presence and place within the four pillars of lifelong learning: learning to know, learning to do, learning to be, and learning to live together (Delors, 1996). Moreover, CONFINTEA V, which was billed as an international adult-education conference that would focus on learning to aid the development and survival of citizens, also demonstrated the inadequacy of international adult education as a forum for advancing the human and civil rights of sexual minorities. Despite the rhetoric about the right to learn, lesbians, gay men, bisexuals, transgender people, and queer people essentially went unnoticed at the conference.

APG: You've presented a bleak picture that suggests lifelong learning is not for all. Is there any hope of a better world for sexual minorities?

RJH: First of all, let me note that CONFINTEAs have mid-term evaluations, which although not official decision-making meetings, are held six years after a conference to assess whether countries are meeting their commitments. At mid-term evaluations, new ideas, which may not have been on the agenda six years prior, can be brought forward.

What happened at the CONFINTEA V Mid-term Review was actually very encouraging and hopeful. For the first time, activist adult educators challenged the reality of no space and place for sexual minorities as participants carried out a mid-term evaluation of the CONFINTEA V agenda. In preparation for the Bangkok meeting, the Gender Education Office of the International Council for Adult Education had conducted a virtual preparatory seminar entitled Education for Inclusion throughout Life. The objectives of the seminar were to (1) advocate for justice in gender relations, (2) promote education for a better world, and (3) advance learning for non-discrimination and inclusion in different spaces and throughout life. With respect to the first objective, I have shown the need for guaranteeing the rights and dignity of lesbians, bisexual women and men, gay men, trans-identified people, and queer people who, in most societies, are denied full citizenship and barred from democratic participation (Hill, 2003a). Gender role expectations—socially constructed notions of feminine and masculine ideals—are often rigidly enforced in societies. Individuals that transgress these expectations are punished in various ways. Regarding the second objective, education related to sexual orientation, gender identity, and human rights should be included in any blueprint of education for a better world. Finally, learning for non-discrimination and inclusion must take into account the fact that some governments and extra-governmental instruments systematically deny sexual-minority people the right to life and work, the right to non-discrimination, the right to be free from degrading and inhumane treatment, the right to construct loving families, the right to pleasure and delight, the right to be free from harassment, the right to privacy, and the right to participate fully in civil society in ways equal to heterosexuals. Advancing learning for non-discrimination and inclusion to transgress these debilitating realities must be a task of lifelong learning and adult education.

Going back to your question, let me say there is always hope and radical possibility. For me, these are the primary beliefs of a critical adult educator. I have told various parts of the journey to sexual-minority inclusion in diverse international adult learning and education arenas from 2001 to 2010 (Hill, 2001a, 2001b, 2003a, 2003c, 2008, 2010; see also Hill & Grace, 2009). In Bangkok, contested but successful negotiations on sexual orientation rights resulted in the first official policy recommendations for lesbian and gay inclusion in the right to education for being, becoming, and belonging (UNESCO, 2003, p. 19). This was followed by another milestone in 2004 during the tenth anniversary of the fall of apartheid in South Africa. I provided a queer presence as part of the Ten Years of Freedom, International Adult Learners Week commemoration—the first democratic election in South Africa, heralding the transition to democracy, was in April 1994—that was held simultaneously with the UNESCO Institute for Education conference on citizenship and adult learning. The South Africa gathering was an especially important occasion since the new post-apartheid country was the first nation in the world to ban discrimination based on sexual orientation.

APG: Could you provide more detail regarding the CONFINTEA V Midterm Review and what happened in Bangkok? How did you participate? What was the outcome in terms of addressing sexual-minority rights?

RJH: Justin Ellis from Namibia, the chairperson of the Governing Board of the UNESCO Institute for Education (now called the Institute for Lifelong Learning, which is located in Hamburg, Germany), reported that the CONFINTEA V Mid-term Review brought together over three hundred representatives of UNESCO member states. This included ministers and senior-level officials, agencies of the UN system, non-governmental and civil-society organizations, and academic and research institutions from more than ninety countries (CONFINTEA V, 2003b). The review, organized in collaboration with the UNESCO Asia and Pacific Regional Bureau for Education, and with support from the Department of Non-formal Education of the Thai Ministry of Education, aimed to assess the accomplishments and the difficulties encountered during the first six years of executing the CONFINTEA V agenda. This was done through a series of thematic and regional reviews, and plenary sessions. Participants examined recent trends and new developments in practices and policies of lifelong learning and adult education. The group also began the task of preparing for CONFINTEA VI by proposing strategies for the advancement of future lifelong-learning programs. One significant thematic review focused on democracy. Dr. Lean Chan Heng, University of Science, Peneng, Malaysia, chaired the session, and I was the rapporteur. As a queer activist/scholar, I arrived in Bangkok with a stated agenda, which I also brought to the Democracy Thematic Review. My goals were to expand the parameters of lifelong learning and adult education by: (1) using education for citizenship and education for civil and human rights as anti-oppression tools to build knowledge, skills, resources, and capacity in human-rights advocacy based on sexual orientation and gender identity; (2) discussing language and broadening the definition of discrimination so that grounds for protection against prejudice in workplace and other sociocultural settings include sexual orientation and gender identity; (3) engaging in public pedagogy to cast members of sexual minorities as persons and citizens who are *not sick*, criminal, or sinful; and (4) engaging in public pedagogy to draw attention to sexual-minority human rights and any violations—social oppression, torture, arbitrary arrest, and extortion are commonplace—across governments and civil society.

After several days of formal and informal meetings, caucuses, and networking on sexual-minority justice, both the Democracy Thematic Review and the Gender Thematic Review took up the language of sexual-minority inclusion in lifelong learning and adult education. One of the regional re-

views, largely under the leadership of Latin American women at the conference, acted similarly. The democracy workgroup issued the following statement, "[We recommend] promoting human-centered values such as peace,
human rights, solidarity and justice, [and the elimination of] discrimination
based on sexual orientation and gender identity" (CONFINTEA V, 2003b,
n.p.). This position was carried into the all-conference discussions. In the
end, the CONFINTEA V Mid-term Review efforts resulted in 38 recommendations. Recommendation 7 called for UNESCO member states, civil
society organizations, non-governmental organizations, and others to include sexual minorities in all lifelong-learning efforts; it also called for equal
rights for sexual minorities.

This recommendation was the *only* controversial agenda item at the final
session during the ratification of the recommendations. A government minister and representative from Uganda objected to the language, stating that it
would require the Government of Uganda to implement policies contrary to
state laws where homosexuality is prohibited. Sadly, Uganda does not stand
alone. Globally, more than 70 countries have a complete ban on homosexuality, with sentences upon conviction ranging from imprisonment to public
flogging and death. In at least 7 nations, same-sex relations are punishable
by execution; Chechnya, Iran, Iraq, Mauritania, Saudi Arabia, Sudan, and
Yemen implement capital punishment for homosexuality. Same-sex relations are unsympathetically handled in Bangladesh, Egypt, Malaysia, and
Pakistan; in these jurisdictions maximum jail sentences range from 3 to 20
years. In some countries such as Mexico, El Salvador, Colombia, and Brazil,
right-wing death squads target lesbians, gay men, and trans-identified people in "social cleansing" campaigns. For example, the seemingly open Brazilian sexual attitudes stop at heterosexuality. The group Ontario Consultants
on Religious Tolerance (2008) reports that "gay positive groups estimate ...
[that] more than 2,680 gays and lesbians were murdered in Brazil between
1980 and 2006" (para. 1).

In response to the Ugandan objection, I argued that in light of CONFIN-
TEA V's focus on *the rights of all*, the erasure of language to abet sexual-minority inclusion would constitute an act of violence and injustice by members of the mid-term review. I requested that, in the name of human rights
and social justice, the chair not eliminate this point. After these brief but
contentious petitions to the chair, a recess was called. During the break, with
the assistance of Alan Tuckett from the National Institute of Adult Con-

tinuing Education in the United Kingdom, the language issue was resolved. In the end, the controversial wording of Recommendation 7 was retained, with the parenthetical phrase *where licit*. Based on the Democracy Thematic Review recommendations, the following assembly approved final statement was commended to the official drafting committee:

> We therefore call upon member states, bi- and multilateral agencies, non-governmental and civil-society organizations and social movements ... to adopt inclusive policies and take concrete measures and provide adequate resources in support of education programs mainstreaming and catering to the learning demands of persons with disabilities as well as groups with special needs such as indigenous people, migrants and refugees, minorities (including sexual minorities, where licit), [and] prisoners. (CONFINTEA V, 2003a, n.p.)

During the CONFINTEA V Mid-term Review it became apparent, once again, that views on "homosexuality" flew in the face of some religious traditions, cultures, and governments, especially in Christian and Muslim countries in Africa, the Middle East, and, to some extent, Asia. In an interesting twist, some people claimed that to promote gay rights was a form of neocolonialism caught up in a dominating Western ideology. In the end, two questions worthy of reflection remain: Were activist educators and cultural workers, who sought equal rights for all sexual-minority people at the mid-term review, contributing to globalization by imposing their will on purportedly less powerful nations? Or was the neocolonialist argument a subtly homophobic manoeuvre to sideline concerns with social justice for sexual minorities? Regardless of the answer, Bangkok provided us with the first real victory on the journey that began in the adult-education arena in Jamaica in 2001.

APG: Could you discuss the record of the United Nations on addressing sexual-minority rights?

RJH: The United Nations has only recently begun to recognize lesbian and gay rights. This is due in part to the educational activities of GLOBE, the UN's Gay, Lesbian, or Bisexual Employees Group. In September 1999, GLOBE issued a statement requesting domestic partner benefits for same-sex employees. Five years passed before then Secretary-General Kofi Annan issued an administrative order that provided the partners of lesbian and gay employees with health and other benefits—if their home country allowed it. As a result of GLOBE's efforts, in 2004 the UN recognized employees' same-sex relationships, although workers from the United States and some other countries were excluded (Windsor, 2004).

There has also been some movement to address sexual-minority rights within a few UN agencies, notably the UN High Commission for Refugees and the UN High Commission for Human Rights. The UN High Commission for Refugees recognizes that people subjected to attack, inhumane treatment, and serious discrimination because of homosexuality, and whose governments show an inability or unwillingness to protect sexual minorities, should be recognized as refugees. Accordingly, lesbians and gay men are identified as a particular social group that could be granted refugee status under the UN Refugee Convention. At least 18 sovereign nations (of the 191 member states of the United Nations) now grant asylum to people fleeing persecution based on sexual orientation.

The UN High Commission for Human Rights, which comprises 53 member states, has as its mandate monitoring and protecting human rights globally. Sergio Vieira de Mello, who sadly died in an attack on the UN Headquarters in Baghdad on August 19, 2003, led the first effort to include sexual orientation in the Universal Declaration of Human Rights. This move was a reminder that sexual orientation simply had no obvious relevance to those who framed the declaration that was adopted in 1948. In attempting to end a history of disregard and ignorance of sexual minorities, Vieira de Mello, the late Brazilian-born UN High Commissioner for Human Rights, acted as a friend to all engaged in the struggle for human rights regardless of sexual orientation and gender identity (Hill, 2003b). He was a supporter of gender mainstreaming (including equal rights for women) at the United Nations and in governments and civil society. Prior to his death, Brazil and 19 co-sponsors introduced a draft resolution entitled *Human Rights and Sexual Orientation* that addressed the topic of equal rights for lesbians and gay men. The resolution, recognizing the inherent dignity and the equal and inalienable rights of all people, affirmed that human-rights education is a key in changing societal dispositions and promoting respect for diversity (International Gay and Lesbian Human Rights Commission, 2004; United Nations, 2003a). It disavowed discrimination and expressed deep concern about global violations of human rights against persons based on their sexual orientation. It stressed that human rights and fundamental freedoms are the birthright of all human beings, that the universal nature of these rights and freedoms is beyond question, and that the enjoyment of such rights and freedoms should not be hindered in any way due to sexual orientation. The resolution called upon all member states to promote and protect the human rights of all persons regardless of their sexual orientation. It encouraged the UN High Commission for Human Rights to use all mandated special procedures to address discrimination targeting sexual minorities. Finally, it requested that the UN High Commissioner for Human Rights address any violation of human rights on the grounds of sexual orientation (United Nations, 2003a, 2003b).

Although it did not use such terms as *homosexual, gay,* or *lesbian,* and it avoided criticizing specific governments, the resolution set off an unprecedented storm of debate. The Vatican called on nations to block the resolution, and the US State Department, then headed by Secretary of State Colin Powell, announced that the United States would not support the rights of lesbians and gays, if it came to a vote. After much discussion, voting on the draft resolution on human rights and sexual orientation (document E/CN.4/2003/L.92) was postponed until the next annual meeting in 2004 (United Nations, 2003a). Sergio Vieira de Mello expressed disappointment and called for the commission to strive for greater unity in dealing with human rights. Brazil's UN ambassador, arguing the need to debate sexual preference and human rights and avoid taboos, promised to renew his efforts for lesbian and gay rights in 2004. The next year, the resolution had the support of Brazil, Canada, New Zealand, South Africa, members of the European Union, and a few other member states. Despite the passionate comments of gay activists who reminded the commission about the fear, isolation, and violence that mark the lives of so many sexual-minority individuals globally, the vote on the UN resolution on human rights and sexual orientation was postponed once again for another year, until 2005. However, the resolution was not reintroduced, ending the Brazilian initiative. Sadly, while numerous opportunities are opening up for sexual-minority communities in many nations so that we can (re)claim the right to learn, develop, play, and make meanings that are specific to us (Sanders, 2007), far too few of these opportunities arise through the influence of supranational organizations such as the United Nations or UNESCO.

Nevertheless, there is still hope that the United Nations will help to advance human rights for sexual minorities (Tatchell, 2008). In December

2008, as Lee (2009) recounts, all 27 members of the European Union as well as Australia, Mexico, Japan, and 36 other nations signed a French-sponsored, non-binding UN declaration calling for global decriminalization of homosexuality. The United States was the only Western nation not to sign. Then, in March 2009, the Obama administration, indicating its support of human rights for all, declared it would endorse the declaration, reversing the Bush administration's refusal to do so. Lee also mentions that the Organization of the Islamic Conference and the Vatican were among the groups that opposed the declaration. This is yet another reminder that conservative religious traditions and homophobia remain inextricably linked (Grace, 2008). In the end though, the declaration is a breakthrough document ending official UN silence regarding the matter (Netherlands Mission, 2008).

Fortunately, there is now a certain momentum to US efforts to protect sexual minorities globally. In remarks she made when she received the Roosevelt Institute's Four Freedoms Award in New York City on September 11, 2009, then US Secretary of State Hillary Rodham Clinton stated that the United States would push the UN General Assembly to pass a Security Council resolution condemning violence on the grounds of sexual orientation and gender identity. Secretary Clinton reminded her audience of the global plight of sexual minorities.

In country after country after country, young men and women are persecuted, are singled out, even murdered in cold blood, because of who they love or just based on claims that they are gay. We are starting to track violence against the LGBT community, because where it happens anywhere in the world, the United States must speak out against it and work for its end. Through our annual human rights report we are documenting human rights abuses against LGBT communities worldwide. And we are seeking out partners at the United Nations such as Brazil, France, Sweden and the Netherlands to help us address these human rights abuses. (Rodham Clinton, 2009, p. 3)

This stance represents a significant change in US policy, favouring human rights for sexual minorities internationally within what Secretary Clinton locates as a politics of hope, respect, and conscience ready for challenge and change. It is in this process of advancing the social that globalization might be revised to aid human progress.

APG: How is lifelong learning as an educational and cultural entity presently positioned in work to advance sexual justice and gender justice?

RJH: Sexual justice and gender justice are both intersected and situated. Efforts to advance them through lifelong learning occur in a complex and thorny international context in which unavoidable questions arise. These include: Are the attempts to break cultural prohibitions against gay, lesbian, bisexual, trans-identified, and queer people, which are found in some societies, a form of cultural imperialism, neocolonialism, or ideological colonization? Are they examples of the dark side of globalization, as some suggested during the ICAE's Sixth World Assembly in Jamaica and the CONFINTEA V Mid-term Review in Bangkok? Or, do they constitute the means to internationalize sexual-minority rights and inclusion?

As educators who engage in lifelong learning, we live and work in a disciplinary space (Grace et al., 2004); lifelong learning can be a means to transform the world we inhabit. Does this further Western hegemony and aid neoliberal cultural practices? I think not. A few public pedagogical examples among many too numerous to cite here provide evidence for this conclusion. One example is the local growth—often at risk of life and liberty—of sexual-minority associations and organizations. In one specific case, in 2007 Ugandan sexual minorities launched a public media campaign, Let Us Live in Peace, despite national laws against homosexuality and the alleged harassment of sexual minorities (International Gay and Lesbian Human Rights Commission, 2007a). In another case, sexual-minority activists from Africa met in Johannesburg in May 2007 to challenge state homophobia in 38 countries on the continent (International Gay and Lesbian Human Rights Commission, 2007b). In a third case, the founder of the Nepalese Blue Diamond Society, Sunil Pant, received the 2007 Felipa de Souza Award from the International Gay and Lesbian Human Rights Commission for justice work to assist sexual minorities (International Gay and Lesbian Human Rights Commission, 2007c). Such individuals and groups are coming to voice that which is distinctly oppositional to material forms found and messages conveyed in the McPinking of the globe.

Of course, global struggles for sexual-minority inclusion, and the resultant emergence of social-movement actors to address these struggles, are not relegated to the so-called Second and Third Worlds; North America and Europe witness them as well. In the United States, police mistreatment of sexual minorities, especially transsexuals and sexual minorities of colour, has been challenged by US sexual minorities and is well documented (Amnesty International, 2005). Amnesty International (2006) reports that the lack of respect, protection, and promotion of the human rights of sexual minorities is still an issue in several European Union countries. For example, on May 17, 2006, the Campaign Against Homophobia (Kampania Przeciw Homofobii or KPH) held an equality parade in Toruń, Poland, linked to the International Day Against Homophobia (Amnesty International, 2006). The National Rebirth of Poland (Narodowe Odrodzenie Polski or NOP), a nationalist organization, countered with a simultaneous demonstration during which its members loudly chanted slogans "such as 'gas the queers' (*pedaly do gazu*), 'come closer' (*chodzcie blizej*) or 'there will be a baton for each queer face' (*znajdzie sie kij na pedalski ryj*)" (Amnesty International, 2006, p. 12). The slogan "gas the queers" is a blatant homophobic reminder of the extermination of gays and lesbians in Nazi concentration camps during World War II. Today memorials to the Gay Holocaust can be found in Israel, the United States, Canada, Uruguay, France, Spain, Italy, and Austria, as well as in Germany in former concentration camps including Mauthausen, Dachau, Neuengamme, Buchenwald, and Sachsenhausen (Koymasky & Koymasky, 2013).

APG: Social themes were pervasive in the lengthy preparations for CONFINTEA VI, the sixth UNESCO intergovernmental international conference on adult learning and education that took place in Belém (State of Pará), Brazil, in December 2009. You seemed hopeful in the run up to CONFINTEA VI that sexual minorities would find increasing respect and accommodation there. First of all, I'd like you to give your impressions of the International Civil Society Forum (known as FISC, an acronym for the Portuguese title), which took place prior to CONFINTEA VI in Belém from November 28 to 30, 2009. Its Charter of Principles included foci on the free exchange of experiences, global solidarity, and a globalization that respects universal human rights, social justice, civil social power, transformative educational practices, and lifelong learning as a human right (International Civil Society Forum [ICSF], 2008). To what extent were sexual minorities and our rights and freedoms globally considered in discussions of these principles?

RJH: The International Civil Society Forum was very significant. It made preparations for the participation of civil society at the official CONFIN-TEA VI, and it also collected the voices of social movements, networks, and civil-society organizations that work on the right to education for youth and adults. The leadership from the International Council for Adult Education, heavily involved in the operation of FISC, was very open to addressing sexual-minority issues. I was invited to play a number of roles at the International Civil Society Forum: I produced the opening ceremony slide-presentation representing North America, to which I added queer issues (Hill, 2009a). I conducted a session entitled "Achieving Full Social Inclusion for Lesbian, Gay, Bisexual, Transgender, and Queer People through Lifelong Learning Opportunities: What Can CONFINTEA VI Do?" (Hill, 2009b). I also designed and facilitated a workshop entitled "Building Capacity for a Visible Global Presence: Sexual Minority Rights" (Hill, 2009c).

The final FISC document, favourable to sexual-minority concerns, "developed a strong united position reflecting the views of over 500 people from 80 countries. [It] laid out a consensus position on how the conference could move from rhetoric to coherent action" (International Civil Society Forum [ICSF], 2009, para. 1). FISC fought for and gained both space and recognition for civil society within CONFINTEA VI. The work of FISC, which was "fully endorsed by the heads of 22 national government delegations from all regions, won significant support from another 14 governments…. [It was] debated throughout [CONFINTEA VI]" (ibid., para. 2). In fact, the declaration of FISC was far more progressive than that produced by CONFINTEA VI. It clearly recognized different forms of discrimination that undermine access to education, including those based on sexual orientation and gender identity. At the conclusion of CONFINTEA VI, civil-society educators who formed the FISC consensus committed to continuing the struggle to secure coherent action on the right to education for adults and young people.

APG: CONFINTEA VI was intended to be a forum to advocate for learning for adults focused on their needs in lifelong and lifewide contexts. This broad purpose was reflected in the conference title: Living and Learning for a Viable Future—The Power of Adult Learning. CONFINTEA VI aimed "to draw attention to the relation and contribution of adult learning and education to sustainable development in all its dimensions: social, economic, ecological, and cultural" (Bochynek, 2008, p. 2). Conference planners hoped that a key outcome would be the adoption of a framework for action that keeps the interests of particularly constructed "regions" of the world—Latin America and the Caribbean; Asia/Pacific; Africa; Europe, North America, and Israel; and the Arab States—in dynamic equilibrium with global goals. The framework would contain key strategies and recommendations to re-vitalize and plan adult learning and education in ways that incorporate ele-ments of social learning including literacy, equity, sustainability, mobility, competition, and inclusion. How did CONFINTEA VI play out? What is your assessment of what the conference, in general, actually accomplished? Did the conference have any impact on the rights and global citizenship of sexual minorities? Were we considered to any degree in discussions focused on social cohesion, equity and diversity, democratic citizenship, and per-sonal and community development?

RJH: Stressing the importance of learning and education in creating and sus-taining a viable future, CONFINTEA VI emphasized participation, inclusion, equity, and quality in learning for adults and youth in the Belém Framework for Action that it adopted (Bochynek, 2010). In anticipation of this social dem-ocratic emphasis energizing CONFINTEA VI, and in keeping with my aim to have a focus on sexual-minority rights included in the Belém Framework, I had strategized numerous ways to shape policies with the following goals:

- to use civil- and human-rights education as an anti-oppression tool to build skills and capacity in human-rights advocacy based on sexual orientation and gender identity
- to help facilitate education about sexual-minority human rights issues in all regions
- to broaden the definition of discrimination—that is, prejudice based on per-sonal characteristics where governments, institutions, and people treat others wrongfully—to include sexual orientation and gender identity
- to inform and promote attention to sexual-minority human-rights violations across governments, religious institutions, and civil society
- to facilitate national conversations and networks in order to share materials, skills, or experiences that foster greater sexual-minority presence, voice, and visibility
- to facilitate discussion on sexual-minority human-rights issues across govern-ment and civil society in order to help achieve some common understandings
- to support the right of sexual minorities to be free from discrimination at

work and the right to be free from social oppression
- to support the right of sexual minorities to enjoy full citizenship
- to support the right of sexual minorities to enjoy full immigration status
- to support the right of sexual minorities to seek asylum from oppressive states where their rights are denied
- to support the right of sexual minorities to be free from torture, arbitrary arrest, and extortion
- to support the right of sexual minorities not to be labeled as sick, criminal, or sinful
- to support the right to possess gay, lesbian, bisexual, and transgender publications, including cultural, scientific, and research materials
- to support the right of youth to age-appropriate expressions of sexual orientation and gender identity, without fear (Hill, 2008)

These points are grounded, in part, in the Charter of the United Nations (1945), the Universal Declaration of Human Rights (1948), the European Convention on Human Rights and its Five Protocols (1950, 1952, 1963, 1966), the Vienna Declaration (1993), the International Covenant on Civil and Political Rights (1996), and the International Covenant on Economic, Social, and Cultural Rights (1996).

I could barely suppress my surprise and delight when I received the preliminary draft of the Belém Framework for Action and found that the rights of sexual minorities were embedded in it. The language prevailed in the final document, recognizing our rights:

Inclusive education is fundamental to the achievement of human, social and economic development. Equipping all individuals to develop their potential contributes significantly to encouraging them to live together in harmony and with dignity. There can be no exclusion arising from age, gender, ethnicity, migrant status, language, religion, disability, rurality, *sexual identity or orientation*, poverty, displacement or imprisonment. (CONFINTEA VI, 2009, p. 5; emphasis added)

In so many ways, this inclusion is part of the communal quest for *full* global citizenship and inclusion for sexual minorities that still remains ahead of us. My hope is that adult educators and learners are inspired and propelled by our victories. Reflecting back, these include the UN gay rights statement that links sexual-minority issues with social justice, which was "the result of an inspiring collective global effort by many LGBT and human rights organisations. Our collaboration, unity, and solidarity have won us this success" (Tatchell, 2008, para. 12). Importantly, since 2001 international adult education has become more integral to our efforts to secure sexual-minority rights. At both FISC and CONFINTEA VI in late 2009, including the right to lifelong learning for sexual minorities continued this momentum. We have continued to make our way, to swim against strong currents and treacherous riptides where homophobia and transphobia remain deterrents to civility, liberty, and even life itself. We remain determined.

APG: We have reached the end of a telling exchange. Is there a final message that you would like to leave with lifelong and adult educators?

RJH: Let me end with a personal vignette, going back to the end of the CONFINTEA V Mid-term Review. I was riding the escalator on my way to exit the UN building. I passed another participant with whom I had conversed during the conference, although he had not spoken publicly at the sessions on democracy that we mutually attended. He wore a name tag indicating that he was from a region whose delegates largely opposed the sexual-minority activism that I had linked to practices of lifelong learning and international adult education at the mid-term review. As we passed this final time, our eyes connected and the government delegate smiled warmly at me, nodded, and slightly raised an arm with his fist clenched in solidarity. While my fight as a Western activist-educator in Bangkok may well have been a sign of imperialism and decadence to some, nevertheless, I believe that for others it was a way to inclusion in the human family. If lifelong learning and international adult education are to remain relevant, it is vital that we build a lived and knowable community that involves deliberate and deliberative global engagements with others based on respect for difference as a universal human right (Grace & Hill, 2004). Here, Rita Ceballos and Paulo Freire speak to me. Latin American popular educator Ceballos (2006) succinctly reminds me that, "in the end, people and their communities are the real subjects and protagonists of their own process [toward empowerment]" (p. 329). Freire (2004) urges me to engage in lifelong learning as critical action when he declares, "Fighting for the currency of the dream, of the utopia of criticalness, and of hope constitutes fighting to refuse the negation of dreams and of hope, a struggle founded in just rage and in effective political-ethical action" (p. 102).

Beyond Paralysis of the Social: Possibilities for Lifelong Learning as Critical Action

In the preceding exchange, Hill makes it clear that we continue to live in a world where sexual-minority citizens commonly experience disenfranchisement, dislocation, and ongoing threats to our safety, security, and, in many cases, our very existence. In an era when neoliberal pragmatism has permeated formal education and learning agendas, there is paralysis of the social as mainstream lifelong learning is primarily reduced to its economistic form. Such limited learning is not a significant intervening force in making the lives of citizens better (Aronowitz, 2005a, 2005b; Edwards, 2000b; Field, 2006; Grace, 2007). Still, in the grand scheme of things, the social and the economic do not have to be in opposition. There can be synchronicity, as demonstrated in a major social step forward that MERCOSUR (Mercado Común del Sur, or Southern Common Market)—the regional trade and integration agreement among a number of Latin American countries—took in August 2007 when its human-rights committee called on member countries to recognize and prohibit discrimination against sexual minorities (International Gay and Lesbian Human Rights Commission [IGLHRC], 2007d). The issuing of this declaration is the first significant region-wide step to promote sexual-minority rights in Latin America. The declaration includes emphases on advancing public awareness and education strategies as well as increasing participation of sexual minorities at all levels of public education (IGLHRC, 2007d). While all the Southern Common Market human-rights representatives signed the declaration, nearly two years later it still had not passed as a resolution (Marcelo Ernesto Ferreyra, email communication, March 2, 2009). Still, placing such importance on public pedagogy and education in diverse contexts provides impetus for lifelong learning as critical action that is about community-based knowledge building, advocacy, outreach, and formal, informal, and non-formal learning, all of which make a difference in the lives of sexual minorities as disenfranchised citizens.

We can find other inspiration by looking at informal learning venues outside mainstream lifelong learning that engage in excellent examples of community-based education and cultural work incorporating inclusive and transformative kinds of pedagogy intended to make the world better for sexual minorities. One Canadian site that exemplifies best practices in community education, advocacy, and outreach work is the Casey House Foundation in

Toronto. Founded in 1988, Casey House has functioned for more than two decades as a self-sustaining HIV/AIDS hospice that has supported about eight thousand people living with HIV/AIDS and their families. It provides exceptional treatment, palliative care, and informal and non-formal education through community programming. At the Toronto Gay Pride Parade in 2008, Casey House staff and supporters carried a banner with a key message to mark the hospice's twentieth anniversary: Recognize, Remember, Educate, Celebrate, Inspire, and Imagine. Colin Harris, development coordinator with Casey House Foundation, shared the meaning of these words:

> "Recognize" the contributions of those who have been involved with Casey House over the last 20 years. "Remember" the struggles of the Hospice being built and the lives of those who have passed on. "Educate" the current generation of young people about the history of Casey House and its place in the community. "Celebrate" the lives of those who have passed on and the joy of living today. "Inspire" to make your dreams come true. "Imagine" that one day that there will be a cure for HIV/AIDS. (email communication)

Toronto Gay Pride 2008 was also the site where another superb example of inclusive and potentially transformative lifelong learning was launched: a multi-year project focused on the theme Global Human Rights for Queers: What Out is About. Rau (2008) recounts that the project utilized the subtheme Dying for Justice during Pride to draw attention to the dangers faced by sexual minorities living in Jamaica. She relates that the international grand marshal for the Pride parade was Gareth Henry, a queer Jamaican activist and cultural worker who led the fight for change in his home country until death threats forced him to leave. International human rights for queers constituted a major theme at Toronto Gay Pride 2008. This was apropos since, as Rau indicates, the city is home to a diverse multicultural sexual-minority community whose members come from many nations that persecute sexual minorities on the grounds of sexual orientation and gender identity. Global Human Rights for Queers is *must-do* lifelong learning and cultural work in light of Hill's account of sexual minorities subsisting in dangerous, life-threatening circumstances in many nations. It is vital to engage in such public pedagogical projects to link learning to advocacy focused on holding every nation accountable when it threatens, tortures, or executes its sexual-minority citizens. This includes nations in the Global South. Even though globalization has relegated these nations with their poor and thus apparently inadequate consumers to second-class global citizenship (Jarvis, 2007), this calamity of class cannot be used to excuse internal calamities of exclusionary culture and tradition that permit violence emanating from the ignorance and fear embodied and embedded in hetero-sexism, homophobia, and transphobia.

Calling for Lifelong Learning as Critical Action for Sexual Minorities

Much of the educational and cultural work for social justice and transforma-tion of the plight of sexual minorities globally has taken place in local sites outside of international organizations, as well as outside of mainstream life-long learning and adult education (Grace, 2006a; Hill, 1995, 2003c; Hill & Grace, 2009). In their institutionalized and systematized forms, these two educational formations have either tended to erase sexual minorities from their social discourses through silence and inaction, or they have reacted in a homophobic manner whenever sexual minorities have transgressed their ex-clusionary spaces and contravened their traditional prescriptions of who has place (see, for example, Grace, 2001; Grace & Hill, 2004; Grace, Hill, & Wells, 2009). Transgression of heteronormative educational space is requisite if the notion of *lifelong learning for all* is to have true rather than rhetorical meaning and value. As inclusive educators strive to achieve the kind of better world that Paulo Freire (2004) worked to create, we must challenge any kind of education or learning that leaves minorities out. In the case of sexual minorities, educa-tors focused on our inclusion have to continue to interrogate the heteronor-mative culture-knowledge-language-power nexus and advocate for our hu-man and civil rights. This requires that they work within a pedagogy of place as they bring aspects of criticality—ethics and the political ideals of moder-nity: democracy, freedom, and social justice—to bear on lifelong learning as critical action that recognizes, respects, and accommodates sexual minorities in policy-making, policy implementation, and practice (Grace, 2006a). Here the goal is to make both heterocentric and subaltern queer knowledges public in the work to achieve safety and security as well as space and place for sexual minorities who occupy a spectral community of queer others (Grace, 2001).

Because education, social action, and cultural work to aid sexual minori-ties has moral and political implications, especially for politico-religious con-servatives who subscribe to unquestioned traditions that also permeate their politics, and because sexual minorities have historically been arbitrarily associated with pathology and deviance, engaging in educational and other work to make life better for us is often construed as provocative, risky, and even dangerous (Grace, 2008). Still this work is vital and a duty despite the possibility of threatened or actual retaliation. When others try to inhibit or negate this work, it should make us angry. Within a politics and pedagogy of indignation, which fired up Freire (2004), anger can be the force used to pull the trigger that enables lifelong learning as critical action: "Anger is a tool that will enable all those who yearn for social justice to recapture our human dignity and avoid falling into cynicism, even when confronted with the inescapable injustice and cruelty now unleashed under the banner of a 'new world order' guided by neoliberal policies and ironclad globalization" (Macedo, 2004, p. xi). When Freire (2004) spoke of anger as a catalyst for cultural work for social transformation, he essentially conceptualized this anger as just ire that can be harnessed as a force to guide ethical decision-making, choosing, acting, and educating, all of which have limits. Freire believed that educators had to be hopeful as they worked to make the world better. It is in this context that he spoke about the right to be angry: "I have the right to be angry and to express that anger, to hold it as my motivation to fight.... My right to feel anger presupposes, in the historic experience in which I participate, that tomorrow is not a 'given,' but rather a challenge, a problem. My anger, my just ire, is founded in my revulsion before the negation of the right to 'be more,' which is etched in the nature of human beings" (pp. 58–59).

Perhaps the best example of Freire's expression of just ire is found in the last essay that he wrote. As his wife, Ana Maria Araújo Freire relates, Freire wrote these words on April 21, 1997, about the barbaric murder of Galdino Jesus Do Santos, a Pataxó Indian in Brasilia. She states, "In them [Paulo] serenely analyzed the 'meanness' of Galdino's death, but he did so with a degree of firmness, depth, clarity, and indignation I had only read or felt in his writings a few times" (Freire, 2004, p. 48). That firmness, depth, clarity, and indignation are the hallmarks of Freire's expression of just ire. They are captured in this excerpt:

What a strange notion, to kill an Indian for play, to kill someone. I keep thinking here, submerged in the abyss of a profound perplexity, stunned before the intolerable perversity of these young men who dehumanize themselves, about the environment where they *devolved* instead of *evolving*. I wonder about their homes, their social class, their neighborhood, their school. I think, among other things, about what sort of testimony may have been given them about thinking and about how to think. I wonder about the place given to the poor, to beggars, Blacks, women, rural workers, factory workers, and to Indians in that thinking.... I can guess the reinforcement that way of thinking received at many moments during a school experience where the Indian remains minimized. I see the *almightiness* of their liberties, exempt of any limits, liberties on the verge of permissiveness, disdainful of all and everything.... The fact in itself that this tragic transgression of ethics has taken place warns us how urgent it is that we fight for more fundamental ethical principles, such as respect for the life of human beings. (pp. 46–47)

Following Freire, lifelong educators committed to critical action need to be deeply concerned about the almightiness of disdainful, unrestrained liberties that, in the case of sexual minorities, dismiss or deny our rights as they pertain to being, becoming, belonging, and acting in the world. When we are its targets, this permissiveness exacerbates our historical plight to protect and advance our rights in local and global contexts (Grace, 2001; Grace & Hill, 2004; Hill, 2003a, 2003b, 2003c; Hill & Grace, 2009). It is grounded in ignorance that often leads to misunderstanding and fear, which, in turn, can lead to symbolic and/or physical acts of violence against sexual minorities. Symbolic acts of violence include shaming, harassment, name-calling, and rightist politico-religious denunciation; physical acts of violence include a spectrum of criminal acts such as assault and battery, torture, rape, and murder. Incidents of extreme physical violence are well documented in Janoff's (2005) book, *Pink Blood: Homophobic Violence in Canada*. Janoff includes a necrology of victims (1990–2004) who were variously beaten, kicked, strangled, suffocated, stabbed, shot, burnt, bludgeoned, dismembered, run over, or thrown off buildings. Paralleling Freire's concern about the young men who brutally murdered Galdino Jesus Do Santos, Janoff notes that more than 40 percent of the perpetrators of these hate crimes were homophobic teenagers.

Building Critical Pedagogy to Encompass Life and Work for Sexual Minorities

To counter the paralysis of the social that is common in neoliberal forms of lifelong learning, we ought to conceptualize lifelong learning as an organic enterprise that conducts learning for work and advancing economies in tandem with learning for life. This conception would be the basis for more encompassing critical pedagogy that meets the instrumental, social, and cultural needs of citizens as learners, workers, and persons. Such pedagogy would constitute lifelong learning as critical action. It would employ an ecology of learning and work that enables citizens to focus on the self, others, and the life-and-work environments they inhabit as they mediate lifelong learning as a comprehensive, lifewide process (Grace, 1997b, 2006b, 2007). Citizens would begin by discerning how they are positioned in relation to others and the complex culture and society in which they live, learn, and work. This focus on building self-knowledge is a crucial component of an ecology of learning and work. Self-knowledge informs mediation of the difficult social and economic circumstances in which issues of recognition, access, accommodation, disposition, contexts, and relationships of power have import (Aronowitz, 2005b; Grace, 2006c, 2007). For sexual minorities, building self-knowledge involves exploring historical systemic deterrents to developing self-confidence and self-esteem while strategizing to engage in educational activities and cultural work that counter manifestations of heterosexism, homophobia, and transphobia in individual and community contexts.

As critical pedagogy, lifelong learning as critical action would also involve building knowledge of life and work that, in sum, bring matters of context (social, cultural, political, historical, and economic), disposition (attitudes, values, and beliefs/ideologies), and relationship (social hierarchies and issues of domination affecting differences including class, gender, gender identity, sexual orientation, race, ethnicity, age, and ability) to bear on knowledge production, exchange, and dissemination. It would explore inherent tensions in bringing multiple and different knowledges to bear on an ecology of learning and work. Here a turn to history would be integral. To build the critical intelligence needed to be politically strategic in educational and cultural work to make a better world, Freire (2004) accentuated the importance of historical awareness in knowledge building that assists hopeful learners to be reflexive as they make sense of experiences as part of engaging with possibility, ethics, justice, democratic vision, learner freedom, critique, and intervention. This blueprint for critical action helps situate lifelong learning as praxis that brings *the critical* to bear on everyday life. For sexual minorities, it means remembering lesbian and gay history. In turn this history can be a starting point for revising history to be more inclusively queer as we explore the meaning of gay liberation as radicalized critical social action (D'Emilio, 1992; Fone, 2000). Expanding our spectral queer history can be a starting point for thinking about possibilities to enhance sexual-minority presence and place, recognition and respect, and ingenuity and integrity.

As pedagogy particularly focused on the locatedness of minority individuals and collectives and our inclusion in learning for life and work, lifelong learning as critical action would entail creating what Aronowitz (2005a) calls *space for the new*. Here, having turned to history to understand the present as different (Carr, 1961), one could begin to construct this space for the new as one in which the social and the economic would be in dynamic equilibrium. As minorities learn how to make space for the new and advocate for a recognized and respected place in communities, educational settings, workplaces, and other socio-cultural spaces, local needs would be nested within larger national and transnational considerations in addressing dislocation and disenfranchisement in learning and work. Lifelong learning as critical action would be concerned not only with the present, but also with the future so minorities could move forward as global citizens with rights, privileges, and responsibilities in economic and civil contexts. As praxis, it would counter the fatalism of neoliberal pragmatism that blames minorities for their predicaments and requires passive acceptance (and not just ire) in the face of systemic oppression. As Freire (2004) insists, just ire is a right and a necessity to counter subjugation. As an example of the queer expression of just ire, Hill (2009d) relates that the US Queer Nation movement, in its aim to achieve full human and civil rights for sexual minorities, has focused on anti-oppressive education and civil action to bring about social and cultural changes. He describes the form this legitimate anger takes: "Queer nationalists contest traditional values about family, the police state, and the panopticon (surveillance) of authoritarian rule over our lives by religious, usually fundamentalist, institutions. It is a struggle to re/claim self-respect and self-esteem. It is a recovery process to salvage the intimacy that has been denied to us by the dominant culture" (p. 54). In this sense, expressing just ire in processes of reclamation and recovery helps sexual minorities create space for the new where we have visibility and assert our identities and variations against the grain of a history of heteronormative erasure and homophobic and transphobic defilement of our positionalities. Changes may be slow, but we have never been more determined. The desire of sexual minorities to be, become, belong, and act in meaningful and decisive ways places ethical demands on lifelong learning as critical action to make its own new spaces for us, intensifying change.

Concluding Perspective: A Stonewall for All

These days, sexual minorities reject our historical exclusion from mainstream forms of lifelong learning and adult education in local, national, and international contexts (Hill & Grace, 2009). We have grown justly angry at the silence, exclusion, and symbolic and physical violence that heterosexism, homophobia, and transphobia have perennially provoked in culture, society, and education as key replicators of the heteronormative status quo. Indeed, there has been fervent and intense expression of that anger as sustained socio-political action since the Stonewall rebellion in New York on June 28, 1969. The result has been a growing global movement for rights and freedoms for sexual minorities. This movement is vital, as former US Secretary of State Hillary Rodham Clinton remarked in a speech to diplomats at the Palais des Nations in Geneva, Switzerland, on International Human Rights Day, December 6, 2011. She spoke about multiple violations of queer integrity:

> It is a violation of human rights when people are beaten or killed because of their sexual orientation, or because they do not conform to cultural norms about how men and women should look or behave. It is a violation of human rights when governments declare it illegal to be gay, or allow those who harm gay people to go unpunished. It is a violation of human rights when lesbian or transgendered women are subjected to so-called corrective rape, or forcibly subjected to hormone treatments, or when people are murdered after public calls for violence toward gays, or when they are forced to flee their nations and seek asylum in other lands to save their lives. And it is a violation of human rights when life-saving care is withheld from people because they are gay, or equal access to justice is denied to people because they are gay, or public spaces are out of bounds to people because they are gay.... [It is also a violation of human rights] when people cite religious or cultural values as a reason to violate or not to protect the human rights of LGBT citizens. This is not unlike the justification offered for violent practices towards women like honor killings, widow burning, or female genital mutilation. Some people still defend those practices as part of a cultural tradition. But violence toward women isn't cultural; it's criminal. Likewise with slavery, what was once justified as sanctioned by God is now properly reviled as an unconscionable violation of human rights.... In each of these cases, we came to learn that no practice or tradition trumps the human rights that belong to all of us. (Rodham Clinton, 2011, pp. 3–4)

Secretary Clinton's remarks signify the need to recognize gay rights as human and civil rights. There is momentum in the movement to do so. Hari (2009), speaking within a politics of hope and possibility, reflects on the state of the queer quest for freedom: "Everywhere it goes, it wins, in time" (p. 23). Let's hope so. The struggle is far from over, as so many embattled queer people continue the fight for human and civil rights in many nations. As Hari indicates, "There are three great swathes of humanity still untouched by the spirit of Stonewall and terrified, terrorized gay people there are screaming for help. In the Caribbean, majority-Muslim countries, and most of Africa, being gay is a death sentence, yet many people who should be showing solidarity choose not to see it" (p. 23).

Caribbean homophobia and the terror it causes in queer lives is quite pronounced in Jamaica, which Hari characterizes as "Taliban Afghanistan for gay people" (p. 23). In that country, the sentence for gays and lesbians who get caught is ten years of hard labour, though it is more likely they would be lynched for the way they love others. Drawing on cases documented by Dr. Robert Carr of the University of the West Indies, Hari provides this example of the extreme violence marking queer life in Jamaica: "A father found a picture of a naked man in his 16-year-old son's rucksack, so he produced it in the playground and called on the boy's classmates to beat him to death—which they promptly did. No one was ever charged" (p. 23).

The murder of the Jamaican youth is but one example of youth, often under the age of majority, being monstrously targeted by homophobes who may even be their parents or friends. In another example of the heinous forms that homophobic targeting of youth can take, 16-year-old Mahmud Asgari and 18-year-old Ayaz Marhoni were blindfolded and publicly hanged in Iran on July 18, 2005 (Moore, 2010). While the facts of the case remain unclear, one story suggests they were put to death for an alleged crime involving homosexual intercourse; it is also possible that they were executed simply for having consensual gay sex (Kim, 2005). Under Iranian law, engaging in homosexual activity is a capital offence punishable by execution. What adds to the horror of murdering human beings for purported same-sex crimes is the fact that the victims were youth. Their executions were in violation of the UN Convention on the Rights of the Child and the International Covenant on Civil and Political Rights, which ban the execution of minors (Kim, 2005). Iran is a signatory to both agreements (Kim, 2005).

In still another example that assaults the integrity and endangers the lives of sexual minorities, the Ugandan parliament has sought to pass the Anti-Homosexuality Bill, 2009. The bill intends to increase the punishment for homosexuality from the current seven years in prison to death by hanging for certain offences (Johnson, 2010). The Anglican Church of Uganda has strongly supported this bill, upholding its theocratic opposition to homosexuality, which many Ugandans consider to be a Western import. Interestingly, Anglicanism is also a Western import—a fact the Ugandan church underplays. The Church Missionary Society founded the Anglican Church of Uganda in 1877, and church membership is now around eight million members (BBC News, 2008). As an indicator of its conservatism, the Ugandan church severed ties with the US Episcopal Church over the election of the Right Reverend Gene Robinson, the first openly gay bishop in the American Anglican Communion. However, Ugandan Anglicans do not speak with one voice. For example, Canon Gideon Byamugisha believes that passing this bill would sanction "state-legislated genocide against a specific community of Ugandans" (Ford & Pomfret, 2009, p. 1). Indeed violence against gays, including the targeting and murder of gay activists, has escalated since Ugandan lawmaker David Bahati authored the bill (Dixon, 2011). Importantly, Canon Byamugisha found a kindred spirit in the former Archbishop of Canterbury Dr. Rowan Williams, who, in his opposition to the bill, stated, "Overall, the proposed legislation is of shocking severity and I can't see how it could be supported by any Anglican who is committed to what the Communion has said in recent decades. Apart from invoking the death penalty, it makes pastoral care impossible—it seeks to turn pastors into informers" (Sarmiento, 2011, p. 1).

The Anti-Homosexuality Bill of 2009 reportedly came about because three visiting American evangelists—Scott Lively and "ex-gays" Caleb Brundidge and Don Schmierer—incited Ugandan politicians to introduce the despicable legislation. In what amounted to an imperious US evangelical infiltration, Lively, Brundidge, and Schmierer placed the lives of Uganda's sexual minorities in jeopardy by preaching a politico-religious gospel that assaulted the gay movement as "an evil institution whose goal is to defeat the marriage-based society and replace it with a culture of sexual promiscuity" (Moore, 2010, p. A12). Describing this hate-mongering message intended to contain homosexuality, Moore (2010) asserts, "Lively, Brundidge, and Schmierer trade in the homosexual equivalent of the Jewish Blood Libel: the notion that gays recruit, spread disease, molest children and actively conspire against family and society" (p. A12).

Nevertheless, the evangelical anti-gay messengers had willing listeners since, as Canon Byamugisha related, there is a "traditional and cultural abhorrence to same-sex relationships" in Uganda (Ford & Pomfret, 2009, p. 2). Indeed, homophobia and intolerance toward sexual minorities are norms on their way to being institutionalized in that country. For example, R. W. Johnson (2010) relates that Yoweri Museveni, the Ugandan president, has long been telling his country's youth that European homosexuals are recruiting in Africa. Johnson also relates that Ugandan sentiment accuses the West of attempting to bully Africans into accepting homosexuality, which they see as an un-African way of life.

Since its introduction in the Ugandan parliament in 2009, the controversial bill has remained in legislative limbo, although always with the possibility and fear that it could be reintroduced in a subsequent parliament (Dixon, 2011; Kron, 2011). As a deterrent to the revival of this bill and other homophobic assaults on gay rights in African nations, Western nations such as the United States, the United Kingdom, Sweden, and Canada have been pressuring Uganda to recognize gay rights as human and civil rights, making gay rights a new border zone in international diplomacy (Chothia, 2011; Dixon, 2011). Former US Secretary of State Hillary Clinton and Canadian Foreign Affairs Minister John Baird have been among those vocal in castigating the Ugandan government for harassing, and violating the rights of, sexual and gender minorities (Lumu, 2013). Nevertheless, on February 19, 2013, the Anti-Homosexuality Bill, 2009, was reintroduced, targeting not only "offenders," but also those who know, help, or defend sexual and gender minorities (Burroway, 2013, n.p.). Moreover, it topped the list of "business to follow" on the Order Papers in the Ugandan parliament (Burroway, 2013, n.p.).

The proposed Anti-Homosexuality Bill, 2009, known in popular terms as the "Kill the Gays Bill," remains both nebulous and precariously sweeping in terms of what constitutes a punishable offence (see text of the proposed bill in Nathan, 2013). For example, as the text of the bill states, the term *sexual act* includes everything from intercourse to touching to using any object on any orifice. Moreover, it also includes "stimulation or penetration of a vagina or mouth or anus or any part of the body of any person, however slight by a sexual organ, … [which is defined] as a vagina, penis or artificial sexual contraption" (ibid., n.p.). In its obsessive attempts to define, categorize, and explain offences in an effort to target all gays all the time, the bill is an anything-and-everything mishmash. When the offence is same-sex stimulation or penetration, the bill states that the penalty on conviction is life imprisonment. When the offence involves a parent or guardian as offender or includes other conditions that the bill lists under "aggravated homosexuality" (n.p.), the death penalty is to be imposed on conviction. The bill also classifies the "attempt to commit homosexuality" (n.p.) as a felony punishable by a seven-year prison term on conviction. The attempt to commit aggravated homosexuality carries a sentence of life imprisonment on conviction.

As if the proposed bill is not draconian enough, it also includes a fine and up to a three-year prison term on conviction for a person in authority—parents, guardians, pastors, and counsellors are included here—who fails to disclose to authorities within 24 hours that a youth has confided in them about engaging in same-sex activity. Thus the bill advances a politics of relentless surveillance. The bill also chooses to be oblivious to international treaties, protocols, declarations, and conventions, considering them null and void when they contravene "the spirit and provisions enshrined in this Act" (n.p.). Moreover, the bill declares that "definitions of 'sexual orientation,' 'sexual rights,' 'sexual minorities,' [and] 'gender identity' shall not be used in any way to legitimize homosexuality, gender identity disorders, and related practices in Uganda" (n.p.), which virtually eliminates possibilities for health care and counselling.

In the end though, we ought to remember, as Hill and others have indicated, that homosexuality is a global condition. Sexual minorities are everywhere and thus the battles against homophobia and transphobia must be fought everywhere. Wherever there is injustice, as exemplified by the preceding examples, lifelong educators should seek transformation of educational and cultural practices and social relations that variously subjugate, dismiss, defile, or erase sexual minorities as learners, workers, persons, and citizens. Indeed, in light of the homophobic and dangerous milieu for sexual minorities in countries such as Jamaica, Iran, and Uganda, lifelong educators ought to help in advancing a Stonewall for sexual-minority Blacks and Arabs. Not to do this work and to ignore the positive impact that Stonewall has had on many White sexual minorities around the world would be "real racism" (Hari, 2009, p. 23) and a victory for uncivil Black and Arab homophobes who continue to try to reduce homosexuality to a Western construct and import. Therefore, lifelong educators should be willing to strategize and engage in the political, pedagogical, and cultural work necessary to make a better world for sexual minorities. To engage in this work as critical action, exclusionary policies and practices in education, culture, and society have to be exposed; communication in the intersection of the moral and the political has to be enhanced; and the state of the struggle, the extent of transformation, and the need for further social and cultural action have to be monitored (Allman, 1999; Grace, 2006a; Grace et al., 2004). Collectively, this work will enable recuperation of sexual minorities as we and our allies engage in social learning, open dialogue, critical questioning, resiliency building, and cultural work for social change (Grace, 2006a). In sum, these efforts transgress lifelong learning as travesty for sexual minorities. They help constitute lifelong learning as critical action.

Conclusion

Beyond the Vast Economic Debacle

The Canadian Council on Learning (CCL) established an Adult Learning Knowledge Centre in September 2005 (Grace, 2009b). Less than four years later, the CCL, uncertain about its own future in a time of fiscal constraints, announced that the centre would close on July 6, 2009. During the last meeting of the centre's national advisory group the preceding month, the CCL informed us that the federal Conservative government would not maintain the previous Liberal government's commitment to fund the centre's initiatives in grassroots community education for adults. Such decisions are not unusual in Canada, where adult education has a history of being subjected to this kind of government whimsy. The demise of the centre speaks to the perennial problems of sustaining Canadian adult education and its regional social and cultural learning projects when a federal government cuts funding, abrogating its public responsibility for the education of adults. Of course, moving away from providing public funding for education is a norm of neoliberalism, which promotes privatized education that is primarily intended to advance economic interests. This norm, which inhibits the construction of lifelong learning in more holistic terms, has perennially frustrated social and cultural educators. In a social democracy, a government should be accountable to its citizens for the provision of accessible and accommodating forms of instrumental, social, and cultural education. Indeed, government should be a lifeline to lifelong learning as critical action that emphasizes both self-reliance and social responsibility as it advances learning for work, living, citizenship, and nation building (Grace, 2009b; Keizer, 2009). This does not mean that private interests ought to be sidelined in developing lifelong learning. Since they are one of its beneficiaries, certainly in instrumental and economic contexts, they should contribute to funding this development, assisting with the creation of forms and projects that align with a responsible national vision for holistic lifelong learning. To achieve this vision, lifelong educators ought to monitor what is happening, interrogating unscrupulous forms of privatized education that so often emerge in the kind of "rumpus-room economic system" associated with neoliberalism in recent decades (Keizer, 2009, p. 12). As earlier chapters of this book have indicated, within this system lifelong learning has emphasized individuals and their success through competition, with "the privilege of disposable income ... [as a marker of success appearing to be] contingent on the existence of disposable people" (Keizer, 2009, p. 12). Here there is little or no concern with understanding self-reliance outside the economic context. As well, there is little or no emphasis on social responsibility as a basis for creating just and sustainable communities.

The existing vast economic debacle has accentuated these realities as recurring financial crises around the world continue to normalize bewilderment and insecurity for markets, governments, and ordinary citizens. With the global economy reeling, government leaders and economists are left to play daily guessing games as they try to gauge the severity and length of an intense state of economic turmoil. In this haphazard world, the promise of neoliberalism to advance the social as an outcome of advancing the economic—a promise that may have always been mythical—now appears to lack both substance and possibility. Indeed, we are paying a tremendous price for having subscribed to a neoliberal culture driven by financialization, which is about grounding economics in finance instead of production. Foster and Magdoff (2009) locate financialization as a long-term trend that has accelerated since the early 1980s, although it was discernible in the late 1960s. The trend is based on the belief that "finance unleashed ... would continue to propel the economy to greater heights" (Johnson, 2009, p. 52). Thus neoliberal culture has celebrated unregulated profit making and inscribed the interests of the financial sector as the interests of society as a whole. However, the global financial and economic crisis has shown us that the financial sector is massive and mysterious, unpredictable and unreliable. It has resulted in "a synchronized downturn in almost all countries, a weakening of confidence among individuals and firms, and major problems for government finances" (Johnson, 2009, p. 56). What we have witnessed on a colossal scale is the vulnerability of interconnected nations in an era of free markets and deregulation. We have been awestruck by the baffling complexity and fragility of the global economy.

As lifelong educators, it is important to consider what this grave crisis means for us. Certainly, the fact that neoliberals have been able to exercise so much control over education during the past few decades is phenomenal (Grace, 2009b; Mason, 2009). Linking learning to the carrot of individual betterment, at least in material terms, neoliberals have proven to be very successful in moving lifelong learning in a predominantly instrumental direction, encouraging learners to gain the knowledge and skills needed to be productive in an information and technology work culture. In the face of this momentum, we should ask: To what extent have lifelong educators simply been complicit players in the neoliberal learning-for-earning game? And, as a consequence, to what extent have lifelong educators lost control over lifelong learning? As we reflect on profound changes in lifelong learning during the heyday of neoliberalism and move toward the future, we should ask other questions: What will lifelong educators learn from the contemporary global economic and social turmoil? How will they think about the future of lifelong learning? How might we rearticulate lifelong learning to enable social, economic, cultural, and technological transitions that advance inclusion, health, well-being, and security for all in a better world? And since we live in uneasy times when governments have to be innovative, strategic, coordinated, and co-operative, how should lifelong educators respond as governments reorient themselves? Can we put lifelong learning into broader service across instrumental, social, and cultural domains, perhaps mustering greater support from governments in the process?

I begin this chapter by discussing how the vast economic debacle of 2008 unfolded amid a selfish politics of destruction and denial that shook neoliberalism and forced troubled nation-states to act, as financial institutions crumbled and citizens experienced burgeoning debt loads and vulnerability in life, learning, and work. Here I consider Alan Greenspan's perspectives on the emergence of the neoliberal economic model that contributed to what he calls an "age of turbulence" (2008, p. 18). I consider how this model has profoundly affected lifelong learning for individuals across the lifespan. Next, I explore how we might reframe lifelong learning as critical action by emphasizing education for responsible citizenship in this time of converging crises. This would involve helping learners to become political change agents who build abilities and capacities to meet local and larger needs, thus contributing to global homeostasis. To demonstrate this kind of lifelong learning as critical action, I then turn to history to explore the politics and pedagogy of Dr. Martin Luther

King, Jr., whose notion of *conscience for change* captured his understanding of education for responsible citizenship. This historical reflection is followed by a look at possible futures for lifelong learning. I overview two recent major studies informative to constructing lifelong learning as critical action: the UK *Inquiry into the Future for Lifelong Learning*, published in 2009, and the *Education for All Global Monitoring Report 2010: Reaching the Marginalized*. I conclude with a historical reflection on the 1996 Delors report, *Learning: The Treasure Within*, as I consider why lifelong learning for all remains to be achieved.

The Vast Economic Debacle of 2008

The vast economic debacle of 2008 is considered the worst financial collapse since 1929 (Zakaria, 2009). Greenspan (2008) describes this crisis, which began to appear in the United States during the summer of 2007, as "an accident waiting to happen" (p. 507). In the wake of this unwieldy crisis, people grew increasingly appalled as they learned more about "Wall Street's exotic products, outrageous pay, dishonest accounting, and crumbling brokerage firms, as well as the [US] government's demand for $700 billion and later much more to bail them out" (Phillips, 2009, p. lxxii). Regarding this bailout, Barlett and Steele (2009) recount that US Congress passed the *Emergency Economic Stabilization Act* in October 2008, enabling the Treasury Department to access bailout funds. They relate that $239 billion was used over the next three months to bail out 296 of the country's 8,000 banks. Interestingly, they remark that 67 percent of the money went to just 8 of those troubled and troubling financial institutions. On a truly confounding note, they point out that the US government did not track whether or how the banks used this unparalleled financial stimulus for the purpose for which it was intended, which was "to buy up defective mortgage-backed securities and other 'toxic assets' through the Troubled Asset Relief Program, better known as TARP" (p. 206).

This incalculable economic and financial crisis has been marked by a series of unprecedented events that, in tandem, have resulted in the most terrible economic slowdown since the Great Depression. These events include: "the destruction of approximately $50 trillion [US dollars] in assets in the global economy; the nationalization of America's largest mortgage lenders; the largest bankruptcy in history (Lehman Brothers); the disappearance of the investment bank; [and] bailouts and stimulus packages around the world adding up to trillions of dollars" (Zakaria, 2009, p. xi). While the cumulative impact has been massive and unrelenting, Krugman (2009), recipient of the 2008 Nobel Prize in Economics, suggests that the current financial and economic crisis does not signify a depression like the 1930s, but a move into the domain of depression economics. This move is indicated by widespread recession induced by incompetent and greedy financial speculators, as governments fight the uphill battle to generate spending to counteract unemployment and other consequences of the crisis. As Krugman indicates, depression economics mean an inadequate private demand for goods and services, underutilizing the nation's productive capacity and limiting prosperity.

Referring to this dire state of affairs as the Great Financial Crisis, Foster and Magdoff (2009) consider the immense economic meltdown to be a consequence of the stagnation of the real—investment in production to create tangible wealth—and the concomitant proliferation of the unreal—financial bubbles associated with volatile and unstable paper claims to wealth, which, on rupturing, caused "real-world repercussions" (p. 7). This trend toward financialization has resulted in many changes in the economic character of the United States. Geoghegan (2009) links the bloating up of the financial sector to the lack of caps on interest rates, which caused capital to rush from the realm of production to the realm of finance. One major consequence of this process of financialization has been a radically changing work culture. Geoghegan asserts, "Basically, we're all waiters now; we're bowing and scraping and working for the banks" (p. 32). Indeed, the power of workers in the financial sector is greatly reduced compared to the glory days in the manufacturing sector when labour wielded power. Geoghegan explains the subservience of workers in the work culture created by financialization:

We became "knowledge workers," dependent on the financial sector. And knowledge workers, unlike skill-based workers, don't have the bargaining power to get higher wages out of rising productivity. What can they withhold? They can't withhold knowledge. And since they have nothing to withhold, it's much trickier for knowledge-based workers to get a higher wage. And if there are fewer skill-based workers, it becomes harder to raise wages in general. And if it's harder to raise wages, then more of us go into debt. (p. 36)

Phillips (2009) blames the massive global economic crisis on complicitous politics that allowed fiscal malpractice, which left citizens vulnerable to the whims of "the paper entrepreneurialism of finance" (p. xiv). Since the 1990s, such speculative finance has resulted in "a grossly overinflated U.S. financial sector—the increasingly commingled excesses of banking, securities, insurance, and real estate—[that] failed the nation's trust through extreme greed, inexcusable speculative leverage, and a streak of sheer incompetence" (p. xii–xiii). As a dire consequence, financialization has positioned debt, especially private debt, as "one of America's giant industries" (p. xviii). Phillips relates that, from 1994 to 2004, US federal, state, and local debt rose to $6.1 trillion while private debt reached a staggering $31 trillion. Foster and Magdoff (2009) note that the ratio of overall consumer debt to disposable income more than doubled from 1975 to 2005. Zakaria (2009) notes that US household debt alone stood at $14 trillion in 2008. This scenario indicates that we live in "an economy of hallucinated wealth" (Greer, 2008, p. 94). Sadly, what this IOU economy fails to notice is the real process of decline that ordinary citizens experience "in the non-hallucinated economy of goods and services, jobs, and personal income" (Greer, 2008, p. 97). Greer predicts that "we can expect each recession to push more people into poverty and each recovery to lift fewer people out of it.... Poverty, malnutrition, and desperation will be among the few things not in short supply" (p. 97).

Connecting the dots into a world picture, Zakaria (2009) remarks that the American-born crisis of 2008 demonstrated the potential of such debt to create deadly dilemmas dangerous to synchronous global growth. The crisis exposed the downside of globalization as nation after nation fell like tumbling dominoes, toppled by the impact of the ubiquitous financial and economic crisis. Both developed and developing nations became victims of the interdependence nurtured by globalization and an international economic system integrated since the 1970s. Zakaria concludes: "The major side effect of all this success—low inflation, global growth, swift technological advancement—was arrogance, or more technically, the death of risk" in a global economy driven by the information revolution (p. xiv). It was the death of risk that paved the way for an extraordinary and extreme rise in debt and borrowing against the future. This has positioned financial worry as an ever-present, everyday reality for many ordinary citizens who have engaged in bad economic practices such as using predatory lending (e.g., payday loans), failing to control credit-card debt, and taking on risk-filled mortgages. Regarding the latter, Foster and Magdoff (2009) relate, "The bursting of the U.S. housing bubble set off a chain reaction of stagnant and falling home prices, a flood of defaults, and a global economic crisis due to financial contagion and a drop of U.S. consumption" (p. 92).

What has the vast economic debacle meant for neoliberalism? Mason (2009) asserts that the widespread economic and financial meltdown on September 15, 2008, was "a signal moment for neoliberalism" as a product of history that had replaced the state and regulation with the self-interest of neoliberal players playing for big money (p. 119). He describes the crisis as a product of three processes: the "credit crunch" or the big financial freeze that began August 9, 2007; a burgeoning commodities bubble; and the growing confusion of policy-makers. As he interprets it, the crisis is marked by the dynamics of destruction and denial: "destruction of capital that had been badly invested, [and] systematic denial of the scale of the problem by executives desperate to maintain the façade of profitability and competence" (p. 99). In trying to resolve this crisis, the subsequent rescue of global capitalism through the intervention of the state became a watershed moment for neoliberalism. This is because the nature of the rescue is antithetical to the neoliberal tenet to reduce the presence and power of the state in the private sphere (Mason, 2009). Moreover, the vast economic debacle exposed defects in neoliberalism as an ideological economic model. From a Western perspective, Mason lists five negative effects of this model: (1) a greater disparity between rich and poor in developed nations; (2) an ever-increasing debt load for workers who have witnessed a decline in real wages; (3) a redistribution of profits from the traditional production sector to the financial sector where dot-com, housing, and commodity bubbles have melded the unyielding desire for profit with omnipresent risk; (4) a decline in both social capital and volunteerism coupled with mounting personal and financial insecurity and an increase in crime; and (5) a privatization of services and property that were once communal or provided to citizens by the state. In this dim light, the time is right to demand a rearticulation of global capitalism so it becomes, as Mason suggests, committed to advancing social justice and sustainability. As I discuss later in this chapter, this has ramifications for the future of lifelong learning and its construction as a broader instrumental, social, and cultural project.

Greenspan's Age of Turbulence: The Neoliberal Economic Model and its Impact on Lifelong Learning

The neoliberal economic model has generated a culture of unprecedented and uncaring risk that has profoundly affected life, learning, and work since the 1980s. To understand this model and its enormous impact, it is useful to consider the standpoint of perhaps its chief proponent, Alan Greenspan. Described as "the prophet of deregulation" (Mason, 2009, p. 118), Greenspan has long been a staunch advocate of fiscal conservatism and free markets. During his tenure as chairman of the Federal Reserve Board from 1987 to 2006, he was integral in transforming the US economy into a sophisticated and resilient neoliberal formation that incorporated deregulated financial markets, highly flexible labour markets, and, as he viewed it, "major advances in information technology … [that increased the nation's] ability to absorb disruptions and recover" (Greenspan, 2008, p. 8). Greenspan helped position the US economy as the hub of global capitalism during the 1990s. He described this mushrooming economy as open and self-correcting in a world where commerce was forever altered by cheap and ubiquitous communications technologies such as cellphones, personal computers, email, and the Internet. This technological revolution allowed real-time investing and trading in a milieu of "irrational exuberance" that drove globalization and intensified market growth (Greenspan, 2008, p. 177). With his nation driving the global economy, "America's freewheeling, entrepreneurial, so-what-if-you-fail business culture [became] the envy of the world [as] U.S. information technology swept the global market" (p. 183). Still, Greenspan remained cautious. In 1996, in what now seems a premonition of the vast economic debacle to come, he warned, "We should not underestimate, or become complacent about, the complexity of the interactions of asset markets and the economy" (p. 177). In managing the US economy as an inextricable part of a complex, interdependent global economy, Greenspan knew that the Federal Reserve Board often made decisions that involved dealing "with incomplete and faulty data, unreasoning human fear, and inadequate legal clarity" (p. 196); thus, he concluded, "Policy-makers cannot reliably anticipate financial or economic shocks or the consequences of economic imbalances" (p. 528). He used the unruly dynamics driving recessions as an example: "Recessions are tricky to forecast because they are driven in part by nonrational behavior. Sentiment about the economic outlook usually does not shift smoothly from optimism to neutrality to gloom; it's like the bursting of a dam, in which a flood backs up until cracks appear and the dam is breached. The resulting torrent carries with it whatever shreds of confidence there were, and what remains is fear" (p. 212). This human fear factor, in tandem with incalculable risks, has created jeopardy for the globalization of trade and financialization. In this milieu, global citizens have experienced risk and vulnerability as norms. For Greenspan, the resulting economic and social instability has created "an age of turbulence" during which "it would be imprudent and immoral to minimize the human cost of its disruptions" (p. 18). With old identities and securities now in tatters, he feels global citizens are left to make a difficult choice: "To embrace the worldwide benefits of open markets and open societies that pull people out of poverty and up the ladder of skills to better, more meaningful lives, while bearing in mind fundamental issues of justice; or to reject that opportunity and embrace nativism, tribalism, populism, indeed all of the 'isms' into which communities retreat when their identities are under siege and they cannot perceive better options" (p. 18). Undergirding this statement is Greenspan's steadfast commitment to fiscal conservatism, despite both his lip service to social justice, historically expected to be a concern of the state, and some recognition of the human toll of neoliberalism and the vagaries of the marketplace. For him, the neoliberal economic model remains the way forward to prosperity and a better life.

As lifelong educators, we have been deeply affected by this economic model that calls individuals to experience its version of the good life. Indeed, the power of the neoliberal economic model has pressured us to recast lifelong learning in predominantly instrumental terms that have pragmatic value in a world changed by globalization and financialization. Greenspan (2008) links these two forces: "Globalization—the deepening of specialization and the extension of the division of labor beyond national borders—is patently a key to understanding much of our recent economic history. A growing capacity to conduct transactions and take risks throughout the world is creating a truly global economy" (p. 364). As these forces have intertwined, the consequences for transitions in learning and work have been phenomenal. Since the 1990s, the technological boom driving globalization and financialization has made job displacement and insecurity predominant concerns for white-collar workers, which has been the dominant worker population in the United States since 1956 (Bell, 1976; Greenspan, 2008). For these workers, instrumental lifelong learning as an expected and necessary periodic venture is now inextricably linked to work, as learning for new work is often necessary once old jobs become redundant. Indeed, learning for new work is now normalized for displaced workers, as is learning for new workers who lack marketable skills. For example, Greenspan relates that the "'corporate university' is rapidly becoming a permanent fixture in adult job-specific training [as] many corporations dissatisfied with the quality of new hires supplement their education and capabilities, equipping them to compete successfully in world markets" (p. 402). Job displacement and the quest for new or better work have resulted in job turnover and mobility as contemporary realities in today's work world. Greenspan explains these changes within the context of Joseph Schumpeter's idea of "'creative destruction'—the scrapping of old technologies and old ways of doing things for the new—[which] is the only way to increase productivity and therefore the only way to raise average living standards on a sustained basis" (p. 268). As Greenspan sees it, this is the probable message of capitalism. Still, there are limits to innovation and the skilling of workers, as even Greenspan notes: "In economies with cutting-edge technologies, people, on average, seem unable to increase their output per hour at better than 3 percent a year over a protracted period. That is apparently the maximum rate at which human innovation can move standards of living forward" (p. 17). This outcome suggests that human development through learning has to be about more than skills development to create a competitive workforce. Moreover, it gives us cause to think about the limits to learning and the need to construct lifelong learning in more holistic terms.

Greenspan's (2008) perspectives are not particularly helpful as we think about these things. He has been predominantly concerned with the instrumental and the pragmatic in his assessment of the design of learning across the discipline of education. While he judges US higher education to be a versatile and world-class formation that advances the economy in practical, creative, and entrepreneurial terms, Greenspan has been quite critical of what he considers dysfunctional and deficient systems of US primary and secondary education that fail to provide graduates with both the capacity and ability to engage in work that would advance his country's intricate goods-and-services infrastructure. He takes educating down to instrumental basics when he asks, "What do we do to their learning process that requires business recruiters to dismiss vast numbers of 'educated' applicants for modestly skilled jobs because they cannot write coherent sentences or add a column of numbers accurately?" (p. 399). Greenspan does not adequately attend to the social and cultural contexts that shape this educational outcome. Instead, he goes straight to what he perceives to be the neoliberal solution, which is to shape educational policy in keeping with the global forces of competition. Still, he seems to realize that sole promotion of market forces in schools is just one value consideration and is neither a full nor equitable resolution:

I recognize that left to their own devices, market incentives will not reach the education of those children "left behind" (to borrow a term from current U.S. education legislation). The cost of educational egalitarianism is doubtless high and may be difficult to justify in terms of economic efficiency and short-term productivity. Some students can achieve a given level of education far more easily, and therefore at far less cost, than others. Yet there is danger to a democratic society in leaving some children out of sync with its institutions. Such neglect contributes to exaggerated income concentration, and could conceivably be far more costly to the sustaining of capitalism and globalization in the long run. The value judgments involved in making such choices reach beyond the imperatives of the marketplace. (p. 406)

Of course, in his quest to sustain capitalism and the economics of globalization, Greenspan is not only concerned with shaping schoolchildren for the marketplace. He also wants to shape adult learners in relation to learning for new work. As noted throughout this book, part of the neoliberal agenda—and this is exemplified in Greenspan's views on education—has been to control all education, which has included curricular control in predominantly instrumental terms as well as financial control through privatization. As an example of the downside of the latter, Barlett and Steele (2008) discuss the involvement of KeyBank of Cleveland in educational finance schemes that gouged vulnerable adult learners, demonstrating the difficulties a neoliberal model of lifelong learning can cause for students who are hanging on to dreams of prosperity and the good life. During the autumn of 2008, KeyBank—KeyCorp, its parent company ranks as the seventh biggest educational lender in the United States—received $2.5 billion in TARP money. This was despite the shady history of its student-loan business. Barlett and Steele describe the predatory lending strategy that KeyBank used to victimize students:

Over the years, thousands of students have secured education loans from Key-Bank to attend a broad range of career-training schools.... One of the schools was Silver State Helicopters, which was based in Las Vegas and operated flight schools in a half-dozen states. During high pressure sales pitches, people looking to change careers were encouraged to simultaneously sign up for flight school and complete a loan application that would be forwarded to KeyBank. Once approved, KeyBank, in keeping with long-standing practice, would give all the tuition money upfront directly to Silver State. If a student dropped out, Silver State kept the tuition and the student remained on the hook for the full amount of the loan, at a hefty interest rate. The same rule applied if Silver State shut itself down, which it did without warning on February 3, 2008.... Silver State Helicopters was a flight school, but it might more accurately be thought of as a Ponzi scheme.... As long as there was a continual source of loan money, keeping the scheme afloat, all was well. KeyBank bundled the loans into securities ... and sold them on Wall Street. But when Wall Street failed to buy at an adequate interest rate, the money supply evaporated.... Without the loans—in other words, without the cooperation of Wall Street—the school had no income. (p. 261)

Thus the evaporation of financing resulted in the evaporation of education. Adult learners found themselves displaced even before they could find a place of work. For them, a neoliberal model of education meant no education, just increasing debt.

The American Dream in Reverse: A Time for Continuity, A Time for Expansion

Students who obtained education loans for flight school from KeyBank fell prey to the "nakedly predatory" way the lending institution had sought out and funded the unscrupulous Silver State Helicopters school in a money-spinning partnership that financially abused students (Barlett & Steele, 2008, p. 261). In a real sense, this scheming crushed the American Dream for these students. The *American Dream*, a term coined by historian James Truslow Adams in 1931, has been "more or less [the] Official National Dream" (p. 120). It is a dream of a better, richer, and fuller life, which is historically embodied and embedded in the second sentence of the Declaration of Independence, which describes such inalienable rights as life, liberty, and the pursuit of happiness (Kamp, 2009). To assess the current status of the dream, Kamp reflects on President Barack Obama's January 30, 2009, address in which he reviewed the dismal state of the US economy, which had just experienced grave job losses and the worst contraction of its gross domestic product in almost three decades. Kamp recounts that the "man who normally exudes hopefulness for a living, pronounced ... [the economic calamity] a 'continuing disaster for America's working families,' a disaster that amounts to no less, he says, than 'the American Dream in reverse'" (p. 120).

Perhaps those US citizens long caught up in the cycle of poverty did not even think about the American Dream or its condition. For them, the days after September 15, 2008, were just more dreamless days without. And for those Americans who believed they could bridge the distance between the dream and reality, the vast economic debacle assaulted their confidence and their ability to continue to dream. Kamp captures the nihilistic mood:

> As the safe routines of our lives have come undone, so has our characteristic optimism—not only our belief that the future is full of limitless possibility, but [also] our faith that things will eventually return to normal, whatever 'normal' was before the recession hit. There is even worry that the dream may be over—that we currently living Americans are the unfortunate ones who shall bear witness to that deflating moment in history when the promise of this country began to wither. (p. 120)

Still, Kamp asserts that the erosion of the American Dream, or whatever US citizens have believed it to be, did not start with the current economic crisis. It began in the 1990s when escalating institutional and personal debt spurred the realization that expectations were excessive and unattainable despite easy credit and a prolonged bull market.

Rather than dwelling on the end of the American Dream, at least as it applies to comfortable middle-class Americans, Kamp believes the way forward is to revise it so it is more realistic, achievable, and no longer a "vague and promiscuously used term" (p. 120). While not forgetting those who still need the promise of the dream, he suggests rearticulating the American Dream by linking it to continuity:

> And what about the outmoded proposition that each successive generation in the United States must live better than the one that preceded it. While this idea is crucial to families struggling in poverty and to immigrants who've arrived here in search of a better life than that they left behind, it's no longer applicable to an American middle class that lives more comfortably than any version that came before it.... I'm no champion of downward mobility, but the time has come to consider the idea of simple *continuity*: the perpetuation of a contented, sustainable middle-class way of life, where the standard of living remains happily constant from one generation to the next. (p. 180)

Presented this way, the American Dream requires attention to scale, self-control, and a decent chance, which are all ideas that should be deliberated in the construction of a holistic model of lifelong learning. Kamp relates that John Truslow Adams helped set reasonable parameters to the American Dream in a long-forgotten iteration in which he depicted it as "'that dream of a land in which life should be better and richer and fuller for every man, with opportunity for each according to his ability or achievement'" (p. 123). Of course, Kamp's Americentric rethinking of the dream of a nation is not enough in the era of globalization, when we need the dream of a better world. If there is to be a rearticulation of the American Dream, then it should be extended to envision a Global Dream whereby the United States truly and fully accepts its international responsibility to contribute to improving the world in ways that reduce the blurring of globalization with Americanization. Currently, the United States does not come close to providing its fair share to aid human development and education in developing nations (UNESCO, 2010). This dereliction of global duty should be impetus for the superpower to rethink its responsibility as the hub of global capitalism. The United States should help global citizens to dream in personally and communally meaningful contexts, without subjecting them to its imperialism as a superpower.

Lifelong Learning as Critical Action in a Time of Converging Crises

In 1968, Aurelio Peccei founded the Club of Rome to seek constructive solutions to what he called "'the global problematique'—the spiral of converging crises" associated with unchecked industrial development and the belief that unregulated economic growth could solve any societal problem (Greer, 2008, p. 4). As indicated throughout this book, the global problematique has grown worse during the emergence of neoliberalism as a pervasive ideology and economic model. This is because neoliberalism has generally been marked by an episodic pattern in which a startling crisis is followed by an incomplete recovery. Greer (2008) calls this process "the Long Descent—the declining arc of industrial civilization's trajectory through time" (p. 32). He contends that this descent fits neither the myth of progress nor the myth of apocalypse, which are the two dominant myths that have been used to make sense of the world. As Greer describes it, the myth of progress locates human history as a story of continuous social and economic improvement tied to the development of science, the gradual triumph of reason over nature, and limitless technological growth. In contrast, the myth of apocalypse holds that "human history is a tragic blind alley" (p. 37) shaped by urban sprawl, excessive governmental bureaucracies, corporate greed, and overly materialistic citizens. Subscribers to the myth of progress assume there are no limits to where science and technology can take us. They seem to forget that people are more important than techno-scientific advances. Subscribers to the myth of apocalypse believe that there will be a tragic, abrupt, cataclysmic, and unmitigated end to industrial civilization mired in neoliberalism. They appear to succumb to nihilism.

Greer asserts that each myth, which is hegemonic and unchangeable to its subscribers who generally accept its presuppositions, is insufficiently in tune with historical social, economic, and environmental patterns that demonstrate the complexity of human existence. As he sees it, the Long Descent contests both the myth of progress and the myth of apocalypse. It sorely challenges a culture of entitlement driven by the long-held belief of citizens in Western nations that "they deserved to get whatever they wanted without having to pay the full price for it" (p. 147). With reference to North America, Greer concludes that this culture has contributed to the disintegration of democratic politics. Citizens are not participating in grassroots political processes to the degree that would show a valuing of democracy and popular involvement in it. This political absence points to a key role for lifelong learning as critical action: to revitalize education for citizenship, reminding learners of the history of the involvement of churches and other local community organizations in skill building and networking that enabled political processes in local and national contexts. Greer speaks to this involvement of civil society: "Institutions of civil society created a context in which individuals could orient their lives to the politics of the day and act in ways that could influence policy all the way up to the national level. People who wrestled with the nuts and bolts of the democratic process in community organizations needed no further education when time came for the precinct caucuses that chose candidates and party platforms" (p. 147). By emphasizing education for citizenship so learners can become political change agents, lifelong learning as critical action can help citizens be proactive in creating options for life, learning, and work. In the process, this can help to revitalize learning and work cultures, politics, civil society, and the environment in the interest of survival for all.

How might we shape lifelong learning as critical action so it incorporates important political and pedagogical dimensions of proactive education for citizenship? Korten's (2006) suggestion asks us to respond to the current spiral of converging crises by changing "the stories by which we define ourselves" (p. 18).

In this light, he calls for a "Great Turning" in which we convert crises into opportunities by learning "to live in creative partnership with one another and the living Earth" (p. 3). This holistic form of lifelong learning as critical action would (1) accommodate human diversity, (2) focus on the intelligence and ingenuity of human beings, (3) demand that corporations be publicly accountable when they cause social upheaval and environmental damage, and (4) seek rejuvenation of local communities and their economies and initiatives. For Korten, this is education for responsible citizenship that builds "Earth Community" as "the egalitarian democratic ordering of relationships based on the principle of partnership" that collaboratively shapes cultures, economies, and politics (p. 20). Such lifelong learning as critical action would prioritize quality education for all that is linked to quality work and quality life. In this regard, it would focus on the politics and pedagogy of providing health care, eradicating poverty, protecting the environment, supporting the arts and public broadcasting, and meeting the needs of baby boomers (Korten, 2006). To enable the Great Turning, lifelong learning as critical action should also have a rearticulated instrumental focus that advances "the idea that the proper defining purpose of business is to serve life and community" (p. 16). In promoting this idea, Korten uses the example of the Master of Business Administration program offered by the Bainbridge Graduate Institute of the Positive Futures Network: This program's "mission is to transform business education.... [It develops] managers for businesses that seek to advance positive social and environmental outcomes as a core business purpose" (p. 16). As Korten sees it, such a program helps to develop life-serving economies that nurture communities on a foundation of responsible citizenship that adapts to local needs. He describes how prosperity is measured in these communities:

> Prosperity is measured by the quality of our lives and the realization by each person of the creative potential of their humanity. A high-performing economic system supports the development of this potential, provides every person with an adequate and dignified means of livelihood, maintains the healthy vitality of the planetary ecosystem that is the source of all real wealth, and contributes to the building of community through strengthening the bonds of affection, trust, and mutual accountability. (p. 303)

In keeping with this notion of creating prosperous communities, lifelong learning as critical action would highlight an ecology for living that nurtures *care of self as critical action* (handwritten)

individual agency and betterment; viable and sustainable ecosystems; and strong, interactive communities. Korten speaks to the importance of building healthy communities that care for and serve individuals, focusing on their development and well-being so they can live intentionally, creatively, and happily. Within these communities, the diversity of individuals ought to be respected, cultivated, accommodated, and utilized. Indeed, "a diversity of age, gender, culture, religion, and race provides an invaluable contribution to the resilience and creative potential of human communities" (p. 294). Truly valuing diversity begins by nurturing dialogue and enabling experiences across differences so individuals can create "communities of congruence" that explore relational differences in local learning scenarios such as study groups (p. 317). Here, lifelong learning as critical action can nurture education for citizenship that exposes "the political process to a greater diversity of voices and parties" and alters "public priorities in favor of people, families, communities, and the planet" (p. 320). Conservatives and liberals do not have to be at odds in this learning process: "A politics of mature citizenship properly honors both the conservative values of freedom and individual responsibility and the liberal values of equity and justice for all. It brings together a conservative concern for community and heritage with a liberal concern for inclusiveness and the creation of a world that works for the whole of life and children yet to come. It recognizes the importance of local roots combined with a global consciousness" (p. 339). Within this political *métissage*, lifelong learning as critical action can be a more intricate construct that engages children, youth, and adults in learning framed as crucial active participation in community life. Korten maintains that such an engagement has to involve learners in proactive learning, action research, and community-service projects in which they hone skills as writers, analysts, team members, communicators, and citizens who focus on communities and their histories, ecologies, and day-to-day interactions and practices. In this process, lifelong learning as critical action comes alive.

Conscience for Change

It is important that lifelong learning as critical action reflexively engages history, deconstructing the involvement of social activists and cultural workers who tackled past crises as it helps citizens as learners to confront the converging crises shaking the world today. For example, as we focus on the challenges of creating prosperous communities in contemporary times, we can turn to history to reflect on the politics and pedagogy of Dr. Martin Luther King, Jr., which invigorated his kind of lifelong learning as critical action. As Korten (2006) relates, Dr. King "worked with a higher-order vision of how truly trans- formational change comes about—not from the barrel of a gun, but from liv- ing the change that we seek" (p. 315). One can find an insightful synopsis of Dr. King's politics and pedagogy in the series of half-hour Massey Lectures that he delivered for the Canadian Broadcasting Corporation starting in No- vember and ending on Christmas Eve 1967, just a few months before his assas- sination. He called the radio lecture series *Conscience for Change*.

The Massey Lectures, named for the first Canadian-born governor general, Vincent Massey, began in the winter of 1961 as an intellectual forum for lead- ing thinkers to discuss complex ideas "that link our political, social, and moral worlds—how we live together in modern societies and define our responsi- bilities towards each other as global citizens" (Lucht, 2007, p. xi). The CBC broadcast each annual series over several weeks in an effort to build public awareness and understanding of issues of the day. When Dr. King (2007) gave his radio lectures, he captured the intensity of Black rage in 1960s America as he exposed "the chaos of neglect" (p. 172) that marked life in both urban Black communities and the United States at large. Dr. King could have been speaking about current conditions when he said, "The cities are gasping in polluted air and enduring contaminated water; public facilities are outworn and inadequate; financial disaster is an annual crisis" (p. 172). Dr. King wor- ried about the accumulating "elements of social catastrophe" (pp. 172–173) in his country, asserting that the US government was incessantly "preoccupied with war and ... determined to husband every resource for military adven- tures rather than for social reconstruction" (p. 173). In this regard, he was particularly concerned about the plight of Black youth, whom a seemingly impenitent US government invariably subjected to one of two tragedies: the horrors of segregation at home or the fiasco of the Vietnam War. In his Massey Lectures, Dr. King declared that many visible and invisible fences had been constructed in the United States to restrict Black youth to certain neighbour- hoods, schools, jobs, and social intersections. He warned, "With most of their lives yet to live, the slamming of doors in their faces can be expected to induce rage and rebellion" (p. 171). This dilemma was exacerbated by the travesty of Black youth who were being sent to die in the Vietnam War in numbers hugely disproportionate in relation to the total US youth population. Dr. King starkly depicted what he saw as his country's heartless manipulation of poor youth who could only grow more cynical as they juxtaposed experiences of a miserable life at home with experiences of war as a "process of death" (p. 184). Still, the US government used the nation's youth, primarily those who were Black, poor, or otherwise marginalized, to justify the sacrifice in Vietnam as a struggle for someone else's liberty. Dr. King recounts:

> [The United States] was taking the Black young men who had been crippled by our society and sending them 8,000 miles away to guarantee liberties in Southeast Asia which they had not found in Southwest Georgia and East Harlem. And so we have been repeatedly faced with the cruel irony of watching Negro and White boys on TV screens as they kill and die together for a nation that has been unable to seat them together in the same schools. We watch them in brutal solidarity burning the huts of a poor village, but we realize they would never live on the same block in Detroit. (p. 179)

Just as he interrogated what was happening to youth in his present, Dr. King would have encouraged those engaging in contemporary lifelong learning as critical action to probe the complex condition of youth living in neoliberal times. He would have asked lifelong educators to use what we learn to inform education for citizenship for youth that addresses their alienation and helps them build lives with meaning, purpose, security, and a sense of place that respects human dignity and integrity. Dr. King (2007) indicated why such education is important so youth can truly participate in local communities and in a nation as a democracy:

> When an individual is no longer a true participant, when he no longer feels a sense of responsibility to his society, the content of democracy is emptied. When culture is degraded and vulgarity enthroned, when the social system does not build security but induces peril, inexorably the individual is impelled to pull away from a soulless society. This process produces alienation—perhaps the most pervasive and insidious development in contemporary society.... Alienation is a form of living death. It is the acid of despair that dissolves society. (pp. 193–194)

Still, Dr. King did not subscribe to the myth of apocalypse. His substantial lectures are grounded in a politics of hopeful possibility that provide a rich basis for nurturing lifelong learning as critical action. Dr. King called for transgression that "rock[ed] the *status quo* to its roots" (p. 166) in order to transform culture and society in ways that acknowledged, accommodated, and thus respected Black personhood and citizenship. To achieve the goal of "ripping gaping holes in the edifice of segregation" (p. 167), he promoted "disciplined non-violence" (p. 167) as an imperative for critical action. In his social activism and cultural work, Dr. King recounted the heavy burden of Black history and the extent of latent racism among the White majority, even among Whites who were outraged by incessant brutality toward Blacks. He reminded us to focus on systemic issues and the insidious ways that power could be used to oppress as we strategize to transgress. He taught us never to underestimate the nature, intensity, and pervasiveness of evils such as racism in mainstream culture and society. As we build an inclusive politics and pedagogy to invigorate lifelong learning as critical action, Dr. King's messages remain vital. While many countries now have laws, legislation, and policies to protect persons against discrimination and violence on grounds such as race, gender, and sexual orientation, still racism, sexism, and heterosexism remain pervasive in their cultures and societies. If, as educators, we wish to cast lifelong learning as critical action in inclusive terms not limited by demography or geography, then, in the spirit of Dr. King, we ought to ask: How might lifelong learning as critical action be constructed to help learners climb over fences whether they are visible or invisible?

In answer to this question, Dr. King (2007) would likely have begun by saying that this construction cannot happen in isolation, but would have to be part of larger social democratic change. In his Massey Lectures, Dr. King called on the United States to engage in such change by undertaking "a radical revolution of values" (p. 185), creating a more democratic basis for judging the degree to which its policies were fair and just. He asserted that if the United States did not act to enable equity and justice, it would "surely be dragged down the long, dark, and shameless corridors of time reserved for those who possess power without compassion, might without morality, and strength without sight" (p. 187). From this perspective, Dr. King would have encouraged lifelong educators to have a healthy scepticism of policy-makers. Since so much of lifelong learning is directed by policy edicts, critical lifelong educators need to interrogate both government and corporate policy-making and how their outcomes affect the development and delivery of lifelong learning for all. As Dr. King reminded us in relation to the oppression of Black US citizens, even purportedly democratic policy-makers who should protect all citizens in a social democracy can be the problem: "The policymakers of White society have caused the darkness; they created discrimination; they created slums; they perpetuated unemployment, ignorance, and poverty.... The slums are the handiwork of a vicious system of the White society; Negroes live in them but they do not make them, any more than a prisoner makes a prison" (p. 169). Here Dr. King did not castigate all Whites. He felt it was important to have White allies participate in his non-violent strategizing and action to make a better world. He concluded, "It is not the [White] race *per se* that we fight but the policies and ideology that leaders of that race have formulated to perpetuate oppression" (p. 170). This speaks to another important tenet of lifelong learning as critical action: the need for coalition building.

Dr. King (2007) supported coalition building. He believed that ordinary citizens across differences could transform self and structures by strategizing in community regarding how to deal with government. He felt that government had a "proneness to adjust to injustice" (p. 186) and a penchant for constructing political myths that it propped up "with the power of new violence" (p. 183). He challenged Black Americans as historically oppressed and disenfranchised citizens "not only [to] formulate a program [for social reform] but [also to] ... fashion new tactics which do not count on government good will but instead serve to compel unwilling authorities to yield to mandates of justice" (p. 173). Dr. King saw active resistance by a coalition of Black and White youth as central to this work. He spoke to the "new spirit of resistance" (p. 195) in which bold, resourceful Black youth acted and built alliances with White youth whom they inspired. The coalition building created a wealth of social spirit and awakened a conscience for change. Within the politics of resistance and the youth-mentoring-youth process at play, Black youth engaged one another and White youth in lifelong learning as critical action. Here they developed leadership skills and strategies for non-violent resistance that included sit-ins and freedom rides. Black youth learned the power of elucidating Black identity and representation, which they linked to teaching others about Blackness and initiating cultural work for social change in their communities and nation. Interestingly, as Dr. King noted, the learning that they initiated in their struggle to address deep, systemic problems occurred primarily in informal contexts: "Many [Black youth] left school, not to abandon learning, but to seek it in more direct ways. They were constructive school dropouts; a variety that strengthened the society and themselves" (pp. 195–196). This historical exodus of youth from formal schooling, paralleled, for example, by the contemporary exodus of youth from formal lifelong learning in countries such as

Canada, challenges schools, colleges, and other formal learning sites to reflect on how they might do a better job in the areas of social and cultural education (Grace, 2007).

In sum, Dr. King (2007) promoted an ecology of learning and living that linked self, others, and local and global communities. This ecology advocated the dignity, worth, and integrity of all citizens; ethical and just learning and community practices; the right to engage in quality work and earn a living for a better life; and life, liberty, social justice, and the pursuit of happiness as the collective inheritance of all citizens in a democracy. Engaging this ecology, which highlighted the interdependence of individuals and nations as "an inescapable network of mutuality, tied in a single garment of destiny" (p. 211), was Dr. King's remedy for alienation and despair. Adhering to the premise that "justice is indivisible" (p. 180), he believed that passionate and unyielding social activism and cultural work in local communities had to be inextricably linked to global survival and building a better world. He tied his beliefs in the agency of individuals and "the sacredness of human personality" together as a counterforce to the oppression and exploitation of ordinary citizens (p. 213). Dr. King's ecology of learning and living was also grounded in the notion of agape, a Greek word for the kind of love that sees others, values service, and demands nothing in return. Dr. King described agape as "understanding, creative, redemptive good will" (p. 214) for all citizens. Agape involves struggle, persistence, the "privilege to love," and working "passionately and unrelentingly for first-class citizenship" for racial, ethnocultural, sexual, and other minorities who comprise a nation's citizens and immigrants (p. 214). Ultimately, Dr. King's ecology of learning and living was grounded in a politics and pedagogy of hope that realized both the life in dreams and the fallibility of myths such as White superiority or unlimited technological progress. This politics and pedagogy challenged "a system that has created miracles of production and technology to create justice" (p. 176). As Dr. King saw it, this required putting both materiality and an accompanying poverty of spirit in a realistic place by realizing the limits to technological advancement. Despite many challenges and threats, Dr. King remained committed to his politics and pedagogy of hope: "Yes, I am personally the victim of deferred dreams, of blasted hopes, but in spite of that ... I still have a dream, because, you know, you can't give up in life. If you lose hope, somehow you lose that vitality that keeps life moving, you lose that courage to be, that quality that helps you to go on in spite of [it] all. And so to-day, I still have a dream" (p. 216).

Futures for Lifelong Learning: Collective Challenges Beyond a Tumultuous Now

The apparent failure of neoliberalism to ensure prosperous local communities interconnected within a secure global economy should prompt lifelong educators long affected by the dictates of this ideology and economic model to reflect on possible futures for lifelong learning beyond the current vast economic debacle. We should think deeply about a few basic questions: What challenges does lifelong learning face today? What messages emanate from these challenges for lifelong educators? What are possible futures for lifelong learning? Recently, two major studies have focused on such questions, as both reflected on possibilities for lifelong learning across educational and community sectors: the UK *Inquiry into the Future for Lifelong Learning* and the *Education for All Global Monitoring Report 2010: Reaching the Marginalized*. While the UK *Inquiry* is more insular, raising the learning concerns of a nation, the *Global Monitoring Report* speaks more broadly to contextual millstones impeding the global progress of education for all in both developed and emerging nations. Both studies provide insights and impetus for thinking about what lifelong learning ought to encompass as we move forward in times of social, cultural, economic, and political flux.

The UK Inquiry into the Future for Lifelong Learning

Starting from the premise of expanding the parameters of lifelong and life-wide learning to focus more on social, cultural, and environmental contexts, the UK Inquiry into the Future for Lifelong Learning began its work in 2007. The commission for the independent inquiry intended to explore basic and vital questions focused on such core concerns as content and method in adult learning, the benefits of learning for various interest groups, what kinds of knowledge have worth, and supports and fiscal responsibility for learning. The inquiry started with a most ambitious goal: to conduct "the most wide ranging and potentially far reaching review of its kind since the Adult Education Committee, established to advise the Ministry of Reconstruction at the end of the First World War, secured an emphasis on the social purpose of adult education in developing a notion of responsible citizenship" (Inquiry into the Future for Lifelong Learning, 2008, p. 1). The inquiry aimed to make recommendations for a strategic framework for action, with the intention of raising the profile of adult learning and education in personal and social contexts. Achieving this goal would mean making the best use of policy and practice to ensure "a future characterized by economic prosperity, social justice, social cohesion and personal wellbeing, and environmental sustainability in the United Kingdom" (p. 1). The terms of reference for the inquiry suggested a future for lifelong learning that would focus on its instrumental, social, and cultural complexities. The inquiry would speak to the intricate nature of holistic lifelong learning by focusing on (1) technological change; (2) prosperity, employment, and work; (3) environmental sustainability; (4) demography and social structure; (5) well-being and happiness; (6) migration and communities; (7) poverty reduction; (8) citizenship and belonging; (9) crime and social exclusion; and (10) the roles of public, private, and voluntary sectors. The inquiry commissioners sought to work in the intersection of these themes. For example, the inquiry would consider workplace learning beyond the instrumentality of obtaining skill sets to develop "a structured sensitivity to skills policy" (p. 3) that accommodates learners by addressing their relational, geographical, sectoral, and occupational differences. Calling for "a radical, practical, and imaginative rethink of the best ways of enabling adults to learn" (p. 1), Tom Schuller, director of the inquiry, declared that the inquiry would have the opportunity to confront a key paradox evident in an international context: "All countries are aware of the challenges that our education systems face due to demographic, social, and economic change, but very few are really committed to lifelong learning to meet these challenges at a strategic level" (p. 1). Schuller added that such a commitment is necessary in times when learners need to be resilient, resourceful, and resolved in the face of the uncertainty and risk that mark their private and public lives.

Of course, the inquiry ultimately took place in the midst of the vast economic debacle that only served to reinforce the need for more complex forms of lifelong learning as critical action that would exceed the kind of learning that was in vogue during the heyday of neoliberalism. The vast economic debacle demonstrated the need to revitalize lifelong learning as holistic learning that attends to home, work, and community ecologies as well as matters of context, disposition, relationship, geography, health, and well-being. This revitalization requires governments to rethink what they have largely relinquished under neoliberalism: public responsibility for lifelong learning.

The *Inquiry into the Future for Lifelong Learning* report was released in 2009. Alan Tuckett (2009), chief executive of the National Institute of Adult

Continuing Education (NIACE), which independently sponsored it, recounts how the inquiry conducted its work while the United Kingdom moved from a period of economic prosperity to a period of economic uncertainty marked by "the sharpest recession we have seen for 30 years" (p. xiii). Since the direction that lifelong learning takes in nations seems to change with the economic weather in neoliberal times, the inquiry found itself grappling with new questions. Tuckett relates that these strategic questions focused on (1) the social and economic aspects of lifelong learning, (2) concerns regarding public and private investment in education and training and, correspondingly, (3) the distribution of resources. As Tom Schuller and David Watson (2009), who co-authored the main report, indicate, these questions were tied to gauging the value that policy-makers and the public placed on lifelong learning as a practice with social, cultural, and economic import. How we answer these questions has implications for the kinds of policy-making and practices that can take lifelong learning into the future, hopefully as quality learning linked to quality living and quality work.

As it explored the meaning, dimensions, and value of lifelong learning in the United Kingdom, the inquiry was guided by a broad vision that focused on individual, social, cultural, and economic contexts: "Our vision is of a society in which learning plays its full role in personal growth and emancipation, prosperity, solidarity and global responsibility. We believe that learning is intimately connected with the achievement of freedom of choice, control over individual and group destinies, health and wellbeing, dignity, cultural identity and democratic tolerance. As a consequence, we begin from the premise that the right to learn throughout life is a human right" (p. 8). This encompassing vision suggests that lifelong learning could be a refuge for all learners, providing a way out of circumstances that place limits on life and its various aspects, including work and living in community. It aligns with Schuller and Watson's (2009) assertion that "in some measure, educational venues are the main surviving public spaces where people from different backgrounds come together as active participants in a common venture" (p. 13).

To enhance this participation and its functionality, the inquiry supported creating a framework for a citizens' curriculum. Such a framework could advance education for responsible citizenship as learners build knowledge and skills to mediate a contemporary world where flexibility, mobility, and perceived or present dangers to security and even existence are normalized. Schuller and Watson relate that the suggested framework would encompass learning opportunities so learners can build capacities in the digital, health, financial, civic, and employability dimensions of their lives. Developing these capacities would help individuals to gain control as they engage in endogenous development through learning that attends to local and national needs, labour-market changes, and human diversity. Ultimately, it would also help individuals not only to be savvy in instrumental or everyday functional terms, but it would also provide a basis, and hopefully the level of understanding and comfort necessary, to take learning further in possibly transformative ways that could enhance human integrity and security. Of course, as Schuller and Watson assert, lifelong learning needs to be integrated with concerns for the whole of life if individuals are to reach this plateau. Recognizing this, just as Dr. Martin Luther King, Jr. did in the 1960s, they reiterate a key critical notion: encompassing lifelong learning embodied and embedded in social democratic principles can be a source of opportunity and possibility. They reflect, "We know that learning alone cannot bring about these personal and social goods. They depend also on social justice and the absence of poverty, principles in both personal and social life, and security. However, we see a further role for learning in supporting such aspects of a modern, inclusive, self-critical and harmonious society. We believe in the possibilities of learning *through* life, in both senses of the word" (p. 9).

If lifelong learning is to be a source of opportunity and possibility, as Schuller and Watson hope, then we need to grapple with a perennial and unresolved question: What is *lifelong learning?* Indeed, we have to come to terms with the term. As Schuller and Watson (2009) relate, "Any definition of lifelong learning is problematic" (p. 9). There are questions regarding which learners belong and which learners are prioritized across the spectrum of lifelong learners. There are also questions concerning which institutional and social contexts engender valuable lifelong learning and fairness in learning, work, and society. Furthermore, there is this fundamental question: How might lifelong-learning policy-makers and practitioners enable lifelong learning as critical action focused on equity, freedom, and justice for all learners? In the end, as Schuller and Watson remark, the goal of lifelong learning should be to help people to be agents who take charge of their lives. This is all the more important now that the vast economic debacle appears to have gravely wounded, if not shattered, the promise of neoliberalism tied to individual betterment. Since 2007, individuals have been left questioning and wanting as the promise of individual prosperity and control gave way to feelings of helplessness and hopelessness as money and jobs evaporated. There is a substantial role for lifelong learning as critical action to play in countering this nihilism.

Education for All Global Monitoring Report 2010: Reaching the Marginalized

While a developed nation such as the United Kingdom has the luxury of working toward a broader construction of lifelong and lifewide learning, many emerging nations around the world still struggle to have even basic education for their citizens. Lack of education is a key factor in overall marginalization, which is a perennial millstone to human development and is included as one of its core indicators (UNESCO, 2010). Furthermore, "marginalization in education is the product of a toxic cocktail of inherited disadvantage, deeply ingrained social processes, unfair economic arrangements and bad policies" (UNESCO, 2010, p. 10). It is also the product of the social and political apathy of so many educated global citizens who assume that getting an education is automatic. These privileged citizens tend to forget or ignore that education is a human right often denied to marginalized citizens. Moreover, most governments in developed nations, through their political unresponsiveness, institutionalize the plight of the marginalized globally "by failing to address extreme and persistent educational disadvantages that ... are rooted in the deeply engrained social, economic and political processes, and unequal power relationships" (p. 8). The *Education for All Global Monitoring Report 2010: Reaching the Marginalized* profoundly reminds us of this systemic exclusion (UNESCO, 2010). As Irina Bokova (2010), director general of UNESCO, declares, the report amounts to a call for collaborative action to craft inclusionary, sustainable systems that advance universal primary education and increase enrolments in secondary and tertiary education, with an emphasis on gender equality on a global scale. Speaking to the particular vulnerability of education in times of financial and economic turmoil, Bokova reminds us that education is a productive site at the heart of human development:

> Education is at the front line. Not only do schools teach literacy and lay the groundwork for productive lives, they also play a crucial role in promoting tolerance, peace and understanding between peoples, and in fighting discrimination of all kinds. Schools are the place where indigenous groups can learn to read and write in their mother tongue, where cultural diversity can thrive, and where children can try to escape the hardships of conflict and displacement. (p. i)

Bokova's declaration of what schools can do goes to the holistic heart of what lifelong learning as critical action aims to achieve.

Like the UK *Inquiry into the Future for Lifelong Learning* report, the *Education For All Global Monitoring Report 2010* (EFA-GMR 2010) has been released in troubled times, when the world is still reeling from a global financial and economic crisis that continues to have a deep impact on human development, including education. As a consequence of the vast economic debacle, there is slower economic growth, resulting in a cumulative negative effect on budgets in emerging nations. This predicament exacerbates the worldwide tragedies of hunger and poverty, which, in turn, exacerbates the risk of educational exclusion at the primary level and beyond. The EFA-GMR 2010 team suggests what could be the disastrous outcome of this situation: "Ultimately, the world economy will recover from the recession, but the crisis could create a lost generation of children in the world's poorest countries whose life chances will have been irreparably damaged by a failure to protect their right to education" (p. 3). Most regrettably, as the EFA-GMR 2010 team critiques, children become hostages to the global economic misfortune: "Children living in the urban slums and the rural villages of the world's poorest countries played no part in the reckless banking practices and regulatory failures that caused the economic crisis. Yet they stand to suffer for the gambling that took place on Wall Street and other financial centres by losing their chance for an education that could lift them out of poverty" (UNESCO, 2010, p. 19).

Creating a lost generation of children would have dire consequences for these already severely disadvantaged nations. For their citizens, relentless marginality in a global context would likely mean a continuation of the cycle of poverty; poor health and well-being; unemployment; reduced citizenship through nonparticipation in political processes that affect daily life, learning, and work; and isolation from the global economy, where having knowledge and skills is requisite to any mainstream measure of success. The ultimate severity of this scenario demands that universal primary education be prioritized. While the EFA-GMR 2010 team estimates that this bedrock education would have a global price tag of $16 billion US dollars over the next five years, they put the total cost in perspective when they note that it represents a mere 2 percent of the amount mobilized to salvage just four major US and UK banks during the global financial and economic crisis.

If universal primary education is not assured, then the EFA-GMR 2010 team estimates that 56 million children will be excluded from participation in schooling by 2015. Of course, the problem with achieving universal primary education is more than a matter of access and ensuring enrolment. Retention is a major issue, as the following example indicates: "Millions of children enter primary school only to drop out before completing a full primary cycle. Some 28 million pupils in sub-Saharan Africa drop out each year. In South and West Asia, 13% of children entering school drop out in the first grade" (UNESCO, 2010, p. 6). In addition to tackling the retention issue, the EFA-GMR 2010 team emphasizes that good quality primary schoolteachers are needed, and they must be more equitably deployed to the most disadvantaged schools and poorest regions of emerging nations. How education is delivered is also a key concern. For example, about 221 million children experience a language of instruction in school that differs from the language they speak at home, impeding their progress in formal schooling and their ability to be lifelong learners. They need bilingual education that respects their cultural integrity and readies them to live and function in globalized contexts. Beyond these concerns, there are also groups of marginalized children victimized by other life circumstances. For example, children who live with HIV/AIDS or who have lives and family situations that have been severely altered by the disease require targeted interventions to protect their right to education as they cope with social discrimination or traumas such as being orphaned or dealing with sick parents. These examples make it clear that an array of larger social, economic, cultural, and other complexities can get in the way of universal education. Addressing educational poverty on such a diverse and immense scale demands "sustained political commitment to social justice, equal opportunity and basic rights" (UNESCO, 2010, p. 11). This commitment lies at the heart of meaningful and functional lifelong learning as critical action that ensures education for all.

If universal primary education is not prioritized, and if there is no substantial effort to improve retention rates in the early years of education in emerging nations, then other sectors of education will be affected. For example, concerns with the future of adult and higher education in these countries would be moot if there is no educational foundation on which to build these sectors. Perhaps most unfortunately in relation to nation building, a lack of primary education also diminishes possibilities for education for responsible citizenship. Even now, so much of education that takes place globally is reduced to literacy education. There are 759 million youth and adults who lack literacy skills; women comprise two-thirds of this population (UNESCO, 2010). This educational poverty is exacerbated by class, ethnic, and gender inequalities.

For example, the EFA-GMR 2010 report indicates that 97 percent of poor Hausa-speaking girls in Nigeria have less than two years of education. Deprivation and Marginalization in Education data, which were developed for the report to highlight the level of exclusion from education in 80 nations, reveals that at least 30 percent of youth aged 17 to 22 in twenty-two nations are entering adulthood with less than four years of schooling, which is the minimum education needed for basic literacy. Since many youth lack even the basic learning skills needed for re-entry educational efforts to help them become functionally employable, they are often excluded from second-chance education. Of course, such education may itself be problematic for youth, as indicated by the case of vocational education in India: "Vocational programmes ... reach only about 3% of rural youth and there is little evidence that they enhance employment prospects. The image of technical and vocational provision as a form of second-class education that provides limited benefits for employment remains largely intact" (UNESCO, 2010, p. 7). Key problems here include a lack of adequate investment and poor quality programming that is not in tune with job markets.

Where does this leave education for all? The EFA-GMR 2010 team stresses that in order to acknowledge that education is a right, so access and accommodation become realities for all vulnerable populations, developed nations have to minimize the risks associated with the global financial and economic crisis and the rise in global food prices. Indeed, the economic crisis and high food prices have certainly taken their toll: There are now over one billion malnourished people trying to subsist in the world (UNESCO, 2010). As the EFA-GMR 2010 team relates, "Hunger undermines cognitive development, causing irreversible losses in opportunities for learning" (p. 24). Such educational poverty is compounded by other problems: "With poverty rising, unemployment growing and remittances [or financial aid from developed nations] diminishing, many poor and vulnerable households are having to cut back on education spending or withdraw their children from school" (p. 1). Thus there is an urgent contemporary need for investment in social protection to alleviate growing risks to education and the futures of children and youth. The EFA-GMR 2010 team concludes, "Social protection, through cash transfers [to safeguard education budgets], nutrition programmes and targeted support in other areas, has been shown in many countries to build the resilience of vulnerable households and strengthen their ability to cope with economic shocks without resorting to damaging measures such as withdrawing children from school" (p. 37). These inequalities are exacerbated in the intersections of relationships of power. For example, the EFA-GMR 2010 team underscores the impact of the intersection of poverty and race, even in a developed nation such as the United States where "African-Americans are twice as likely to be out of school as White Americans, and young adults from poor households are three times as likely to be out of school as those from wealthy homes" (p. 10). In light of the many faces of educational poverty, the EFA-GMR 2010 team sets a clear challenge for the international community, if education for all is to be realized: to "address inequalities, stigmatization and discrimination linked to wealth, gender, ethnicity, language, location and disability" (p. 2). To achieve education for all, we also need to address fallout from such impediments as material poverty, armed conflict, racial conflict, ethnic cleansing, castigation of cultural and sexual differences, and geographical remoteness. To increase access and improve affordability and accommodation for marginalized communities across nations, the EFA-GMR 2010 team challenges national governments to make equity and social expenditures a focus of public expenditures. It also challenges developed nations to provide concessional financing to emerging nations to further human development and the creation of inclusive educational systems. This idea reflects a key tenet of lifelong learning as critical action: to improve education and participation by developing policy and designing strategic interventions that are framed and enabled within a larger social democratic plan that focuses on equity (emphasizing access, accommodation, and retention), justice (passing laws and legislation to protect marginalized populations), and the provision and redistribution of public finance (prioritizing social protection programs) (UNESCO, 2010).

Concluding Perspective: Déjà Vu

Both the *Inquiry into the Future for Lifelong Learning* report and the *Education for All Global Monitoring Report 2010: Reaching the Marginalized* are contemporary reminders that we need holistic and encompassing lifelong learning as critical action to meet the diverse instrumental, social, and cultural needs of lifelong learners and, perhaps most especially, marginalized learners. I believe a turn to critically progressive education, informed by the history of social education, is one alternative to neoliberalized lifelong learning that can help us to meet this need (Grace, 2012). Here learning, constructed as pre-emptive and proactive, is concerned with social cohesion, cultural inclusion, and economic justice as learners secure personal and communal futures. As actors in the learning process, learners achieve their goals as they gain new skills and attitudes as problem solvers and change agents. When the focus turns to the individual, it is as a contributor to the collective and the common good. This requires learners to be creative thinkers as well as producers. Moreover, learners have to be reflexive, keeping thinking and doing in dynamic equilibrium as they advocate for self and others as whole learners. In the end, competency is as much about attitude as it is about skill.

The *UK Inquiry* and the *EFA Global Monitoring Report* reflect perspectives and themes contained in *Learning: The Treasure Within*, the 1996 report of the International Commission on Education for the Twenty-first Century. The fact that much the same complexity of conditions that were identified in this report continue to exacerbate educational poverty begs the question: Why haven't we achieved lifelong learning for all? The answer that commission chair Jacques Delors provided at the time is similar to the answers found in the two recent reports. Locating education as "the necessary Utopia" in times that witnessed boom-and-bust crises and increased risk taking (Delors, 1996, p. 13), Delors focused on the paradox that governments were devaluing education. He related that they made socio-political choices based on competing demands or the availability of resources. These choices did not adequately support educational sectors. He concluded, "Educational policies are being sharply criticized or pushed—for economic and financial reasons—down to the bottom of the agenda" (p. 13).

In the report, Delors also highlighted what is now a perennial concern: the need to grapple with the complexities of globalization in the quest to solve social and economic problems. In his version of lifelong learning as critical action, he emphasized that educational policy-makers needed to link education to sustaining human development, addressing challenges associated with economic and technological progress, increasing mutual understanding among people across differences, and renewing participatory democracy. Delors wanted educational, social, and economic policy-makers to join forces in an effort to resolve the tension between competition, which drove learning for the economy, and equality of opportunity, which drove lifelong learning as a more holistic, flexible, diverse, and accessible venture abetting self-development, environmental awareness, and social cohesion. From this lifewide perspective locating education within larger social democratic and economic concerns, Delors construed education broadly so it would be a passport and a foundation for future learning. In doing so, he wanted to (re)present "the concept of lifelong education so as to reconcile three forces: competition, which provides incentives; co-operation, which gives strength; and solidarity, which unites" (p. 18).

Delors felt that educational policy-makers should attend to the needs of youth in order to make up for any failures of schooling and to reduce the feelings of apathy, exclusion, and hopelessness that were common among youth. This focus remains important since youth, a key focus in this book, are the lifelong learners of today and tomorrow. Like adult learners, they need to mediate a contemporary learning culture that has repositioned the learner. Unfortunately, adult education has failed to acknowledge the blurring divide between being a youth and being an adult (Grace, 2007; Grace & Wells, 2007a). It does not focus adequately on education for young adults who are excluded and thus victimized in so many learning, work, and life spaces. This belies the purpose of education, stated by Delors and the commission when they located education and training activities among "prime movers of development" (p. 72) that should be concerned with human welfare, instability, the precarious nature of work, innovation, both technical and social skill building, problem solving, and human agency in the face of change. From this perspective, Delors and the commission located learning as lifelong and lifewide. In doing so, they positioned learning broadly, associating it with working in economic and cultural contexts, participating as an active citizen, and performing other life roles. In this spacious sense, learning is something personal and creative that is intended to address citizens' needs and desires in keeping with "the changing time-frames and rhythms of individual existence" (p. 100). This viewpoint reflects perspectives in both the *Inquiry into the Future for Lifelong Learning* and the *EFA Global Monitoring Report 2010*. It captures the encompassing sense of learning that drives lifelong learning as critical action. This sense is embedded in the closing poetic reflection:

Individualism
Let it include a focus on listening to individuals
Make it more than just telling or blaming them
Let citizens be, become, and belong
Let them feel they can act
And let them act to make a better life
A holistic life that juxtaposes learning, working, and living

Competition
Downplay it with juxtapositions
So the social and cultural are placed in the mix
And not forgotten in the instrumental fray
There is a need for unraveling complexities and assumptions
To ensure that lifelong learning is also lifewide
Work cannot be insulated from the lives it helps define

Privatization
Explore its social and economic limits for citizens as learners and workers
Remember history and why a welfare state emerged
Keep democracy a beating heart and protect its publics
Don't reduce learning to just a cyclical venture for the already educated
Emphasize ethics and justice so lifelong learning can be for all
For every citizen so they can benefit in all life spaces

Globalization
Think about the prosperity of global citizens
And advance the global economy
But not at the expense of quality life and work and sustainable communities
Think about the health and well-being of global citizens
Think about abused women, sexual and gender minorities, and everyone
    who is unsafe
Think about the ways in which lifelong learning is still an enigma to so many

Today lifelong learning is caught in a vortex of cultural change forces
The reality is it is not a panacea
Think about what this means for citizens everywhere
Think about the ways that parameters and expectations confine lifelong
    learning
Think about new ways to have lifelong learning make a road to hope and
    healing
Do something to lift us out of the vortex
Keep working toward lifelong learning for all

References

Adult Learning Knowledge Centre (ALKC). (2007). *Report on the community connections circle.* Moncton, NB: Author.

Aitchison, J. (2004). Lifelong learning in South Africa: Dreams and delusions. *International Journal of Lifelong Education, 23*(6), 517–544.

Albrow, M. (1996). *The global age: State and society beyond modernity.* Cambridge, UK: Polity Press.

Alexander, B. K. (2008). Queer(y)ing the post colonial through the West(ern). In N. K. Denzin, Y. S. Lincoln, & L. T. Smith (Eds.), *The handbook of critical and indigenous methodologies* (pp. 101–133). Thousand Oaks, CA: Sage.

Allman, P. (1999). *Revolutionary social transformation: Democratic hopes, political possibilities and critical education.* Westport, CT: Bergin & Garvey.

Amnesty International (AI). (2001). *Crimes of hate, conspiracy of silence: Torture and ill-treatment based on sexual identity.* Retrieved August 14, 2001, from http://web.amnesty.org/ai.nsf/Index/ACT400162001?OpenDocument&of=TH EMES\SEXUAL+ORIENTATION

Amnesty International (AI). (2005, September). *USA: Police mistreatment and abuse widespread in lesbian, gay, bisexual and transgender communities nationwide.* Retrieved January 15, 2008, from http://web.amnesty.org/library/Index/ ENGAMR511502005?open&of=ENG-347

Amnesty International (AI). (2006). *Poland and Latvia: Lesbian, gay, bisexual, and transgender rights in Poland and Latvia.* Retrieved May 13, 2013, from http:// www.amnesty.org/library/info/EUR01/019/2006

Apple, M. W. (1988). *Teachers and texts: A political economy of class and gender relations in education.* New York: Routledge.

Apple, M. (1993). *Official knowledge: Democratic education in a conservative age.* New York: Routledge.

Aronowitz, S. (2000). *The knowledge factory: Dismantling the corporate university and creating true higher learning.* Boston: Beacon Press.

Aronowitz, S. (2005a, June). *Remarks for a TV Ontario television debate 6/20/05.* Paper version of remarks made at the Future of Lifelong Learning and Work Conference, Ontario Institute for Studies in Education of the University of Toronto (OISE/UT), Toronto, ON.

Aronowitz, S. (2005b, June). *Social justice in lifelong learning and work.* Keynote presentation made at the Future of Lifelong Learning and Work Conference, OISE/UT, Toronto, ON.

Aronowitz, S., & DiFazio, W. (1994). *The jobless future: Sci-tech and the dogma of work.* Minneapolis, MN: University of Minnesota Press.

Aspin, D. N., & Chapman, J. D. (2000). Lifelong learning: Concepts and conceptions. *International Journal of Lifelong Education, 19*(1), 2–19.

Aspin, D. N., & Chapman, J. D. (2001a). Lifelong learning: Concepts, theories and values. In L. West, N. Miller, D. O'Reilly, & R. Allen (Eds.), *Proceedings of the 31st Annual Conference of SCUTREA: The Standing Conference on University Teaching and Research in the Education of Adults* (pp. 38–41). Nottingham, UK: Pilgrim College, University of Nottingham.

Aspin, D. N., & Chapman, J. D. (2001b). Toward a philosophy of lifelong learning. In D. Aspin, J. Chapman, M. Hatton, & Y. Sawano (Eds.), *International handbook of lifelong learning: Part 1* (pp. 3–33). Dordecht, Netherlands: Kluwer Academic Publishers BV.

Aspin, D., Collard, J., & Chapman, J. (2000). Lifelong learning in Australia. In J. Field & M. Leicester (Eds.), *Lifelong learning: Education across the lifespan* (pp. 171–190). London: RoutledgeFalmer.

August, R. (2009). *Paved with good intentions: The failure of passive disability policy in Canada.* Ottawa, ON: Caledonian Institute of Social Policy. Retrieved November 4, 2012, from http://digitalcommons.ilr.cornell.edu/gladnetcollect/474/

Bagnall, R. (2001). Locating lifelong learning and education in contemporary currents of thought and culture. In D. Aspin, J. Chapman, M. Hatton, & Y. Sawano (Eds.), *International handbook of lifelong learning: Part 1* (pp. 35–52). Dordecht, Netherlands: Kluwer Academic Publishers BV.

Bagnall, R. (2006). Lifelong learning and the limits of tolerance. *International Journal of Lifelong Education, 25*(3), 257–269.

Baird, D. (2012, January/February). Apocalypse soon. *The Walrus, 9*(1), 26–33.

Barlett, D. L., & Steele, J. B. (2009, October). Good billions after bad. *Vanity Fair, 590*, 204–209 & 261–263.

Barros, R. (2012). From lifelong education to lifelong learning: Discussion of some effects of today's neoliberal policies. *European Journal for Research on the Education and Learning of Adults, 3*(2), 119–134.

Battiste, M. (2002). *Indigenous knowledge and pedagogy in First Nations education: A literature review with recommendations.* Prepared for the National Working Group on Education and the Minister of Indian Affairs, Indian and Northern Affairs Canada (INAC), Ottawa, ON.

Bauman, Z. (1996). From pilgrim to tourist—or a short history of identity. In S. Hall & P. du Gay (Eds.), *Questions of cultural identity* (pp. 18–36). London: Sage Publications.

Bauman, Z. (2001). *The individualized society.* Cambridge, UK: Polity Press.

Bauman, Z. (2005). *Liquid life.* Cambridge, UK: Polity Press.

BBC News. (2008). *Anglican Church around the world.* Retrieved February 27, 2013, from http://news.bbc.co.uk/2/hi/3226753.stm

Beck, U. (1992). *Risk society.* Translated by M. Ritter. London: Sage Publications.

Beddie, F. (2004). Learning communities: A catalyst for collective responsibility. In P. A. Danaher, C. Macpherson, F. Nouwens, & D. Orr (Eds.), *Proceedings of the 3rd International Lifelong Learning Conference, Central Queensland University* (pp. 1–7). Rockhampton, Australia: Central Queensland University Press.

Bell, D. (1960). *The end of ideology.* Glencoe, IL: The Free Press.

Bell, D. (1967). The post-industrial society: A speculative view. In E. Hutchings & E. Hutchings (Eds.), *Scientific progress and human values* (pp. 154–170). New York: American Elsevier Publishing Company.

Bell, D. (1976). *The coming of post-industrial society: A venture in social forecasting.* New York: Basic Books.

Blackmore, J. (2007, April 18). *Unprotected participation in lifelong learning and the politics of hope: A feminist reality check of discourses around flexibility, seamlessness, and learner earners.* Paper presented to the Departments of Educational Policy Studies, Political Science, and Sociology, and the Work and Learning Network, University of Alberta, Edmonton, AB.

Blewitt, J. (2011). Lifelong learning and environmental sustainability. In S. Jackson (Ed.), *Lifelong learning and social justice: Communities, work and identities in a globalised world* (pp. 18–41). Leicester, UK: National Institute of Adult Continuing Education.

Bochynek, B. (2008, July). Towards CONFINTEA VI. *UIL Nexus, 3*(2), 2.

Bochynek, B. (2010, January). CONFINTEA VI adopts the Belém framework for action. *UIL Nexus, 5*(1), 1–4.

Bokova, I. (2010). Foreword. In UNESCO, *EFA global monitoring report 2010: Reaching the marginalized* (p. i). Paris: Author.

Boshier, R. (2000). Running to win: The contest between lifelong learning and education in Canada. *New Zealand Journal of Adult Learning, 28*(2), 6–28.

Boshier, R. (2001). Lifelong learning as bungy jumping: In New Zealand what goes down doesn't always come up. *International Journal of Lifelong Education, 20*(5), 361–377.

Brennan, B. (1987). Conversation with John Ohliger. *Australian Journal of Adult Education, 27*(3), 52–56 & 65.

British Ministry of Reconstruction, Adult Education Committee. (1919). *Final report.* (Chaired by Arthur L. Smith and commonly known as "The 1919 Report.") Cmnd 321 (1919). London: HMSO.

Burke, G., Long, M., & Wurzburg, G. (2000). *Reducing the risk of under-investment in adults.* Background paper for the International Conference on Lifelong Learning as an Affordable Investment, Château Laurier, Ottawa, ON, Canada. Retrieved June 18, 2001, from http://www.canada-ocde.gc.ca/index.cfm

Burke, P. J., & Jackson, S. (2007). *Reconceptualising lifelong learning: Feminist interventions.* New York: Routledge.

Burroway, J. (2013, February 19). Uganda's anti-homosexuality bill rises to top of Parliament's "business to follow." *Box Turtle Bulletin.* Retrieved February 27, 2013, from http://www.boxturtlebulletin.com/2013/02/19/53855

Canadian Council on Learning (CCL). (2008). *The 2008 composite learning index: Measuring Canada's progress in lifelong learning.* Ottawa, ON: Author.

Canadian Council on Learning (CCL). (2009). *The state of Aboriginal learning in Canada: A holistic approach to measuring success.* Ottawa: Author.

Canadian Council on Social Development (CCSD). (1999). *Thinking ahead: Trends affecting public education in the future.* Written by Susan Carter for the CCSD. Retrieved February 3, 2004, from http://www.ccsd.ca/pubs/gordon/part2.htm

Canadian Policy Research Networks (CPRN). (2008, Spring). CPRN to conduct youth dialogue for Newfoundland and Labrador. *CPRN Network News, 39*, 1–2.

Candy, P. C. (2000). Learning and earning: Graduate skills for an uncertain future. In K. Appleton, C. Macpherson, & D. Orr (Eds.), *Proceedings of the Inaugural International Lifelong Learning Conference, Central Queensland University* (pp. 7–19). Rockhampton, Australia: Central Queensland University Press.

Carr, E. H. (1961). *What is history?* New York: Vintage Books.

Catts, R. (2004, June 13). *Lifelong learning and higher education: Reflections and prospects.* Keynote paper presented at the 3rd International Lifelong Learning Conference, Yeppoon, Central Queensland, Australia.

Ceballos, R. M. (2006). Adult education for community empowerment: Toward the possibility of another world. In S. B. Merriam, B. C. Courtenay, & R. M. Cervero (Eds.), *Global issues and adult education: Perspectives from Latin America, Southern Africa, and the United States* (pp. 319–331). San Francisco: Jossey-Bass.

Central Queensland University (CQU). (2000). *Lifelong learning conference: Main announcement & registration* (Brochure). Rockhampton, Queensland, Australia: Central Queensland University Library.

Chapman, J., Gaff, J., Toomey, R., & Aspin, D. (2005). Policy on lifelong learning in Australia. *International Journal of Lifelong Education, 24*(2), 99–122.

Charter of the United Nations. (1945). Retrieved December 3, 2008, from http://www.un.org/en/documents/charter/index.shtml

Chasin, A. (2000). *Selling out: The gay and lesbian movement goes to market.* New York: Palgrave.

Chief Public Health Officer. (2012). *The Chief Public Health Officer's report on the state of public health in Canada 2012: Influencing health—the importance of sex and gender.* Ottawa: Office of the Chief Public Health Officer. Available online at http://www.phac-aspc.gc.ca/cphorsphc-respcacsp/2012/index-eng.php

Chothia, F. (2011, December 7). *Gay rights: Africa, the new frontier.* Retrieved December 9, 2011, from http://www.bbc.co.uk/news/world-africa-16068010

CNN. (2001). Falwell apologizes to gays, feminists, and lesbians. CNN.com. Retrieved September 16, 2001, from http://www.cnn.com/2001/US/09/14/Falwell.apology/index.html

Coffield, F. (2002). Breaking the consensus: Lifelong learning as a social control. In R. Edwards, N. Miller, N. Small, & A. Tait (Eds.), *Supporting lifelong learning, volume 3: Making policy work* (pp. 174–200). New York: RoutledgeFalmer.

Collins, M. (1998). *Critical crosscurrents in education.* Malabar, FL: Krieger.

CONFINTEA V. (2003a). *Call for action.* Retrieved September 26, 2003, from http://www.unesco.org/education/uie/pdf/Callforaction.pdf

CONFINTEA V. (2003b). *Recommitting to adult education and learning: A midterm evaluation.* Retrieved September 26, 2003, from http://www.unesco.org/education/uie/pdf/recommitting.pdf

CONFINTEA VI. (2008). *Recommitting to lifelong learning: Proposals from Latin America and the Caribbean.* Final document of the Regional Literacy and CONFINTEA VI Preparatory Conference of Latin America and the Caribbean: From literacy to lifelong learning: Towards the challenges of the 21st century, Mexico City, Mexico, September 10–13, 2008.

CONFINTEA VI. (2009, December 4). *Bélem framework for action: Harnessing the power and potential of adult learning and education for a viable future.* Retrieved April 18, 2010, from http://www.unesco.org/uil/en/UILPDF/nesico/confintea-close/ BelemFramework_Final.pdf

Cotton, W. E. (1968). *On behalf of adult education: A historical examination of the supporting literature.* Boston: Center for the Study of Liberal Education for Adults.

Council of Ministers of Education, Canada (CMEC). (1998). *Report on education in Canada.* Ottawa, ON: Authors. Retrieved August 15, 2003, from http://www.cmec.ca/reports/rec98/texteng.htm

Council of Ministers of Education, Canada (CMEC). (1999). *Education indicators in Canada: Report of the Pan-Canadian Education Indicators Program 1999.* Ottawa, ON: Author.

Council of Ministers of Education, Canada (CMEC). (2012). *Adult learning and education: Canada progress report for the UNESCO Global Report on Adult Learning and Education (GRALE) and the end of the United Nations Literacy Decade.* Toronto: Author.

Coy, P. (2008, October 11). The sky falls on Wall Street. *BusinessWeek.* Retrieved October 29, 2008, from http://www.businessweek.com/bwdaily/dnflash/content/oct2008/db20081010_744839.htm

Cruikshank, J. (2001). Lifelong learning in the new economy: A great leap backwards. In unedited *Proceedings of the 20th Annual Conference of the Canadian Association for the Study of Adult Education* (pp. 49–54). Laval, QC: Laval University.

Cruikshank, J. (2002). Lifelong learning or re-training for life: Scapegoating the worker. In S. Mojab & W. McQueen (Eds.), *Proceedings of the 21st Annual Conference of the Canadian Association for the Study of Adult Education* (pp. 54–58). Toronto: Ontario Institute for Studies in Education, University of Toronto.

Cruikshank, J. (2003a). The changing face of lifelong learning. In D. Flowers, M. Lee, A. Jalipa, E. Lopez, A. Schelstrate, and V. Sheared (Eds.), *Proceedings of the 44th Annual Adult Education Research Conference* (pp. 73–78). San Francisco: San Francisco State University.

Cruikshank, J. (2003b). Lifelong learning and the changing nature of work. In P. Cranton (Ed.), *Proceedings of the 22nd Annual Conference of the Canadian Association for the Study of Adult Education* (pp. 57–62). Halifax, NS: Dalhousie University.

Cunningham, P. M. (1988). The adult educator and social responsibility. In R. G. Brockett (Ed.), *Ethical issues in adult education* (pp. 133–145). New York: Teachers College Press.

Cunningham, P. M. (1991, September). What's the role of adult educators? *Adult Learning, 3*(1), 15–16 & 27.

Deacon, B., Hulse, M., & Stubbs, P. (1997). *Global social policy: International organisations and the future of welfare.* London: Sage.

Delors, J. (1996). *Learning: The treasure within.* Paris: UNESCO Publishing.

D'Emilio, J. (1992). *Making trouble: Essays on gay history, politics, and the university.* New York: Routledge.

Diggins, J. (1988). *The proud decades.* New York: W. W. Norton & Company.

Dixon, R. (2011, May 12). *Uganda lawmakers remove death penalty clause from anti-gay bill.* Retrieved June 28, 2011, from http://articles.latimes.com/2011/may/12/world/la-fg-uganda-gays-20110512

Doughney, L. (2000). Lifelong learning: The implications for the structure of learning communities. In K. Appleton, C. Macpherson, & D. Orr (Eds.), *Proceedings of the Inaugural International Lifelong Learning Conference, Central Queensland University* (pp. 158–163). Rockhampton, Australia: Central Queensland University Press.

Edwards, R. (2000a). Lifelong learning, lifelong learning, lifelong learning: A recurrent education? In J. Field & M. Leicester (Eds.), *Lifelong learning: Education across the lifespan* (pp. 3–11). London: RoutledgeFalmer.

Edwards, R. (2000b). Pedagogies of (dis)location. *The Journal of East London Studies, 4*(20), 22–37.

Edwards, R., Miller, N., Small, N., & Tait, A. (2002). Introduction: Making policy work in lifelong learning. In R. Edwards, N. Miller, N. Small, & A. Tait (Eds.), *Supporting lifelong learning, volume 3: Making policy work* (pp. 1–5). New York: RoutledgeFalmer.

Edwards, R., & Usher, R. (2006). A troubled space of possibilities. In P. Sutherland & J. Crowther (Eds.), *Lifelong learning: Concepts and contexts* (pp. 58–67). London: Routledge.

Engardio, P. (2008, October 12). IMF and G-7 say: No more Lehmans. *Business-Week.* Retrieved October 29, 2008, from http://www.businessweek.com/bw-daily/dnflash/content/oct2008/db20081012_029874.htm

Environics Institute. (2010). *Urban Aboriginal peoples study.* Toronto: Author.

European Convention on Human Rights and its Five Protocols. (1950, 1952, 1963, 1966). Available online at http://www.hri.org/docs/ECHR50.html

Fejes, A. (2008). What's the use of Foucault in research on lifelong learning and post-compulsory education? A review of four academic journals. *Studies in the Education of Adults, 40*(1), 7–23.

Fenwick, T. J. (2001). Navigating the "enterprise" discourses: Women's journeys in learning and work. In L. West, N. Miller, D. O'Reilly, & R. Allen (Eds.), *Proceedings of the 31st Annual Conference of SCUTREA: The Standing Conference on University Teaching and Research in the Education of Adults* (pp. 111–115). Nottingham, UK: Pilgrim College, University of Nottingham.

Fenwick, T. (2004). What happens to the girls? Gender, work and learning in Canada's "new economy." *Gender and Education, 16*(2), 169–185.

Field, J. (2000a). Learning in the Isles: Evolving policies for lifelong learning in the Republic of Ireland and the United Kingdom. In J. Field & M. Leicester (Eds.), *Lifelong learning: Education across the lifespan* (pp. 215–227). London: RoutledgeFalmer.

Field, J. (2000b). *Lifelong learning and the new educational order*. Stoke on Trent, UK: Trentham Books.

Field, J. (2006). *Lifelong learning and the new educational order*. 2nd ed. Stoke-on-Trent, UK: Trentham Books.

Field, J., & Leicester, M. (2000). Introduction: Lifelong learning or permanent schooling? In J. Field & M. Leicester (Eds.), *Lifelong learning: Education across the lifespan* (pp. xvi–xix). London: RoutledgeFalmer.

Fone, B. (2000). *Homophobia: A history*. New York: Metropolitan Books, Henry Holt and Company.

Ford, L., & Pomfret, E. (2009, December 4). Ugandan church leader brands anti-gay bill "genocide." *Guardian*. Retrieved February 11, 2010, from http://www.guardian.co.uk/katine/2009/dec/04/gideon-byamugisha-homosexuality-bill/print

Forrester, K. (2005, June). *Working lifelong learning, young people and competitive advantage: Notes from a European perspective*. Paper presented at the Future of Lifelong Learning and Work Conference, OISE/UT, Toronto, ON.

Foster, J. B., & Magdoff, F. (2009). *The great financial crisis: Causes and consequences*. New York: Monthly Review Press.

Foucault, M. (1982/1997). Technologies of the self. In P. Rabinow, (Ed.), *Michel Foucault—Ethics, subjectivity, and truth: Essential works of Foucault 1954–1984* (Vol. 1) (pp. 223–251). New York: The New Press.

Foucault, M. (1984/1997). The ethics of the concern of the self as a practice of freedom. In P. Rabinow, (Ed.), *Michel Foucault—Ethics, subjectivity, and truth: Essential works of Foucault 1954–1984* (Vol. 1) (pp. 281–301). New York: The New Press.

Fox, J. (2007, November 26). Denmark's difference. *Time* (Canadian Edition), 170(22), 48–49.

Francis, T., & Sasseen, J. (2008, October 12). Federal stakes in U.S. Banks: Details, please. *BusinessWeek*. Retrieved October 29, 2008, from http://www.business-week.com/bwdaily/dnflash/content/oct2008/db20081012_516469.htm

Freire, P. (2004). *Pedagogy of indignation*. Boulder, CO: Paradigm Publishers.

Frideres, J. S. (1997). Civic participation, awareness, knowledge and skills. In Canadian Heritage—Multiculturalism (Ed.), *Immigrants and civic participation: Contemporary policy and research issues* (pp. 33–48). Montreal, QC: Canadian Heritage—Multiculturalism.

Geoghegan, T. (2009, April). Infinite debt: How unlimited interest rates destroyed the economy. *Harper's Magazine*, 31–39.

Giroux, H. A. (1993). *Living dangerously: Multiculturalism and the politics of difference*. New York: Peter Lang.

Giroux, H. A. (1994). *Disturbing pleasures: Learning popular culture*. New York: Routledge.

Giroux, H. A. (2004). *The terror of neoliberalism*. Boulder, CO: Paradigm Publishers.

Gopinath, G. (2005). *Impossible desires: Queer diasporas and South Asian public cultures*. Durham, NC: Duke University Press.

Gouthro, P. A. (2001). Learning across culture, time and space: Canadian and Jamaican women's experiences in learning via distance. In L. West, N. Miller, D. O'Reilly, & R. Allen (Eds.), *Proceedings of the 31st Annual Conference of SCUTREA: The Standing Conference on University Teaching and Research in the Education of Adults* (pp. 133–136). Nottingham, UK: Pilgrim College, University of Nottingham.

Gouthro, P. A. (2009). Neoliberalism, lifelong learning, and the homeplace: Problematizing the boundaries of "public" and "private" to explore women's learning experiences. *Studies in Continuing Education, 31*(2), 157–172.

Government of Newfoundland and Labrador. (2003). *Beyond high school: The report of the follow-up survey of June 2001 high school graduates*. St. John's, NL: Office of the Queen's Printer.

Grace, A. P. (1996). Striking a critical pose: Andragogy–missing links, missing values. *International Journal of Lifelong Education, 15*(5), 382–392.

Grace, A. P. (1997a). *Identity quest: The emergence of North American adult education (1945–70)*. Unpublished doctoral dissertation, Dalhousie University, Halifax, Nova Scotia, Canada.

Grace, A. P. (1997b). Where critical postmodern theory meets practice: Working in the intersection of instrumental, social, and cultural education. *Studies in Continuing Education, 19*(1), 51–70.

Grace, A. P. (1998). Parameters, pedagogy, and possibilities in changing times. In S. M. Scott, B. Spencer, & A. Thomas (Eds.), *Learning for life: Canadian readings in adult education* (pp. 114–124). Toronto: Thompson Educational Publishing.

Grace, A. P. (1999). Building a knowledge base in U.S. academic adult education (1945–1970). *Studies in the Education of Adults, 31*(2), 220–236.

Grace, A. P. (2000a). Building an inclusive pedagogy of lifelong-learning community. In K. Appleton, C. Macpherson, & D. Orr (Eds.), *Proceedings of the Inaugural International Lifelong Learning Conference, Central Queensland University* (pp. 54–59). Rockhampton, Australia: Central Queensland University Press.

Grace, A. P. (2000b). Canadian and US adult learning (1945–1970) and the cultural politics and place of lifelong learning. *International Journal of Lifelong Education, 19*(2), 141–158.

Grace, A. P. (2001). Using queer cultural studies to transgress adult educational space. In V. Sheared & P. A. Sissel (Eds.), *Making space: Merging theory and practice in adult education* (pp. 257–270). Westport, CN: Bergin & Garvey.

Grace, A. P. (2002a). Intersecting instrumental, social, and cultural education to build and sustain inclusive lifelong-learning communities. In K. Appleton, C. Macpherson, & D. Orr (Eds.), *Proceedings of the 2nd International Lifelong Learning Conference, Central Queensland University* (pp. 181–187). Rockhampton, Australia: Central Queensland University Press.

Grace, A. P. (2002b). Lifelong learning: International perspectives on policy and practice. In S. Mojab & W. McQueen (Eds.), *Proceedings of the 21st Annual Conference of the Canadian Association for the Study of Adult Education* (pp. 128–133). Toronto: Ontario Institute for Studies in Education, University of Toronto.

Grace, A. P. (2004a). Lifelong learning as a chameleonic concept and versatile practice: Y2K perspectives and trends. *International Journal of Lifelong Education, 23*(4), 385–405.

Grace, A. P. (2004b). Mediating lifelong learning in Canada in inclusive contexts. In P. A. Danaher, C. Macpherson, F. Nouwens, & D. Orr (Eds.), *Proceedings of the 3rd International Lifelong Learning Conference, Central Queensland University* (pp. 138–143). Rockhampton, Australia: Central Queensland University Press.

Grace, A. P. (2005). Lifelong learning chic in the modern practice of adult education: Historical and contemporary perspectives. *Journal of Adult and Continuing Education, 11*(1), 62–79.

Grace, A. P. (2006a). Critical adult education: Engaging the social in theory and practice. In T. Fenwick, T. Nesbit, & B. Spencer (Eds.), *Contexts of adult edu-*

cation: Canadian perspectives (pp. 128–139). Toronto: Thompson Educational Publishing.

Grace, A. P. (2006b). Keynote address: Reflecting critically on lifelong learning in an era of neoliberal pragmatism—Instrumental, social, and cultural perspectives. In D. Orr, F. Nouwens, C. Macpherson, R. E. Harreveld, & P. A. Danaher (Eds.), *Proceedings of the 4th International Lifelong Learning Conference, Central Queensland University* (pp. 1–16). Rockhampton, Australia: Central Queensland University Press. Available online at http://lifelonglearning.cqu. edu.au/2006/papers-ft/keynote-grace.pdf

Grace, A. P. (2006c). Writing the queer self: Using autobiography to mediate inclusive teacher education in Canada. *Teaching and Teacher Education, 22*, 826–834.

Grace, A. P. (2007). Envisioning a critical social pedagogy of learning and work in a contemporary culture of cyclical lifelong learning. *Studies in Continuing Education, 29*(1), 85–103.

Grace, A. P. (2008). The charisma and deception of reparative therapies: When medical science beds religion. *Journal of Homosexuality, 55*(4), 545–580.

Grace, A. P. (2009a). Resilient sexual-minority youth as fugitive lifelong learners: Engaging in a strategic, asset-creating, community-based learning process to counter exclusion and trauma in formal schooling. In J. Field (Ed.), *Proceedings of the Lifelong Learning Revisited: What Next? Conference of the Scottish Centre for Research in Lifelong Learning, University of Stirling*, Stirling, UK.

Grace, A. P. (2009b). A view of Canadian lifelong-learning policy culture through a critical lens. In J. Field, J. Gallacher, & R. Ingram (Eds.), *Researching transitions in lifelong learning* (pp. 28–39). London: Routledge.

Grace, A. P. (2012). The emergence of North American adult education (1947–1970): With a reflection on creating critically progressive education. *Studies in the Education of Adults, 44*(2), 225–244.

Grace, A. P., & Benson, F. J. (2000). Using autobiographical queer life narratives of teachers to connect personal, political, and pedagogical spaces. *International Journal of Inclusive Education, 4*(2), 89–109.

Grace, A. P., & Hill, R. J. (2004). Positioning queer in adult education: Intervening in politics and praxis in North America. *Studies in the Education of Adults, 36*(2), 167–189.

Grace, A. P., Hill, R. J., Johnson, C. W., & Lewis, J. B. (2004). In other words: Queer voices/dissident subjectivities impelling social change. *International Journal of Qualitative Studies in Education, 17*(3), 301–323.

Grace, A. P., Hill, R. J., & Wells, K. (2009). Art as anti-oppression adult education:

Creating a pedagogy of presence and place. In R. J. Hill & A. P. Grace (Eds.), *Adult and higher education in queer contexts: Power, politics, and pedagogy* (pp. 69–86). Chicago: Discovery Association Publishing House.

Grace, A. P., Rocco, T. S., & Associates. (2009). *Challenging the professionalization of adult education: John Ohliger and contradictions in modern practice*. San Francisco: Jossey-Bass.

Grace, A. P., & Wells, K. (2007a). Everyone performs, everyone has a place: Camp fYrefly and arts-informed, community-based education, cultural work, and inquiry. In D. Clover & J. Stalker (Eds.), *The art of social justice: Re-crafting activist adult education and community leadership* (pp. 61–82). Leicester, UK: NIACE.

Grace, A. P., & Wells, K. (2007b). Using Freirean pedagogy of just ire to inform critical social learning in arts-informed community education for sexual minorities. *Adult Education Quarterly, 57*(2), 95–114.

Graveline, F. J. (2000). Circle as methodology: Enacting an Aboriginal paradigm. *International Journal of Qualitative Studies in Education, 13*(4), 361–370.

Greenspan, A. (2008). *The age of turbulence: Adventures in a new world*. New York: Penguin Books.

Greer, J. M. (2008). *The long descent*. Gabriola Island, BC: New Society Publishers.

Griffin, C. (2000). *Lifelong learning: Policy, strategy and culture*. Paper included in A Global Colloquium Supporting Lifelong Learning presented by The Open University, the Festival of Lifelong Learning, and the University of East London. Retrieved June 21, 2001, from http://www.open.ac.uk/lifelong-learning/

Grossberg, L. (1997). *Bringing it all back home: Essays on cultural studies*. Durham, NC: Duke University Press.

Hari, J. (2009, July 1). Almost everywhere is touched by the Stonewall riots now. *The Independent*, no. 7087, p. 23.

Harpur, P. (2012). Embracing the new disability rights paradigm: The importance of the Convention on the Rights of Persons with Disabilities. *Disability & Society, 27*(1), 1–14. Retrieved from http://dx.doi.org/10.1080/09687599.2012.631794

Harvey, D. (2005). *A brief history of neoliberalism*. New York: Oxford University Press.

Hill, R. J. (1995). A critique of heterocentric discourse in adult education: A critical review. *Adult Education Quarterly, 45*(3), 142–158.

Hill, R. J. (2001a). Contesting discrimination based on sexual orientation at the ICAE Sixth World Assembly: "Difference" is a fundamental human right. *Convergence, 34*(2–3), 100–116.

Hill, R. J. (2001b, June). *Notions of citizenship and democracy in the queer lifeworld*.

Paper presented at the 6th World Assembly, International Council for Adult Education (ICAE), Ocho Rios, Jamaica, West Indies.

Hill, R. J. (2002). Contesting rights in the new world (dis)order: Spiritual vignettes in a queer voice. In J. Pettitt (Ed.), *Proceedings of the 43rd Annual Adult Education Research Conference* (pp. 383–390). Raleigh, NC: North Carolina State University.

Hill, R. J. (2003a, August). Inclusion of sexual minorities in the discussion on gender justice: The Gender Education Office (GEO) virtual seminar. In P. Alonso (Ed.), *International Council for Adult Education, Gender Education Office (GEO) virtual seminar, Education for inclusion throughout life: Preparatory process towards CONFINTEA V + 6, Paving the way to Bangkok* (pp. 130–134). Norad, Norway: Royal Ministry of Foreign Affairs.

Hill, R. J. (2003b, August 20). In memoriam: Sergio Vieira de Mello (1948–2003)— Amigo de la paz y los derechos humanos. *La Red Va, 6* (276), (Boletín publicado en correo electrónico, en español y portugués por la REPEM [Red de Educación Popular Entre Mujeres de América Latina y el Caribe, Montevideo, Uruguay]).

Hill, R. J. (2003c). Turning a gay gaze on citizenship, sexual orientation, and gender identity: Contesting/ed terrain. In C. Medel-Anonuevo et al. (Eds.), *Citizenship, democracy and lifelong learning* (pp. 99–139). Hamburg, Germany: The United Nations Educational, Scientific, & Cultural Organization (UNESCO), Institute for Education (UIE). Available online at http://www.unesco.org/education/uie/pdf/uiestud35.pdf

Hill, R. J. (2005a). The impact of gender and race on learning in the workplace. Keynote address at the 35th Annual Standing Conference on University Teaching and Research in the Education of Adults (SCUTREA) Pre-Conference: It's a Man's World? Gender, Learning and Work, University of Sussex, Brighton, UK.

Hill, R. J. (2005b). Making difference count: Queer cultural competency in lifelong learning. *Proceedings of the 35th Annual Standing Conference on University Teaching and Research in the Education of Adults Conference* (SCUTREA): Diversity and Difference in Lifelong Learning. Brighton, UK: University of Sussex.

Hill, R. J. (2007). Breaking open our times (and other liberatory acts). In K. B. Armstrong, L. W. Nabb, & A. P. Czech (Eds.), *North American adult educators: Phyllis M. Cunningham archive of quintessential autobiographies for the 21st century* (pp. 153–158). Chicago: Discovery Association Publishing House.

Hill, R. J. (2008). Sexual minority rights (lesbian, gay, bisexual, transgender, two-spirit, and queer): Will comprehensive policy considerations find a voice? *Con-*

vergence, 40(3), 169ff. Available online at http://www.icae.org.uy/eng/convergence34.pdf

Hill, R. J. (2009a, November 28). North America: Adult learning and education for personal and social transformation. Role: Designer of Opening Ceremony Presentation (DVD) representing North America: Canada and the US at the International Civil Society Forum, UNESCO, Bélem do Para, Brazil. Available online at http://public.me.com/bobhill51

Hill, R. J. (2009b, November 29). Session: Education for inclusion/educación para la inclusión/education pour l'inclusion/educação para a inclusão. Title: Achieving full social inclusion for lesbian, gay, bisexual, transgender, and queer people through lifelong learning opportunities: What can CONFINTEA VI do? The International Civil Society Forum (FISC), UNESCO, Bélem do Para, Brazil, November 29, 2009. Available online at http://www.fisc2009.org/eng/index.php

Hill, R. J. (2009c, November 30). Building capacity for a visible global presence: Sexual minority rights. International Civil Society Forum (FISC), Bélem do Para, Brazil. Available online at http://www.fisc2009.org/eng/index. php?option=com_content&view=article&id=108:build-capacity-for-sexual-minority-rights&catid=3:noticias&Itemid=11 & http://public.me.com/bobhill51.

Hill, R. J. (2009d). Que(e)rying intimacy: Challenges to lifelong learning. In R. J. Hill & A. P. Grace (Eds.), *Adult and higher education in queer contexts: Power, politics, and pedagogy* (pp. 45–68). Chicago: Discovery Association Publishing House.

Hill, R. J. (2010). Achieving full social inclusion for lesbian, gay, bisexual, transgender, and queer people through lifelong learning opportunities: A queer educator's journey. Paper presented at the LGBTQ+A pre-conference of the Adult Education Research Conference (AERC), June 3, 2010, California State University at Sacramento.

Hill, R. J., Daigle, E. A., Graybeal, L., Walker, W., Avalon, C., Fowler, N., and Massey, M. W. (2008). *A review and critique of the 2008 United States "National report on the development and state of the art of Adult Learning and Education"* (ALE). Athens, GA: Authors.

Hill, R. J., & Grace, A. P. (Eds.). (2009). *Adult and higher education in queer contexts: Power, politics, and pedagogy.* Chicago: Discovery Association Publishing House.

Hobsbawm, E. (1994). *Age of extremes: The short twentieth century, 1914–1991.* London: Abacus.

Holst, J. (2006). Globalization and the future of critical adult education. In S. B. Merriam, B. C. Courtenay, & R. M. Cervero (Eds.), *Global issues and adult education: Perspectives from Latin America, Southern Africa, and the United States* (pp. 41–52). San Francisco: Jossey-Bass.

Hornagold, M. (2000). *Lifelong learning is an indigenous practice.* Retrieved September 6, 2000, from http://www.library.cqu.edu.au/conference/papers/hornagold.htm

Horton, M., & Freire, P. (1990). *We make the road by walking: Conversations on education and social change.* Edited by B. Bell, J. Gaventa, & J. Peters. Philadelphia: Temple University Press.

Human Resources Development Canada (HRDC). (1998). *A vision for HRDC.* Retrieved June 18, 2001, from http://hrdc-drhc.gc.ca/dept/mission/mission.shtml

Human Resources Development Canada (HRDC). (2002a). *An analysis of results from the School Leavers' Follow-up Survey, 1995.* Retrieved April 8, 2002, from http://hrdc-drhc.gc.ca/stratpol/arb/publications/books/notenough/c1_e.shtml

Human Resources Development Canada (HRDC). (2002b). *What is behind the declining youth participation rate?* Retrieved April 8, 2002, from http://hrdc-drhc. gc.ca/stratpol/arb/publications/bulletin/vol3n2/v3n2c2e.shtml

Human Resources and Skills Development Canada (HRSDC). (2004). *Youth employment strategy programs.* Retrieved November 18, 2004, from http://www.hrsdc. gc.ca/asp/gateway.asp?hr=en/epb/yi/yep/newprog/yesprograms.shtml&...

Human Resources and Skills Development Canada (HRSDC). (2010). *The Government of Canada's annual report on disability issues.* Retrieved November 4, 2012, from http://www.hrsdc.gc.ca/eng/disability_issues/reports/fdr/2010/page00.shtml

Human Resources and Skills Development Canada (HRSDC). (2012). *Government of Canada initiatives for people with disabilities.* Retrieved November 4, 2012 from http://www.hrsdc.gc.ca/eng/disability_issues/mandate/initiatives.shtml

Inquiry into the Future for Lifelong Learning (IFLL). (2008, February). *The future for lifelong learning: An independent commission of inquiry* (Briefing #2). Leicester, UK: NIACE.

International Civil Society Forum (ICSF). (2008). *ICSF in CONFINTEA VI: Charter of Principles.* Retrieved January 3, 2010, from http://www.fisc2009.org/eng/index.php?option=com_content&view=article&id=29&Itemid=8

International Civil Society Forum (ICSF). (2009, December 6). *Final reactions from the civil society caucus.* Retrieved January 10, 2010, from http://fisc2009english.wordpress.com/

International Council for Adult Education (ICAE). (2008). *ICAE Academy of Lifelong Learning Advocacy IV* (Brochure). Montevideo, Uruguay: Author.

International Covenant on Civil and Political Rights. (1996). Available online at http://www.unhchr.ch/tbs/doc.nsf/0/7359917ff4aa5a06c12570a00052810c/$FILE/G0442208.pdf

International Covenant on Economic, Social and Cultural Rights. (1996). Available online at http://www2.ohchr.org/english/law/cescr.htm

International Gay and Lesbian Human Rights Commission (IGLHRC). (2004, January). UN resolution on sexual orientation and human rights. *Women's Health Journal, 1*, 68–72.

International Gay and Lesbian Human Rights Commission (IGLHRC). (2007a, August). *Ugandan homosexuals launch media campaign: "Let us live in peace."* Retrieved January 15, 2008, from http://www.iglhrc.org/site/iglhrc/section.php?id=5&detail=772

International Gay and Lesbian Human Rights Commission (IGLHRC). (2007b). *African lesbian and gay activists meet in Johannesburg to challenge State homophobia in 38 countries on the continent.* Retrieved January 15, 2008, from http://www.iglhrc.org/site/iglhrc/section.php?id=5&detail=728

International Gay and Lesbian Human Rights Commission (IGLHRC). (2007c). *The Felipa de Souza award.* Retrieved December 18, 2007, from http://www.iglhrc.org/site/iglhrc/section.php?id=76

International Gay and Lesbian Human Rights Commission (IGLHRC). (2007d, August 30). *Latin America: First hurdle for LGBT rights passed within Latin American Economic Union.* Retrieved March 1, 2009, from http://www.iglhrc.org/cgi-bin/iowa/print/460.html

Jackson, S. (2011a). Lifelong learning and social justice: Introduction. In S. Jackson (Ed.), *Lifelong learning and social justice: Communities, work and identities in a globalised world* (pp. 1–10). Leicester, UK: National Institute of Adult Continuing Education.

Jackson, S. (2011b). Sustaining communities: Introduction. In S. Jackson (Ed.), *Lifelong learning and social justice: Communities, work and identities in a globalised world* (pp. 13–17). Leicester, UK: National Institute of Adult Continuing Education.

Jackson, S. (2011c). Sustaining communities: Conclusion. In S. Jackson (Ed.), *Lifelong learning and social justice: Communities, work and identities in a globalised world* (p. 102). Leicester, UK: National Institute of Adult Continuing Education.

Jackson, S. (2011d). Identities: Conclusion. In S. Jackson (Ed.), *Lifelong learning and social justice: Communities, work and identities in a globalised world* (pp.

271

284–290). Leicester, UK: National Institute of Adult Continuing Education.

Janoff, D. V. (2005). *Pink blood: Homophobic violence in Canada*. Toronto: University of Toronto Press.

Jarvis, P. (2000). "Imprisoned in the global classroom" revisited: Towards an ethical analysis of lifelong learning. In K. Appleton, C. Macpherson, & D. Orr (Eds.), *Proceedings of the Inaugural International Lifelong Learning Conference, Central Queensland University* (pp. 20–27). Rockhampton, Australia: Central Queensland University Press.

Jarvis, P. (2006). Beyond the learning society: Globalisation and the moral imperative for reflective social change. *International Journal of Lifelong Education, 25*(3), 201–211.

Jarvis, P. (2007). *Globalisation, lifelong learning and the learning society: Sociological perspectives*. New York: Routledge.

Jarvis, P. (2008). Rediscovering adult education in a world of lifelong learning. *International Journal of Critical Pedagogy, 1*(1). Retrieved May 16, 2010, from http://www.freireproject.org/ojs/index.php/home/article/view/52/20

Jeria, J. (2001). The political economy of adult education: Implications for practice. In V. Sheared & P. A. Sissel (Eds.), *Making space: Merging theory and practice in adult education* (pp. 314–325). Westport, CN: Bergin & Garvey.

Johnson, R. W. (2010, January 12). The battle over homophobia in Africa. *National Post*, p. A12.

Johnson, S. (2009, May). The quiet coup. *The Atlantic, 303*(4), 46–50 & 52–54 & 56.

Johnston, R. (2000). Community education and lifelong learning: Local spice for global fare? In J. Field & M. Leicester (Eds.), *Lifelong learning: Education across the lifespan* (pp. 12–28). London: RoutledgeFalmer.

Kamp, D. (2009, April). Rethinking the American dream. *Vanity Fair, 584*, 118–123 & 177–180.

Keizer, G. (2009, April). Notebook: Shine, perishing Republicans. *Harper's Magazine*, 9–10 & 12.

Kenny, M. (2004). Lifelong learning: Sailing to Atlantis? In P. A. Danaher, C. Macpherson, F. Nouwens, & D. Orr (Eds.), *Proceedings of the 3rd International Lifelong Learning Conference, Central Queensland University* (pp. 20–25). Rockhampton, Australia: Central Queensland University Press.

Kim, H., Gomes, A., & Prinz, C. (2010). *Sickness, disability, and work: Breaking the barriers—Canada: Opportunities for collaboration*. Paris: Organisation for Economic Co-operation and Development. Retrieved November 4, 2012, from http://www.oecd.org/els/socialpoliciesanddata/sicknessdisabilityandworkbreakingthebarriers-canadaopportunitiesforcollaboration.htm

Kim, R. (2005, August 7). Witnesses to an execution. *The Nation*. Retrieved February 11, 2010, from http://www.thenation.com/doc/20050815/kim/print

King, Jr., M. L. (2007). Conscience for change. In *The lost Massey lectures: Recovered classics from five great thinkers* (pp. 163–217). Toronto: House of Anansi Press. (King's lectures copyright 1967).

Kinney, J. (2008, October 20). This is not Bill Clinton's financial crisis. *Business-Week*. Retrieved October 29, 2008, from http://www.businessweek.com/bw-daily/dnflash/content/oct2008/db20081017_373460.htm

Kiviat, B. (2007, November 26). Getting to the top. *Time* (Canadian Edition), *170*(22), 44–45.

Klein, N. (2007). *The shock doctrine: The rise of disaster capitalism*. Toronto: Alfred A. Knopf Canada.

Kligman, S. J. (2003). Education and (re)training and the intersections of diversity: Challenge paper. In Canadian Heritage—Multiculturalism (Ed.), *Intersections of diversity: Developing new approaches to policy and research* (pp. 1–8). Niagara Falls, ON: Canadian Heritage—Multiculturalism.

Korten, D. C. (2006). *The great turning: From empire to earth community*. San Francisco: Berret-Koehler Publishers.

Koymasky, M., & Koymasky, A. (2008). Memorials of the Gay Holocaust. Retrieved May 13, 2013, from http://andrejkoymasky.com/mem/holocaust/ho08.html

Kron, J. (2011, May 13). Antigay bill in Uganda is shelved in parliament. *The New York Times*. Retrieved June 28, 2011, from http://www.nytimes.com/2011/05/14/world/africa/14uganda.html

Krugman, P. (2009). *The return of Depression economics and the crisis of 2008*. New York: W. W. Norton & Company.

Lambeir, B. (2005). Education as liberation: The politics and techniques of lifelong learning. *Educational Philosophy and Theory, 37*(3), 349–355.

Lave, J., & Wenger, E. (1991). *Situated learning: Legitimate peripheral participation*. New York: Cambridge University Press.

Leap, W. L., & Boellstorff, T. (Eds.). (2003). *Speaking in queer tongues: Globalization and gay language*. Chicago: University of Illinois Press.

Lee, M. (2009, March 18). Obama to sign UN gay-rights declaration. *Time* (in partnership with CNN). Retrieved March 26, 2009, from http://www.time.com/time/printout/0,8816,1885989,00.html

Lindsay, S., Robinson, S., Mcdougall, C., Sanford, R., & Adams, T. (2012). Employers' perspectives on working with adolescents with disabilities. *International*

Journal of Disability, Community & Rehabilitation, 11(1). Retrieved from http://www.ijdcr.ca/VOL11_01/articles/lindsay.shtml

Lisman, D., & Ohliger, J. (1978). Must we all go back to school? *The Progressive, 42*(10), 35–37.

Little Bear, L. (2009). *Naturalizing Indigenous knowledge: Synthesis paper.* Saskatoon, SK: University of Saskatchewan, Aboriginal Education Research Centre & Calgary, AB: First Nations and Adult Higher Education Consortium. Retrieved November 4, 2012, from www.ccl-cca.ca

Lucht, B. (2007). Introduction. In *The lost Massey lectures: Recovered classics from five great thinkers* (pp. vii–xvi). Toronto: House of Anansi Press.

Lumu, D. T. (2013, January 10). Uganda: Anti-gay bill hurting economy—govt official. *The Observer* (Kampala). Retrieved February 27, 2013, from http://allafrica.com/stories/201301101384.html

Macedo, D. (2004). Foreword. In P. Freire, *Pedagogy of indignation* (pp. ix–xxv). Boulder, CO: Paradigm Publishers.

MacNeil, R. (1990). Home I'll be. On *Home I'll be* (CD). Virgin Music Canada: Lupin Records.

Mandel, M. (2008, October 28). Mandel: It's not a crisis of confidence. *Business-Week*. Retrieved October 29, 2008, from http://www.businessweek.com/bw-daily/dnflash/content/oct2008/db20081027_860032.htm?chan=top+news_top+news+index+-+temp_dialogue+with+readers

Marwick, A. (1998). *The sixties: Cultural revolution in Britain, France, Italy, and the United States, c.1958–c.1974.* Oxford: Oxford University Press.

Mason, P. (2009). *Meltdown: The end of the age of greed.* New York: Verso.

Maunsell, K. (2010). "Tracing our roots: Imagining our future": A life history of adult education in the Republic of Ireland. In B. Merrill & P. Armstrong (Eds.), *Looking back, looking forward: Learning, teaching, and research in adult education past, present, and future. Proceedings of the 40th Annual Standing Conference on University Teaching and Research in the Education of Adults, University of Warwick, Coventry, UK* (pp. 251–256).

Mayo, M. (2005). *Global citizens: Social movements and the challenge of globalization.* Toronto: Canadian Scholars' Press.

McGrath, B. (2006). "Everything is different here …": Mobilizing capabilities through inclusive education practices and relationships. *International Journal of Inclusive Education, 10*(6), 595–614.

McQuaig, L. (2007, December). Mission not yet accomplished: How Iraq figures in Big Oil's dreams. *The Walrus, 4*(10), 40–47.

Merriam, S. B., & Caffarella, R. S. (1999). *Learning in adulthood: A comprehensive guide*. 2nd ed. San Francisco: Jossey-Bass.

Mezirow, J. (1991). *Transformative dimensions of adult learning*. San Francisco: Jossey-Bass.

Milana, M. (2012). Political globalization and the shift from adult education to lifelong learning. *European Journal for Research on the Education and Learning of Adults, 3*(2), 103–117.

Miller, N., & West, L. (2001). Once upon a time, on the road from adult education to lifelong learning. In L. West, N. Miller, D. O'Reilly, & R. Allen (Eds.), *Proceedings of the 31st Annual Conference of SCUTREA: The Standing Conference on University Teaching and Research in the Education of Adults* (pp. 13–18). Nottingham, UK: Pilgrim College, University of Nottingham.

Mojab, S. (2006). War and diaspora as lifelong learning contexts for immigrant women. In C. Leathwood & B. Francis (Eds.), *Gender and lifelong learning: Critical feminist engagements* (pp. 164–175). London: Routledge.

Moore, J. (2010, January 12). Coming-out wars: The seeds of hatred. *National Post*, A12.

Morton, D. (Ed.). (1996). *The material queer: A LesBiGay cultural studies reader*. Boulder, CO: Westview Press.

Murray, S. O. (1995). *Latin American male homosexualities*. Albuquerque, NM: University of New Mexico Press.

Murray, S. O., & Roscoe, W. (Eds.). (1997). *Islamic homosexualities: Culture, history, and literature*. New York: New York University Press.

Murray, S. O., & Roscoe, W. (Eds.). (1998). *Boy-wives and female husbands: Studies in African homosexualities*. New York: Palgrave/St Martin's Press.

Murray, R., & Viljoen, F. (2007). Towards non-discrimination on the basis of sexual orientation: The normative basis and procedural possibilities before the African Commission on Human and Peoples' Rights and the African Union. *Human Rights Quarterly, 29*(1), 86–111.

Myers, K., & de Broucker, P. (2006, June). *Too many left behind: Canada's adult education and training system* (Research Report W/34, Work Network). Ottawa, ON: Canadian Policy Research Networks.

Napier, I. (2002). The lifelong learning exchange in Singapore and its parallels in large public companies. In K. Appleton, C. Macpherson, & D. Orr (Eds.), *Proceedings of the 2nd International Lifelong Learning Conference, Central Queensland University* (pp. 36–42). Rockhampton, Australia: Central Queensland University Press.

Nash, R. (2003). Pierre Bourdieu: The craft of sociology. In M. Peters, M. Olssen, & C. Lankshear (Eds.), *Futures of critical theory: Dreams of difference* (pp. 187–196). Lanham, ML: Rowman & Littlefield.

Nathan, M. (2013). *Ugandan Parliament resumes with anti-gay bill 8th on agenda: Keeping guard over the Kill the Gays Bill*. Retrieved February 27, 2013, from http://oblogdeeoblogda.me/2013/02/05/ugandan-parliament-resumes-with-anti-gay-bill-8th-on-agenda/

Nesbit, T. (1999). Mapping adult education. *Educational Theory, 49*(2), 265–279. Retrieved February 5, 2005, from http://web32.epnet.com

Netherlands Mission. (2008). *Human rights: Statement on human rights, sexual orientation and gender identity at high level meeting*. Retrieved January 2, 2009, from http://www.netherlandsmission.org/article.asp?articleref=AR00000530EN

Newman, F., Couturier, L., & Scurry, J. (2004). *The future of higher education: Rhetoric, reality, and the risks of the market*. San Francisco: Jossey-Bass.

Ohliger, J. (1968). Accent on social philosophy. *Adult Leadership, 17,* 124.

Ohliger, J. (1971). *Lifelong learning or lifelong schooling? A tentative view on the ideas of Ivan Illich with a quotational bibliography*. Occasional Papers No. 24. Syracuse, NY: Syracuse University Publications in Continuing Education and ERIC Clearinghouse on Adult Education.

Ohliger, J. (1990). Forum: You shall know the truth and the truth shall make you laugh. *Journal of Adult Education, 19*(1), 25–38.

Olds, L. (n.d.). *A memoir of my journey in adult education: The making of a popular educator*. Unpublished manuscript.

Olssen, M. (2006). Understanding the mechanisms of neoliberal control: Lifelong learning, flexibility and knowledge capitalism. *International Journal of Lifelong Education, 25*(3), 213–230.

Ontario Consultants on Religious Tolerance. (2008). *Hate speech in Brazil. Gay bashing problem*. Retrieved January 2, 2009, from http://www.religioustolerance.org/braspeech1.htm

Organisation for Economic Co-operation and Development (OECD). (2000). Financing lifelong education in tertiary education. Background paper for the International Conference on Lifelong Learning as an Affordable Investment, Château Laurier, Ottawa, ON, Canada. Retrieved June 18, 2001, from http://www.canada-oecd.gc.ca/ index.cfm

Organisation for Economic Co-operation and Development (OECD) & Human Resources Development Canada (HRDC). (2000a). Conference overview. International Conference on Lifelong Learning as an Affordable Investment, Château Laurier, Ottawa, ON, Canada. Retrieved June 18, 2001, from http://www.canada-oecd.gc.ca/index.cfm

Organisation for Economic Co-operation and Development (OECD) & Human Resources Development Canada (HRDC). (2000b). Draft annotated programme. International Conference on Lifelong Learning as an Affordable Investment, Château Laurier, Ottawa, ON, Canada. Retrieved June 18, 2001, from http://www.canada-oecd.gc.ca/index.cfm

Pagé, M. (1997). Reaction to a paper by J. Frideres, in contribution to the discussion of proposed future strategic research on the civic participation of immigrants and new citizens. In Canadian Heritage—Multiculturalism (Ed.), *Immigrants and civic participation: Contemporary policy and research issues* (pp. 49–60). Montréal, QC: Canadian Heritage—Multiculturalism.

Partridge, J. (2000). Lifelong learning—How literate do people need to be? In K. Appleton, C. Macpherson, & D. Orr (Eds.), *Proceedings of the Inaugural International Lifelong Learning Conference, Central Queensland University* (pp. 209–215). Rockhampton, Australia: Central Queensland University Press.

Pendlebury, S., & Enslin, P. (2000). Lifelong learning for a new society: The South African case. In J. Field & M. Leicester (Eds.), *Lifelong learning: Education across the lifespan* (pp. 149–157). London: RoutledgeFalmer.

Phillips, K. (2009). *Bad money: Reckless finance, failed politics, and the global crisis of American capitalism.* New York: Penguin Books.

Philpott, D. F., & Cahill, M. (2008). A pan-Canadian perspective on the professional knowledge base of learning disabilities. *International Journal of Disability, Community & Rehabilitation, 7*(2). Retrieved November 4, 2012, from http://www.ijdcr.ca/VOL07_02_CAN/articles/philpott.shtml

Queer Peace International. (2009). Queer Peace International is…. Retrieved February 24, 2009, from http://www.queerpeace.org

Quirk, M. (2007, December). Bright lights, big cities. *The Atlantic, 300,* 32–33.

Rau, K. (2008, June 19). Human rights come to the fore: Pride adopts a more international focus. *Xtra,* No. 617, p. 9.

Rodham Clinton, H. (2009). Remarks upon receipt of the Roosevelt Institute's Four Freedoms Award at the Roosevelt Institute's Four Freedoms Medals Gala Dinner. Retrieved September 17, 2009, from http://www.state.gov/secretary/rm/2009a/09/129164.htm

Rodham Clinton, H. (2011). Remarks in recognition of International Human Rights Day, December 6, 2011. Washington: US Department of State.

Rubenson, K. (2000). Revisiting the map of the territory. In T. J. Sork, V. L. Chapman, & R. St. Clair (Eds.), *Proceedings of the 41st Annual Adult Education Research Conference* (pp. 397–401). Vancouver: University of British Columbia.

Rubenson, K. (2002). Lifelong learning for all: Challenges and limitations of public policy. In S. Mojab & W. McQueen (Eds.), *Proceedings of the 21st Annual Conference of the Canadian Association for the Study of Adult Education* (pp. 242–248). Toronto: Ontario Institute for Studies in Education, University of Toronto.

Sanders, D. (2007, May). Human rights and sexual orientation in international law. Retrieved January 15, 2008, from http://www.ilga.org/news_results.asp?FileCat egory=7&ZoneID=7&FileID=1078

Sarmiento, S. (2011, May 11). Uganda's anti-gay bill is far from dead. *The Guardian* (UK). Retrieved June 28, 2011, from http://www.guardian.co.uk/commentis-free/ belief/2011/may/11/uganda-anti-gay-bill

Saskatchewan Ministry of Education. (2008). *Post-secondary education: In support of First Nations and Inuit students.* Saskatoon, SK: University of Saskatchewan, Aboriginal Education Research Centre & Calgary, AB: First Nations and Adult Higher Education Consortium. Retrieved November 4, 2012, from http://www. ccl-cca.ca

Saunders, R. (2007, November). *Towards an effective adult learning system: Report on a series of regional roundtables.* Ottawa, ON: Canadian Policy Research Networks & Adult Learning Knowledge Centre, Canadian Council on Learning. Retrieved January 7, 2008, from http://search.ccl-cca.ca/NR/rdonlyres/ EB7A1C34-CFC4-469A-A604-F3BF0727C74D/0/OverallReportonRoundtab-lesENG.pdf

Schmitt, A., & Sofer, J. (Eds.). (1992). *Sexuality and eroticism among males in Moslem societies.* Binghamton, NY: Haworth Press.

Schuller, T., & Watson, D. (2009). *Learning through life: Inquiry into the future for lifelong learning.* Leicester, UK: National Institute of Adult Continuing Education.

Scott, P. (2000). The death of mass higher education and the birth of lifelong learning. In J. Field & M. Leicester (Eds.), *Lifelong learning: Education across the lifespan* (pp. 29–42). London: RoutledgeFalmer.

Senn Breivik, P. (2000). Information literacy and lifelong learning: The magical partnership. In K. Appleton, C. Macpherson, & D. Orr (Eds.), *Proceedings of the Inaugural International Lifelong Learning Conference, Central Queensland University* (pp. 1–6). Rockhampton, Australia: Central Queensland University Press.

Small, N. (2001). Lifelong learning: A new route to an old destination? In L. West, N. Miller, D. O'Reilly, & R. Allen (Eds.), *Proceedings of the 31st Annual Conference of SCUTREA: The Standing Conference on University Teaching and Research in the Education of Adults* (pp. 367–370). Nottingham, UK: Pilgrim College, University of Nottingham.

Solomon, D. (Ed.). (1964). *The continuing learner.* Chicago: Centre for the Study of Liberal Education for Adults.

Stromquist, N. P., & Monkman, K. (2000). Defining globalization and assessing its implications on knowledge and education. In N. P. Stromquist & K. Monkman (Eds.), *Globalization and education: Integration and contestation across cultures* (pp. 3–25). Lanham, MD: Rowman & Littlefield.

Sutherland, P., & Crowther, J. (2006). Introduction: "The lifelong learning imagination." In P. Sutherland & J. Crowther (Eds.), *Lifelong learning: Concepts and contexts* (pp. 3–11). London: Routledge.

Tatchell, P. (2008). 66 countries sign UN gay rights statement. Retrieved January 10, 2009, from http://www.petertatchell.net/international/UNmakeshistory.htm

Thomas, A. M. (1998). Learning our way out. In S. M. Scott, B. Spencer, & A. Thomas (Eds.), *Learning for life: Canadian readings in adult education* (pp. 354–364). Toronto: Thompson Educational Publishing.

Thomas, C. (2004). Rescuing a social relational disability. *Scandinavian Journal of Disability Research, 6*(1), 22–36.

Tobias, R. (2004). Lifelong learning policies and discourses: Critical reflections from Aotearoa, New Zealand. *International Journal of Lifelong Education, 23*(6), 569–588.

Tossebro, J. (2004). Introduction to the special issue: Understanding disability. *Scandinavian Journal of Disability Research, 6*(1), 3–7.

Tough, A. (1971). *The adult's learning projects: A fresh approach to theory and practice in adult learning.* Toronto: Ontario Institute for Studies in Education.

Tuckett, A. (2009). Foreword. In T. Schuller & D. Watson (Eds.), *Learning through life: Inquiry into the future for lifelong learning* (pp. xi–xiv). Leicester, UK: National Institute of Adult Continuing Education.

Tuijnman, A. (2002). Themes and questions for a research agenda on lifelong learning. In R. Edwards, N. Miller, N. Small, & A. Tait (Eds.), *Supporting lifelong learning, volume 3: Making policy work* (pp. 6–29). New York: RoutledgeFalmer.

Tutton, M. (2008, June 24). Lost generation? Exodus of youth presents "scary" challenge on aging East Coast. *The Telegram,* A7.

United Nations. (2003a, April 17). *Promotion and protection of human rights.* Retrieved February 25, 2009, from http://daccess-dds-ny.un.org/doc/UNDOC/ LTD/G03/138/18/PDF/G0313818.pdf?OpenElement

United Nations. (2003b, April 25). *Commission on Human Rights adopts resolution on situation in Iraq*. Press Release HR/CN/1047. Retrieved February 25, 2009, from http://www.un.org/News/Press/docs/2003/hrcn1047.doc.htm

United Nations Educational, Scientific, & Cultural Organization (UNESCO). (2001). *The Cape Town statement on characteristic elements of a lifelong learning higher education institution*. Retrieved May 13, 2013, from http://www.unesco. org/education/uie/pdf/ct-statement.pdf.

United Nations Educational, Scientific, & Cultural Organization (UNESCO). (2003, September 6 –11). *Recommitting to adult education and learning: Synthesis report of the CONFINTEA V Midterm Review Meeting, Bangkok, Thailand*. Available online at http://www.unesco.org/education/uie/pdf/recommitting. pdf

United Nations Educational, Scientific, & Cultural Organization (UNESCO). (2010). *EFA global monitoring report: Reaching the marginalized*. Paris: Author.

Universal Declaration of Human Rights. (1948). Available at http://www.un.org/ en/documents/udhr/

Verry, D. (2000). *Financial resources for lifelong learning: Evidence and issues*. Background paper for the International Conference on Lifelong Learning as an Affordable Investment, Château Laurier, Ottawa, ON, Canada. Retrieved June 18, 2001, http://www.canada-ocde.gc.ca/index.cfm

Vienna Declaration. (1993). Available at http://www.unhchr.ch/huridocda/huridoca.nsf/(symbol)/a.conf.157.23.en

Wain, K. (2000). The learning society: Postmodern politics. *International Journal of Lifelong Learning 19*(1), 36–53.

Walters, S. (2006). Realizing a lifelong learning higher education institution. In P. Sutherland & J. Crowther (Eds.), *Lifelong learning: Concepts and contexts* (pp. 71–81). London: Routledge.

Welton, M. (1998). Educating for a deliberative democracy. In S. M. Scott, B. Spencer, & A. Thomas (Eds.), *Learning for life: Canadian readings in adult education* (pp. 365–372). Toronto: Thompson Educational Publishing.

Wexler, P. (1992). *Becoming somebody: Toward a social psychology of school*. London: The Falmer Press.

Wildemeersch, D., & Salling Olesen, H. (2012). Editorial: The effects of policies for the education and learning of adults—from "adult education" to "lifelong learning," from "emancipation" to "empowerment." *European Journal for Research on the Education and Learning of Adults, 3*(2), 97–101.

Wilson, A. L., & Cervero, R. M. (2001). Walkabout: On the nature of practice in a lifelong learning world. In L. West, N. Miller, D. O'Reilly, & R. Allen (Eds.), *Proceedings of the 31st Annual Conference of SCUTREA: The Standing Conference on University Teaching and Research in the Education of Adults* (pp. 435–438). Nottingham, UK: Pilgrim College, University of Nottingham.

Windsor, D. (2004, January). *UN to provide same-sex partner benefits to non-US workers*. Retrieved January 24, 2004, from http://www.gaypasg.org/index.htm

Wolin, S. S. (1996). Fugitive democracy. In S. Benhabib (Ed.), *Democracy and difference: Contesting the boundaries of the political* (pp. 31–45). Princeton, NJ: Princeton University Press.

Zakaria, F. (2009). *The post-American world*. New York: W. W. Norton & Company.

About the Author

André P. Grace completed a PhD in Educational Foundations at Dalhousie University, Halifax, Nova Scotia, Canada. He engaged in post-doctoral studies with Dr. Henry A. Giroux at the Waterbury Forum for Education and Cultural Studies, Pennsylvania State University, State College, USA. Currently, he is a professor and director of the Institute for Sexual Minority Studies and Services in the Faculty of Education, University of Alberta. In national research projects funded by the Social Sciences and Humanities Research Council, Dr. Grace has used qualitative methodology focused on explorations of the self, others, and culture to examine the positionalities and needs of students and teachers across sexual and gender minority differences. He has also studied educational interest groups in political analyses of their impacts on inclusion and accommodation of sexual and gender minorities in education and culture. Dr. Grace keeps his research and service in dynamic equilibrium. He is co-founder of Camp fYrefly, a national summer leadership camp for sexual and gender minority youth, and he is national consultant on sexual and gender minority issues for the Canadian Teachers' Federation. Dr. Grace has served as external reviewer to the Chief Public Health Officer's Reports Unit on the State of Public Health in Canada for the 2011 and 2012 national reports. He is a past president of the Canadian Association for the Study of Adult Education, and a past chair of the Steering Committee for the US national Adult Education Research Conference. Dr. Grace's work in educational policy studies primarily focuses on comparative studies of policies, pedagogies, and practices shaping lifelong learning as critical action, especially in the contexts of OECD (Organisation for Economic Co-operation and Development) countries. Within this research he includes a major focus on sexual and gender minorities and their issues and concerns regarding social inclusion, cohesion, and justice in education and culture. With Tonette S. Rocco, Florida International University, he received the 2009 Phillip E. Frandson Award for Literature in the Field of Continuing Higher Education from the US University Continuing Education Association for their co-edited book *Challenging the Professionalization of Adult Education: John Ohliger and Contradictions in Modern Practice*. At the 2010 Standing Conference on University Teaching and Research in the Education of Adults, University of Warwick, United Kingdom, Dr. Grace received the Ian Martin Award for Social Justice for his paper *Space Matters: Lifelong Learning, Sexual Minorities, and Realities of Adult Education as Social Education*.

Copyright Acknowledgements

Chapter 3

André P. Grace, "Lifelong Learning Chic in the Modern Practice of Adult Education: Historical and Contemporary Perspectives," *Journal of Adult and Continuing Education,* vol. 11, no. 1 (2005), 62–79. Reproduced with the permission of the copyright holders, the National Institute of Adult Continuing Education.

Chapter 4

André P. Grace, "Lifelong Learning as a Chameleonic Concept and Versatile Practice: Y2K Perspectives and Trends," *International Journal of Lifelong Education,* vol. 23, no. 4 (2004), 385–405. Reproduced with the permission of the copyright holders, Taylor & Francis.

Chapter 5

Excerpted from Rita MacNeil, "I'll Be Home," from the album *I'll Be Home,* recorded by Virgin in 1990.

Index